THE ARTHURIAN LEGEND IN THE LITERATURES OF THE SPANISH PENINSULA

BY

WILLIAM J. ENTWISTLE

PHAETON PRESS

NEW YORK

1975

Originally Published 1925
Reprinted 1975

Library of Congress Cataloging in Publication Data

Entwistle, William James, 1895-1952.
The Arthurian legend in the literatures of the Spanish Peninsula.

Reprint of the 1925 ed. published by J. M. Dent, London and Dutton, New York.
Includes index.
1. Arthurian romances--History and criticism.
2. Romance literature--History and criticism.
3. Literature, Medieval--History and criticism.
I. Title.
PN685.E6 1975 809'.933'51 75-6563
ISBN 0-87753-059-9

PREFACE

THE work which these lines preface arose from a suggestion by Professor E. G. Gardner. Certain investigations which he had undertaken with regard to Dante's use of the Arthurian novels led easily to the project of an introductory treatment of the Spanish, Portuguese and Catalan romances of the same order, the more so as they have not been discussed at length in any English or American work. The present writer, through some minor enquiries into disputed or doubtful points, had gained a stance in the subject, and it was originally intended to link his notes to the results obtained by distinguished Spanish scholars. But when the project came to be examined more closely, the requirements of synthetic treatment induced a number of fresh observations even in the explored territory of the Peninsular romances and gave a higher relief to some facts than had been allowed by specialist investigators of individual novels. The general theory here offered, and the greater number of the dates which support it, are novel, and, except where force of circumstances has exacted a disclaimer, for all statements in this work the writer must accept personal responsibility. For the same reason more space has been allotted to the notes than was at first intended, and by them the scholar will be able to check each step of the argument; absolute accuracy is perhaps hardly to be expected in matter so novel, and the author has endeavoured to moderate the tone of the work from exposition to suggestion. In the treatment of the constituent parts an effort has been made to state facts before deductions, and to give priority to the more certain over the less secure inferences; which method, though it may impose a crab's progress on the subject itself, should serve as a safeguard for the cautious or sceptical reader. A short appendix is added in order to give the reader due notice of such studies in Spanish Arthurianism as have been printed or come to hand since the completion of the author's manuscript.

The writer takes this opportunity of putting on record his indebtedness to the distinguished name already mentioned, and to those which are cited in the notes throughout the volume, and apart from whose researches this synthesis could not have been planned. Of other obligations, not less deep though less germane to this occasion, the author would be understood to be none the less sensible. He owes thanks also to the courteous and scholarly librarians and officials of the Biblioteca Nacional, Centro de Estudios, Escorial, John Rylands and Christie collections, and the British Museum, who will recognise his indebtedness in the citations of books; likewise to the trustees for the Fullerton, Reid and Carnegie scholarships, through whose generosity he had the leisure to lay a basis for these studies. He is also deeply sensible of the kindness of Mr. J. M. Dent, whose interest has given to this book the facilities for its publication.

CONTENTS

THE ARTHURIAN LEGEND

I

INTRODUCTORY REMARKS

THE history of the Arthurian novels within the Iberian Peninsulà is one of attractive simplicity. They form a literature of restricted types and homogeneous expression, which arose at an era that is known or can be ascertained, and derive from one general current of inspiration. The limits of discussion are definite and recognisable, and the topics of controversy are not historically remote; for the range of debate is limited to such concrete matters as the time and manner of their introduction, their classes and pedigree, their influence and general direction, and any special circumstances of their appeal to Peninsular taste. Such matters can be decided by the ordinary procedure and evidence of textual or historical criticism; they allow small scope for dubiety or conjecture. We are not faced in Spain by any question as to the origins of the various cycles, nor do we receive any opportunities for studying their growth and development. We can at once proceed to assume the existence of the French prose Arthurian literature of the early thirteenth century, which is expanded and amplified to some extent by our Spanish texts, as the universal basis of our discussion, but we do not require to ask ourselves how that literature came into being, nor are our specific interests affected by the complicated and insoluble problems connected with the Breton Lays and the finished novels, the historicity of Arthur or Tristram, the proportions of the final product which belong to the different racial ingredients, the names and precedence of the heroes, the attributions of authorship, or the conflicting theories of composition. Those controversies find their conclusion in the great prose cycles which are accessible to all students; and it is with the prose cycles of France, translated literally and without imaginative addition into the Peninsular literatures of the fourteenth century, that the special province of this work begins.

Spain has but little to add to our knowledge of the Arthurian cycles. Her *Tristan*, *Merlin* and *Grail* postulate originals which are no longer extant in a French dress, but which fall within fixed limits of deviation from the normal types of romance and might be inferred from other evidence. One ballad joins to the name of Tristan a charming lovers' allegory from universal folk-lore; another gives to Lancelot for ally the figure of a typical Spanish go-between, the duenna Quintañona, and the third preserves the memory of one of his least famous adventures. A son of Tristan carried the fame of his father into battle with the Moors of Spain, where he lived for no more than one edition of the romance, though he had vitality enough to reach the public of Italy in *I due Tristani*; and Sagramor, as one of the younger knights of the Round Table, obtained a new romance of his own from the pen of Jorge

Ferreira de Vasconcellos. Spain may have been the passive source of some details of the *Parzifal*, but the Spanish setting of that romance by Wagner and Wolfram is entirely foreign to the thought of that nation. Allusions to facts of date antecedent to the established cycles are rare and difficult to determine as such: the work of Geoffrey of Monmouth was kept in circulation by the language in which it was composed and by the pseudo-historical repute which it obtained; but the Breton lays are, at most, but faintly reflected in the story of *Cifar* and the first five lyrics of the *Cancioneiro Colocci-Brancutti*.

But if the romances of the Peninsular cycles offer comparatively little of interest to the student of Arthurian origins; and if (as must likewise be conceded) they are frequently of little intrinsic significance; yet the circumstances of their progress, their accompaniments, and their results, together with the great measure of assurance with which we can affirm these circumstances, have invested them with an importance in the history of European literature which need hardly yield precedence to the romances of Germany, England, Italy, or perhaps of France itself. Circulating at first in the courts of Lisbon, Toledo, Pamplona and Barcelona during the later years of the thirteenth century, most probably as French manuscripts, they were translated in or before the first half of the fourteenth, and for some two hundred and fifty years continued to fertilise the literature and society of the Spanish kingdoms. They formed an antithesis to the real and literal trend of national thought; they coalesced with and guided its peculiar exaltation when influenced by love, honour and religion; they gradually expanded the doctrines and practice of polite society from the immediate entourage of the monarch to the least leisured classes. During all this period they were accompanied by their derivative romance, *Amadis de Gaula*, a native creation of unknown authorship, nationality or date, whose name was bracketed during the whole mediæval period as an equal third to Lancelot and Tristan, and to whose progeny these heroes ultimately resigned their identity and interest. The invention of printing brought a brief revival to the Arthurian fictions, which was followed by their total extinction; but to the *Amadis* it gave an enormous expansion of influence. For the native romance, which had preferred independent imitation to literal translation, became prolific in the mind of the new public of printed books; it expressed the truth of life as a century of hope and chivalry and achievement was willing to see it,—unheard-of earths and enchanted scenes, princesses the reward of valour and empires the prize of a strong arm, brave hearts and unsullied faith and the wiles of the Evil One, endless adventure and scorn of reality, swelling phrases of love and honour and the militant extension of the holy Faith. And so the endless succession of Peninsular romances passed hot from the presses into the hands of the readers, until the profusion of supply glutted the demand. The rarefied emotions of discovery and conquest cooled and settled, and faith itself was mortified by humiliations. Charles V., Philip II., Philip III.—the names themselves are sufficient to illustrate the progress of disenchantment. Realistic novels, never entirely absent in Castile, which had for fifty years flowed beneath the optimism of their rivals, appeared in increasing numbers and bitterness, until the chivalrous strain was lost and engulfed. But just before all memory of them was lost, Cervantes, the best of the optimists and the most veritable of the realists, caught up both strains in the first and greatest of novels. In the *Don Quixote* no *a priori* interpretation is forced upon nature, the soul of the idealist and the insistent body of the realist are brought together as complementary parts of the same world, and the hard dualism of mediæval romance yields to the blended light and shade of the modern novel. The work of Cervantes has many affinities, but for its pedigree we can cite the author's own affirmation that Don Quixote derives from Amadis as Amadis from Arthur.

It is the third of these names, the earliest portion of the trilogy, which forms the subject of this work. Since the last general exposition of the Peninsular history of the Arthurian cycles by Sr. Menéndez y Pelayo in his great work on the origins of the Spanish novel, there has been considerable research; texts are generally more accessible, though some that are of great interest still are buried in outlying manuscripts; and the student may now consult important articles and reports. The decline of the theories of Gaston Paris in the country of their birth restores in some measure the autonomy of the Spanish cycles, which can be studied with more corporate and literal attention when the dazzle of brilliant preconceptions dims them no more. It is hardly possible to produce a definite treatment of all the problems connected with our subject, even if in Arthurian studies definitive treatments can be; for in addition to the remoteness of certain texts, the Spanish Arthurian romances lack discussion and suffer from the incuriosity of both nationals and strangers; but it seems to the author that facts are now available sufficient to lay down resolutely the larger lines of their development and influence, lines which to some extent reverse the contentions of the accepted exposition, and which would substitute an evidential history of their progress for a theory which appears to us too largely conjectural and preconceived.

II

THE THEORY OF PORTUGUESE PRIORITY

THE greater part of the Arthurian matter which has survived in the literatures of the Iberian Peninsula is to be found in Castilian impressions of the latest fifteenth or early sixteenth century, to which we can add sundry manuscripts in Castilian or Portuguese of approximately the same general date, and an important fragment in Catalan which bears the date 1380 in its colophon. This, together with a single leaf from a *Tristan* in Castilian and a reference in the colophon of one of the Portuguese romances, takes us back into the fourteenth century: but it is, generally speaking, true that most of what actually survives is in Castilian, is very late, and provides few indications as to its pedigree. To connect these dying romances—for they were soon snowed under by the immense novelistic output of the Caroline and Philippine eras in Spain—with their French originals of the thirteenth century, and to specify the time and manner of their introduction, the influences they felt or exerted, and their mutual relations, these are the objects of Arthurian research in the Peninsula. In such questions two generations of able minds have already been exercised, and our own day still awaits the long-announced and authoritative essay of D.

Adolfo Bonilla y San Martín,[1] who must either quench or rekindle the long debate. The beginnings of the discussion were illustrated by the labours of Pascual de Gayangos,[2] Amador de los Ríos and Milá y Fontanals. The catalogue of the whole chivalresque literature of Spain which was achieved by the former was a contribution of fundamental importance to all the knightly cycles of the Peninsula, and was utilised in illustration of *Don Quixote* by Ormsby;[3] and both Ormsby and the late Professor Fitzmaurice-Kelly[4] appear to have been following Gayangos when they conjectured a connection between the *Baladro del Sabio Merlin* and the *Historia di Merlino* of Messer Zorzi. Amador de los Ríos added to the subject a noteworthy competence in the study of Spanish manuscripts, and Milá y Fontanals displayed a more scientific spirit as well as an accurate knowledge of his native Catalan. These three distinguished scholars sifted the libraries for examples of, and the literature of Spain for references to, the *matière de Bretagne*, so that theory began to forge a chain of allusion between the surviving romances and their distant French originals. A parallel research in Portugal conducted by Varnhagen[5] and the ingenious Theophilo Braga

[1] In the third volume (Essays) which is to complete his edition of the *Libros de Caballerías* (*Nueva Biblioteca de Autores Españoles*, tt. vi. and xi.). Meanwhile his views are to be inferred from the preface to his *Tristan de Leonis* (*Sociedad de Bibliófilos Madrileños*, t. vi.) and his *Leyendas de Wagner* (Madrid, 1913).

[2] Gayangos, *Libros de Caballerías* (*Bibl. de Aut. Esp.*, t. xl.); Ríos, *Historia Crítica de la Literatura Española*, t. v.; Milá, *De la poesía heroico-popular castellana*, cap. x.

[3] *Don Quixote*, trans. J. Ormsby (London, 1885), *cf.* vol. iv., app. 2.

[4] Ormsby, *loc. cit.*; Fitzmaurice-Kelly, *Historia de la Literatura Española* (Madrid, 1921), p. 121, and earlier editions; *cf.* Gayangos, *Libros de Caballerías*, Intro. p. x, notes 5–7.

[5] *Da Litteratura dos Livros de Cavallarias* (Vienna, 1872).

emerged into a coherent and documented statement in the pronouncements of Dona Carolina Michaëlis de Vasconcellos;[1] whose conclusions—accessible to the English reader in the *Portuguese Literature* of Mr. Aubrey Bell,[2]—though impugned by G. Baist[3] in the same publication, were substantially adopted by the great Spanish critic of last generation, D. Marcelino Menéndez y Pelayo,[4] for his synthesis of scholarly opinion with regard to the entry and progress of Arthurian chivalry in Spain and Portugal. His exposition is of masterly sweep and lucidity, and his thesis is conciliatory, offering certain *a priori* attractions to critics on both sides of the border. Its cardinal position is that the *matière de Bretagne* was received from France not by the central kingdom but by the western; and so while conceding that Portuguese priority which the Portuguese critics claimed and yet claim, assigning as cause the strong Celtic infusion which is supposed to be found in their blood, it is acceptable to the Castilian because it adopts from Milá the attribution of the Castilian retardation to the obstacles presented by a more robust sense of reality and a self-conscious nationalism. Their passage to Portugal, like that of the Carolingian epics, was marked by the Pilgrims' Way to Santiago, that first cradle of Spanish Christian culture; but in respect of mere acquaintance with the romances, Catalonia, by virtue of its linguistic affinities with Provence and Languedoc, preceded either of the other Spanish kingdoms.

[1] *Grundriss der romanischen Philologie*, ii., 2, pp. 212 *ff.*, and elsewhere.
[2] Oxford, 1922, pp. 62–64. [3] *Grundriss*, ii., 2, pp. 416, 438, etc.
[4] *Origenes de la Novela*, i., pp. clix – clxxxiv, *Antologia de Poetas Liricos Castellanos* t. xii.

This theory, in which racial characteristics are permitted to play so imposing a rôle, finds a convenient basis in the speculations of Gaston Paris. In them the Celtic element, whether insular or continental, is prominent as containing not only the suggestions for, but also the primitive and veritable form of, the stories which came to be grouped into the French cycles; it is, therefore, particularly easy to step from the Gallic to the Lusitanian Celts, from the Arthurian novels of France to those of Galicia-Portugal. To lead up to this racial and temperamental affinity and to set the Peninsular novels in their European frame, Menéndez y Pelayo's exposition is fittingly prefaced by an admirable summary of the views of Gaston Paris, quarried out of the *Littérature Française au Moyen Âge*, the *Histoire Littéraire de la France* (t. xxx.), and the fifteenth, sixteenth and seventeenth volumes of *Romania*; but with that introduction we will venture to dispense, both because criticism north of the Pyrenees has somewhat changed its ground within more recent times, and because theories of Arthurian origins have no necessary relevance to the history of the Peninsular romances. In so doing, we but follow the lead of the learned English exponent of these views, Dr. Henry Thomas of the British Museum, whose introductory lecture to his *Spanish and Portuguese Romances of Chivalry* (1920) [1] summarises in a few pages present knowledge and opinion concerning Spanish and Portuguese Arthurian cycles. "Through the medium of the Provençal *troubadours* the Celtic legends reached Cata-

[1] H. Thomas, *Spanish and Portuguese Romances of Chivalry* (Cambridge, 1920), pp. 21–27.

lonia at an early date. . . . But these legends also followed the same route as the Charlemagne legends, and found an equally natural outlet in Galicia and Portugal, where there existed not only a flourishing school of lyric poetry, but also, we may assume, a kindred spirit — a heritage from early Celtic inhabitants, increased by communication with more thoroughly Celtic lands. . . . These lyrics (the five *Lays de Bretanha* of the *Cancioneiro Colocci-Brancutti*) are free translations from the French, and show how familiar the *matière de Bretagne* must have been to the Galician and Portuguese *trovadores* even in the thirteenth century. . . . During the fourteenth century they (the Arthurian romances) began to be translated into Castilian. There are two fragments of a Spanish *Tristan* in existence which are even ascribed to the first third of that century, but the period to which most of the translations belong is the latter part of the fourteenth and the fifteenth century. . . . The first type to establish itself successfully was the romance of chivalry in the sixteenth century." As a pendant to this theory it is usual to accept, with greater or less reserve, the hypothesis of the Portuguese origin of the great Arthurian derivative, the romance of *Amadis de Gaula*, by adopting one or other of the shadowy Lobeiras as its author; for by this device the whole chivalresque current is made to flow uniformly from the west to the centre of the Peninsula.

The intimate relations of politics, culture and speech which bound Catalonia to Provence made the literature of the Spanish Marches peculiarly responsive to foreign moods; and it was not many years after Bernard de Ventadorn had uttered the first allusion to Tristan and Iseut (1154) [1] that the Catalan-born troubadour Guiraut de Cabrera [2] appears in the full possession of the main strands of romance (*c.* 1170). His poem is an attack on the jongleur Cabra for his inefficient performances in song and on the viol, and for his ignorance of the most reputable subjects for verse. Guiraut speaks of Cardueill, Erec, Viviana, and perhaps Merlin, of Gawain, Arthur, Tristan, Iseut, and perhaps of Lancelot; but it might be reasonable to infer, from the pride which their knowledge seems to inspire in the troubadour, that these fashionable novelties were still the property of

[1] L. Sudré, *Les allusions à la légende de Tristan*, in *Romania*, t. xv.
[2] Milá y Fontanals, *De los Trobadores en España*, pp. 273 *ff*.

"Cabra juglar,
Non puesc mudar
Qu'eu non chan, pos a mi sab bon;
E volrai dir
Senes mentir,
E comtarai de ta faison.
Mal saps viular
E pietz chantar
Del cap tro en la fenizon;
Non sabz finir,
Al mieu albir,
A temperadura de Breton
. . . .
Non sabs d'Erec
Con conquistec
L'esparvier for de sa rejon
. . . .
Ni de Cardueill.
. . . .
Ni de Tristan
C'amava Yceut a lairon,
Ni de Gualvaing,
Qui ses conpaing
Fazia tanta venaison
. . . .
Ni d'Arselot la contençon."

But Arselot (according to Crescini, *Inchiesta del San Graal*, Intro.) is from *Arselot et Riquelme*, and not from *Lancelot du Lac* as Milá suggested.

a restricted circle. In such a restricted orbit it is quite probable that they moved for some centuries more, or even for the whole duration of Catalan literature; for although allusions to the *matière de Bretagne* can be combed out of the poetry of the next three centuries in some abundance, and though the romances themselves occupied much of the leisure of Pedro the Ceremonious, count of Barcelona and king of Aragon, nothing positive could be affirmed at the time when Menéndez y Pelayo finished writing (1905) concerning vernacular romances of this cycle, nor do we even now have access to more than an isolated story of the Holy Grail and a single leaf which describes Lancelot's skirmish with Sir Carados. We might even say, were it not for our fear of negative evidence, that the Breton legends proved uncongenial to the practical Catalan mind.

There was, however, one part of the Peninsula in which the Breton fictions found a second fatherland, whether on account of an occult affinity of ethnic origins, or by ancient communication with Celtic lands, or owing to the absence of a national epic capable of withstanding the impulse of imported narratives. Favoured by the prestige of lyric poetry, by courtly fashion, by the influence of chivalrous customs, they quickened the germ of indigenous inspiration; and from that trunk, already to all appearance rotten and dry, there sprang the prolific vegetation of *Amadis de Gaula*, the first type of the idealistic novel in Spain. It will be easily understood that I refer to the kingdoms of Galicia and Portugal, whose primitive Celticism (at least as a powerful element in its population, as also in Asturias and Cantabria) it would be an excess of scepticism to doubt, though we would not by any means adopt the dreams and fancies forged on this topic by the imagination of local archæologists. If the persistence of this primitive stratum be not conceded, not merely do noteworthy customs, beliefs and superstitions remain unexplained which yet live, as well as such singular instances of atavism as the rebirth of the Messianism of Arthur in King Sebastian, but enigmatic remains the development of chivalric literature, which was so deeply rooted there, which without effort conquered the imagination as if this was prepared for its reception, and which was imitated after a few generations with so much originality.

There, too, lyrical poetry was the vehicle of the Welsh and Armorican traditions.[1]

In the north-western corner of the Peninsula the native *cossantes* and the influence of Provençal models had combined to produce a technique of lyrical poetry and a dialect which was at the service not only of Galicians or Portuguese, but also of Leonese, Castilians, and even Italian strangers. Their references to contemporary literature are rare, but those which they dedicate to the Breton legends have been frequently collected and are now generally known. The earliest in date of these references stands under the name of Alfonso the Wise,[2] king of Leon and Castile, whose *Cantigas de Santa Maria* mention Brutus, Arthur and Merlin, and who in a love song of the *Cancioneiro* alludes to the similar sufferings of Tristan. His grandson, D. Diniz of Portugal, cites both Tristan and Iseult, and others mention Merlin, Cornish songs, and the Blatant Beast.[3] By these poems the circulation of Arthurian novels among the contributors to the Portuguese song-books of the early fourteenth century appears to be certified; but they yield in interest to the five curious lyrics, self-styled *Lais de Bretanha*, with which the collection known as the *Cancioneiro Colocci-Brancutti* commences (Nos. 1–5). These are ascribed by their

[1] Menéndez y Pelayo, *Orígenes de la Novela*, t. i., p. clxxi.

[2] *Cantigas de Santa Maria*, Nos. 35 and 108; *Cantigas de las Fiestas de Santa Maria*, No. 9; *Canzoniere Portoghese Colocci-Brancutti*, No. 468 (360).

[3] *Cancioneiro da Vaticana*, Nos. 115, 930, 1007 and 1140.

rubrics to Tristan himself, and their antiquity is supported by the assertion that one of them was "the first that was made"; and these *lais* have been held to prove the existence of a prose *Tristan* in a Portuguese dress as early as the thirteenth century.[1] The final ordering of the *Cancioneiros* was the work of the bastard son of King Diniz, D. Pedro, count of Barcellos,[2] who includes in his own *Nobiliario* or Book of Lineages (*Livro das Linhagens*) a chapter which is wholly devoted to Arthurian pseudo-history, in which he mentions not only Arthur, Lear and Merlin, but also Gawain, Lancelot and Avalon. To the supposed Galician original we might attribute the mention of Tristan and Merlin in the poem whereby Rodrigo Yáñez[3] celebrates the triumph of Castilian and Portuguese arms at the Río Salado in 1340. During the fourteenth century the Arthurian temperature continued to rise in Portugal. As early as 1359 Lançarote began to appear as a christian name, and we meet frequently such names as Lançarote, Tristão, Percival, Arturo, as also Iseu, Ginebra, Viviana, etc.[4] In the reign of Fernando the Handsome, Nun' Alvares Pereira chose as his model the hero of the Holy Grail, Sir Galahad;[5] and about the same time, doubtless, the passionate attachment of Pedro the Justiciar and Ines de Castro began to be con-

[1] C. Michaëlis de Vasconcellos, *Lais de Bretanha*, in *Revista Lusitana*, t. vi., and in *Cancioneiro da Ajuda*, t. ii. Of the second *lai* the rubric says, "Esta cantiga he a primeira que achamos que foy feita."

[2] *Livro das Linhagens*, titulo ii., in *Portugaliæ Monumenta Historica . . . Scriptores*, ed. Herculano.

[3] *Poema de Alfonso Onceno*, coplas 405, 242–5, and 1808–41.

[4] Th. Braga, *Curso de historia de litteratura portugueza*, 1885, pp. 144–8. (*As novelas da Tavola Redonda em Portugal.*)

[5] Fernam Lopes, *Chronica del Rei D. João I.*, ed. Braacamp Freire, 1915, p. 60.

strued in terms of the Tristan legend. For the historian of King John I. of Portugal the whole range of quotation is familiar from of old; so that, for example, *à propos* of the siege of Coria in 1385, he can quote the names of Galahad and Lancelot, Tristan, Keu and Arthur. These customs of chivalry were imitated in the Lovers' Wing (*Ala dos Enamorados*) which fought at the battle of Aljubarrota (1385), in the Order of the Knights of the Honeysuckle (*Cavalleiros da Madreselva*), and in the story of the twelve knights who visited England[1] at the request of John of Gaunt in order to support the honour of the English ladies.

We hear of works on Tristan, Merlin and Galahad as contained in the library of the unfortunate D. Duarte,[2] son of John I. and of Philippa of Lancaster, his wife, but nothing is said as to their language. There actually remain to us in Portuguese three books—a history of the *Destruction of Jerusalem* or of the *Emperor Vespasian* (1496), which was considered to have been the original of the corresponding Castilian work (1499) until the discovery by Haebler of another Castilian incunable of date approximately 1486; a manuscript entitled *Joseph Abaramatia*, written by a Dr. Alvarez in the reign of John III. of Portugal, but based on the work of an Astorgan schoolmaster, Joam Samchez, whose own language can only be inferred from the copy; and a *Historia dos cavalleiros da Mesa Redonda* which belongs to the fifteenth century, and is related to certain Spanish romances in a fashion about which it is

[1] Camões, *Os Lusiadas*, VI., vv. 43–69.

[2] D. Duarte, *Leal Conselheiro*, 1842, ed. J. I. Roquete, pp. xx–xxi (No. 29, *Livro de Tristam*; No. 32, *Merlim*; No. 35, *O livro de Galaaz*).

possible to dispute. The prominence which Grail romances assume in the relics of Portuguese Arthurian literature may actually imply a greater interest among them than among Castilians in the more visionary sections of the *matière de Bretagne*: but that they were the unique possession of the Portuguese people up to the middle of the fifteenth century is in itself improbable and an entirely improper deduction from a passage in the *Mar de Historias* of Fernán Pérez de Guzmán. The manuscript of the Grail cites its other parts (the *Joseph* and the *Merlin*) as also the *Conto*, *Livro* or *Romanço do Brado* (*Conte del Brait*), the *Estoria de Tristam*, the *Estoria Grande de Lançarote*, and the *Estoria de Parcival*, which are all probably to be considered as French romances and not as Portuguese; and "were we able to draw a conclusion from works later rehandled and printed in Spanish, there would be found further *Merlim* (*Baladro* and *Prophecias*, 1498 and 1500); *Joseph de Arimathia* (=*Vespasian*, 1496 Port. and 1498 Span.); *Santo Graal* or *Galaaz* (1515, 1535); *Tristan* (1501, 1528, 1533, 1534); *Lanzarote* (1528?); and *Parcival* (1526); and a separate *Artus* (1501)."[1] In this fashion quite a noteworthy but hypothetical literature might be evolved, but "unhappily most of the early Portuguese versions of the Breton legends have been lost."[2]

To the feverish poetry of amorous delirium, to the gallantry that was frequently adulterous, to the distant and fantastic adventures of the *matière de Bretagne* a firm resistance was offered by the soul

[1] *Grundriss der romanischen Philologie*, ii. 2, p. 214, n. 4.
[2] A. F. G. Bell, *Portuguese Literature*, p. 63.

of Castile, clear, practical and austere, preoccupied by the reconquest of its soil, the defence of its faith, and the assertion of its nationality. The introduction of the Breton cycle into Castile was not early; bound up with a new chivalry which was at once less heroic and more refined than the Carolingian, it did not conform with the grave character of Castilian knighthood.[1] Allusions to it are rare before the fourteenth century. The earliest of these is found in the *Anales Toledanos Primeros*,[2] fasti which conclude with the year 1219, and it consists of the bare statement that "Arthur fought Mordred in Camlan in the Era 580," *i.e.* in the year 542. Some fifty years later than the *Anales*, the *Grande et General Estoria* of Alfonso the Wise "extracts from the chronicle of Geoffrey of Monmouth, which the king entitles the *Estoria de las Bretañas*, all the feats attributed to the son of Sylvius, without forgetting the stories of Corineus and Locrinus, of Lady Gwendolen and Mandon, Ferrex and Porrex, Brennus and Belinus," etc.;[3] and the *Gran Conquista de Ultramar*, which was completed under the reign of his successor, finds leisure to note the "Round Table in King Arthur's days," as well as to give at length the story of the Swan Knight (*à propos* of Godfrey de Bouillon). Don Juan Manuel mentions in his *Libro de la Caza*[4] (written before 1325) falcons named Lanzarote and Galvan, the latter having pertained at one time to D. Enrique, brother of Alfonso X. The name of

[1] Milá y Fontanals, *De la poesía heroico-popular castellana*, cap. x., *Del Ciclo Bretón*.

[2] *España Sagrada*, t. xxiii. p. 381.

[3] Amador de los Ríos, *Historia Critica de la Literatura Española*, t. v. p. 29.

[4] Ed. Baist, p. 42.

Lanzarote is given to a child before a Spanish font in 1344; while the previous year offers an allusion to Tristan from the *Cantiga de los Clerigos de Talavera* of the ribald Archpriest of Hita.[1] A translation of Egidio Colonna's *De Regimine Principum* executed in Castilian before 1350 by Johan García de Castrogeriz[2] brackets *Tristan* with *Cifar* and *Amadis*, the two earliest indigenous romances of chivalry; and the author of the *Poema de Alfonso Onceno* is, as we have already shown, familiar with the harp of Tristan and the prophecies (or at least prophetical recipe) of Merlin. Towards the end of this same fourteenth century, between 1367 and 1403, the turncoat and chancellor D. Pero López de Ayala brackets *Lancelot* and *Amadis* among the books wherewith he destroyed many valuable hours—presumably those of his early youth; but his penitence did not sink so deep as to prevent him from recurring to the Arthurian conventions and to Merlin for the climax of his *Cronica del Rey Don Pedro*, perhaps the most highly worked, though hardly the most effective, piece of mediæval Spanish prose.[3] D. Pero López de Ayala left his work uncompleted in the reign of Henry III. of Castile, and Gutierre

[1] Juan Ruiz, *Libro de Buen Amor*, copla 1703:

> "Ca nunca fue tan leal Blanca Flor a Frores,
> Nin es *agora* Tristan con todos sus amores."

[2] *Revue Hispanique*, t. xv. p. 815.

[3] Pero López de Ayala, *Rimado de Palacio*, copla 162:

> "Plogome otrosi oyr muchas vegadas,
> Libros de devaneos e mentiras probadas,
> Amadis, Lanzalote e burlas asacadas,
> En que perdi mi tiempo a muy malas jornadas";

and *Cronica del Rey Don Pedro*, año xviii. cap. 22 and año xx. cap. 3.

Diez de Games,[1] who writes in the reign of that monarch, likewise mentions the fashionable interest in Merlin. "With the coming of each new king, they make a new Merlin: they say that that king is to cross the sea and destroy all Mohammedanism, and win the Holy Places, and become Emperor; and thereafter we see things turn out as God wills them." And such a new Merlin was Alfonso Alvarez de Villasandino,[2] the false prophet of the conquest of the Moors, the reunion of Christendom, and other marvels. As a result of his researches in Normandy and Brittany during the years 1405–6, which the author had spent very happily harrying the south coast of England and the island of Jersey, Diez de Games propounded an account of the first settlement of England by Brutus, Æneas' grandson, together with the history of his wife Dorothea, and other delectable fictions which are not to be found in Geoffrey of Monmouth's work. In the reign of John II. of Castile, a Jew named Juan Alfonso de Baena collected the poetical *nugæ* of the court into the notorious *Cancionero de Baena* (1445); which, whatever real merit it may have excluded from its covers, is a veritable arsenal of Arthurian citations.[3] One of its oldest contributors, Pero Ferrús (*d.* 1379), addressing the chancellor Ayala, speaks of Arthur, Lancelot, Galahad and Tristan in addition to the Carolingian peers, and mentions explicitly the three books of

[1] Gutierre Diez de Games, *Cronica de Don Pedro Niño*, ed. Llaguno, pp. 29–30.

[2] *Cancionero de Baena*, No. 199.

[3] *Cancionero de Baena*, No. 305. *Cf.* Menéndez y Pelayo, *Historia de la poesía lírica castellana en la Edad Media*, t. i. p. 385. *Cancionero de Baena*, Nos. 38, 149, 124, 199, 209, 226, 249, 301, 305, 331=533, 485, 572, 116 and 234.

Amadis. "The undigested erudition of Pero Ferrús," says Menéndez y Pelayo, "has to-day the advantage of showing us the precise time at which the novels of the Breton cycle entered Spain, and the culminating point to which their prestige and influence attained." The allusions name constantly the chivalresque trinity of Lancelot, Tristan and Amadis, and their ladies, Guenevere, Iseut and Oriana, and we further meet with Arthur, Galahad, Merlin, the Grail, King Ban, Bademagus, Joseph of Arimathia (who is more famous than the Virgin's husband!), and Brius *sans pitié*; and the references are found equally among the old Conservatives of the type of Villasandino and among the new school of Italian allegorists who followed Francisco Imperial. The illustrious Marquis of Santillana, the most notable exile from Baena's book of quips, is equally acquainted with Tristan, Lancelot and Gallehault;[1] and his relative, Fernán Pérez de Guzmán,[2] who had already contributed notices of Guenevere and Iseut to the *Cancionero*, discussed both Merlin and the Holy Grail in his *Mar de Historias*. Tristan and Lancelot are known to the other picaresque archpriest of mediæval Spain, him of Talavera,[3] and the books of the Grail cycle and of Sir Lancelot were to be seen in the hands of Isabel the Catholic.[4]

[1] Santillana, *Triunfete de Amor*, in *Obras*:

"Vi Tristan e Lançarote
E con el a Galeote,
Discreto e sotil mediante."

[2] *Cancionero de Baena*, No. 572, and *Mar de Historias*, capp. xcvi. and civ.

[3] *El Arcipreste de Talavera*, parte IV. cap. vi.

[4] Nos. 142, 143 and 144 of her library, according to Clemencín's inventory in *Memorias de la Academia de Historia*, t. vi.

Two popular ballads are dedicated to Lancelot and one to Tristan, both being of respectable antiquity;[1] but Durán has argued that so small a number proves the indifference of the general public, and it is even possible that the later fifteenth century saw a general decline of interest in the chivalresque themes, if we may measure opinion by the frequency of lyrical citations.[2] It is as if the manuscript circulation was exhausted and the new public of the printing presses had not begun.

Such is the long, allusive approach to the surviving Spanish romances; but before taking the final step it would be well to consider the weight of the evidence offered for the priority of Portugal. It is not easy to say how far Menéndez y Pelayo is wedded to his exposition, for he is rather a historical critic of literature than a literary historian, and we feel that he is not curious to determine the *minutiæ* which go to form documented history.[3] It is quite possible that, as a historical dogma, Portuguese priority is hardly a matter of interest to him, and that his intention was artistic—to clear away his French, Catalan and Portuguese notes before reaching his true theme of the Castilian novels—even as he has preferred to direct his Arthurian criticism toward the French stage in order to reserve his Castilian observations for the national romances, *Amadis*, *Cifar*, *Tirant lo Blanch*. The Portuguese

[1] Durán, *Romancero General*, Nos. 351, 352 and 353.

[2] G. Baist, *Grundriss der romanischen Philologie*, ii. 2, p. 441.

[3] A curious instance of his detachment from detail is contained in the reference to the *Baladro del Sabio Merlín* (*Origenes de la Novela*, I. p. clxxxiii). He is content to direct the reader to G. Paris and Ulrich, *Merlin*. Yet they gained their knowledge of the *Baladro* from or by Menéndez y Pelayo himself (*cf. Merlin, Roman en Prose*, I. p. lxxiii).

apologists, such as Th. Braga, Snra. de Vasconcellos, J. J. Nunes and Mr. A. F. G. Bell, are of necessity more deeply implicated; yet their theory has certain grave weaknesses. The greater number of the supposed Portuguese texts have to be hewn by mere hypothesis out of the Castilian relicts themselves. Extant in Portuguese, the reader will recollect, we have only two sections of the *Holy Grail*, and they are both objects of controversy. Not that we wish to deny the existence of vernacular romances of the Round Table in the western kingdom, nor to subscribe to the sweeping assertion of G. Baist that "the Castilians employ narrative and prose, the Portuguese the lyric, they translate Castilian prose."[1] It is altogether probable that a considerable and early literature of novels has been lost not only in Portugal, but also in Spain and Catalonia; but it must be confessed that what is itself hypothetical is a shifty foundation for the further hypothesis of Portugal's Arthurian priority. The circumstance that both Portuguese fragments pertain to the cycle of the Grail has tempted some scholars, notably Amador de los Ríos and O. Klob, to torture in this sense a passage from the *Mar de Historias* of Fernán Pérez de Guzmán.[2] Pérez de Guzmán (1376?–1460?) says of the

[1] *Grundriss der romanischen Philologie*, ii. 2, p. 441.

[2] For this discussion see Ríos, *Hist. Crit. de la Lit. Esp.*, t. v. p. 76; O. Klob in *Zeitschrift für rom. Phil.*, xxvi. p. 180; G. Baist, in *Zeitschrift für rom. Phil.*, xxxi. pp. 605–7; and my note in *Modern Language Review*, xviii. pp. 206–8. Pérez de Guzmán, *Mar de Historias*, cap. xcvi. (Del stõ grial), reads: "Del imperio de leon año d'l señor de dccxxx fue en bretaña avn hermitaño fecha vna marauillosa reuelacion segun se dize: la qual diz que le reuelo vn angel d' vn grial o escudilla que tenia josep abarimatia en que ceno nuestro señor jp̃u xh̃o el jueues dela cena. Dela qual reuelacion el dicho hermitaño escriuio vna estoria q̃ es dicha del sancto grial: esta historia no se halla en latin sino en

Grail that "this story is not found in Latin but in French," implying (according to Ríos) that it was not current in Castilian, or rather (according to Klob) that the Peninsular rendering was still confined to Portuguese territory. That these implications are dubious has already been noted by Baist: if true, we might still inquire into the competence of the writer, seeing that to establish a negation requires a high certificate of bibliographical attainment. But it so happens that the whole of the passage in question has descended to the Castilian, through Giovanni Colonna and Vincent de Beauvais, from the ancient Helinandus of Beauvais[1] (*c.* 1227), who not only makes the statement concerning the language of the *Grail*, but also is the begetter of the characteristically "Castilian" distrust of fabling when he discriminates between the more and the less verisimilar and useful (*verisimiliora et utiliora*) portions of the story. Pérez de Guzmán's passage implies, if anything, that the Grail-story was of some interest for Castile—and why not in Castilian? That the first part, the *Joseph Abarimatia*, was well known is a tolerable inference from the caution of Nicolás de Valencia that the Blessed Virgin was mated "with St. Joseph, not him of Arimathea";[2] and that the second part, the *Merlin*, might be used to alleviate the strain of reading Holy Writ appears from the "complete vernacular Bible with a little of the book of Merlin"

frances: and dizese que algunos nobles la escriuieron. La qual quanto quier q̃ sea deleitable de leer and dulce: enpero por muchas cosas estrañas que enella se cuentã asaz deuele ser dada poca fe."

[1] For Helinandus, see Migne, *Patrologia*, t. ccxii. p. 815, and *Modern Language Review*, *loc. cit.*

[2] *Cancionero de Baena*, No. 485:

"Con santo Joseph non de Abazimatia."

which stood in the Count of Benavente's library about the year 1440.[1]

If the texts are insufficient to sustain the Portuguese thesis, still less can be demanded of the allusions. In respect of absolute priority, the entry in the *Anales Toledanos Primeros* anticipates all other Castilian or Portuguese citations by almost half a century; and the name of Alfonso X., who heads the list of allusions in the *Cancioneiros*, belongs impartially to either literature. We find, it is true, a mass of references in these song-books at an earlier date than a similar mass can be noted in Castile; but that phenomenon is obedient, not to the presence or absence of Arthurian novels, but to the gravitation from Galicia to Castile of the courtly lyric —the most natural repository of allusions to the Arthurian *amour courtois*. They might, indeed, be wholly referred to the influence of a Provençal convention;[2] and their existence is quite an insufficient guarantee of the presence of prose-romances in the vernacular. Similar difficulties are presented by the attempt to transmute the five *lais de Bretanha* into a Portuguese *Tristan* of the thirteenth century.

The theory, therefore, must stand or fall by its first principle, the Celtic descent of the Portuguese people. "It was but natural that a Celtic people living by the sea, delighting in vague legends and in foreign novelties, should have felt drawn towards these misty tales of love and wandering adventure,

[1] R. Beer, *Handschriftenschätze Spaniens*, para. 67, No. 29: "Brivia complida en romance con un poco del libro de Merlin, en papel cebti mayor, con tablas de madero cubierto de cuero blanco."

[2] Baist, *Grundriss der rom. Phil.*, ii. 2, p. 438: "Wenn Alfonso X. einmal Tristan, Iseu und Artus nennt, so ist dass nur Reflex der provenzalischen Dichtung."

which carried them west as far as Cornwall and Ireland, and also east, through the search for the Holy Grail. It was natural that they should undergo their influence earlier and more strongly than their more direct and more national neighbours the Castilians, whose clear, definite descriptions in the twelfth-century *Poema del Cid* would send those legends drifting back to the dim regions of their birth. (Even to-day connection with and sympathy for Ireland is far commoner in Galicia than in any other part of Spain.)"[1] The last phrase of special pleading recalls the story of Florián de Ocampo,[2] the Spanish archæologist of the sixteenth century, who was wrecked off Waterford and was well received by the Irish, who affirmed that they also were Spaniards (by race at least, for they had to speak in signs); but Ocampo remembered that Ireland had been colonised by one of the paulo-post-diluvian kings of Spain, Brigus by name. And who can doubt King Brigus, who is not only certified by "Berosus" and Annius Viterbiensis, but also by the very name of all the Brigidas or Bridgets of the distressful country? We do not question some Celtic element in Galicia; but we still lack proof that it is more there than elsewhere in the Peninsula. Woe, indeed, to the man whom ambition or profession should drive to the study of Hispanic origins in the authors of antiquity! Yet these authors have hardly anything more probable to say than the doctrine of Pliny,[3] that the

[1] Bell, *Portuguese Literature*, p. 63.

[2] Cirot, *Les Histoires Générales d'Espagne*, p. 121.

[3] The reader will find almost all that can be known about the Hispanic Celts (as well as a little more) in D'Arbois de Jubainville, *Les Celtes en Espagne*, in *Revue Celtique*, xiv. and xv.

Celtici of the Anas are an offshoot of the main body of Celts in Castile, and that the Galician Celts are a defeated remnant of the Lusitanian. The main strength of Celtic place-names or tribal appellations lines the hills that overlook the Ebro valley; thence they string out lineally down the Tagus and the Douro, and find their outposts south of the Tagus estuary and close to Finisterra. The argument from culture may be equally unfortunate. The Messianism of Arthur and Sebastian, for example, on which Menéndez y Pelayo rests some weight, is hardly conclusive evidence of Celtic persistence when we further consider the Messianism of the Mahdi, the Buddha and the Messiah. Furthermore, our unbelieving generation has been taught to distinguish between race, language and culture, three human factors which often combine in a movement of civilisation, but which can never be argued to imply each other; and the evidence for the Hispanic Celts is chiefly linguistic (toponymic, in fact), and so not racial. If, however, the Celt is to be admitted into our argument (albeit that in most arguments the Celt is a fallacy), let him not merely be the Celt of Nerium, but also the Celts of Segontia, Segobriga and Segovia. And there is still one more suspicion to be whispered against this Celtic nationality of Portugal, namely, that it exists on sufferance. The Castilian has been too much preoccupied with the "Iberian" and the Goth (who present a convenient antithesis to the Celts or Franks of France) to devote much interest to his own Celtic origins. These he is quite willing to concede as a badge of distinction to his Portuguese neighbour. Yet the Celt, *teste* D'Arbois de Jubainville, abounded on the Central Plateau. The Galician might find a more peculiar mark in the Suevi of his kingdom, who are neatly distinguished from the Castilian's Visigoths, and who, being almost wholly unknown, afford a more excellent basis for theory—for any theory.

III

THE INTRODUCTION OF ARTHURIAN ROMANCE INTO CASTILE AND PORTUGAL

Our knowledge, perhaps, does not entitle us to bring the whole body of Arthurian literature in Spain and Portugal within the scope of a single theory. To do so we would require to obtain from the texts all the particulars of their origin, authorship and history; and the texts are far from committing their secrets to the first searcher. Some facts we shall obtain, and by working from them through hints and analogies we may reach probable conclusions over the whole field.

It is particularly instructive in this sense to consider the fortunes of the *Historia Regum Britonum* of Geoffrey of Monmouth in the Iberian Peninsula. He enjoys an absolute priority over the prose novels, which follow him in France at two removes, being separated from him by a mass of Arthurian verse; and he enjoys a relative priority in Spain, both because the language in which he writes (Latin) entitles him to an earlier hearing than would French, and because his standing as a historian is one that would more promptly attract notice than if he had given himself out to be a mere novelist. Thus the first use of his work, as we hope to prove, in Castile is contemporary with the composition of the prose cycles in France. Now it happens that we can discuss the introduction of the *Historia* into the Peninsula with some feeling of assurance. Many historical figures have been named as possible originators or disseminators of Arthurian chivalry in Spain, and so long as it was fashionable to fix one's gaze wholly on the fourteenth century, it was impossible to pass over unnoticed the irruption of Edward the Black Prince in 1367.[1] He may have heated the chivalresque temper which was already exemplified by the order of the Knights of the Scarf,[2] but we can document with reference to him but one effect on Peninsular chivalry: when the Maréchal d'Andreghem, who had been paroled by the English in France, was captured in the opposing ranks at Nájera (1367), he defended himself from an accusation of treachery by contending that a French parole was not binding in a Spanish quarrel; and this precedent has been noted by López de Ayala, Fernam Lopes and Mossen Bernat Boades.[3] With the Prince of Wales it is possible to cite such men as Sir Hugh Calveley who supported the first invasion of Henry of Trastamara (1366), or Bertrand du Guesclin[4] who became in Spain one of the "Worthies"; as well as Edmund earl of Cambridge, later duke of York, who fought or wished to fight in Portugal in the year 1381, and John of Gaunt who was present at the battle of Nájera (1367), conducted some

[1] H. Thomas, *Spanish and Portuguese Romances of Chivalry*, p. 28.

[2] The Caballeros de la Banda, *Cronica de Alfonso Onceno*, cap. xcix.

[3] Ayala, *Cronica de Pedro I.*, año 18, cap. 13; Fernam Lopes, *Chronica de D. Fernando*, cap. x.; Boades, *Llibre dels Feyts d'Armes de Catalunya* (Relación del desafío del senescal de Francia con el príncipe de Gales, en lemosín, Escorial MS. 105, iii. 4).

[4] Amador de los Ríos, *Hist. Crit. de la Lit. Esp.*, t. v., cites him in connection with the Spanish Arthurian novels.

campaigns in Galicia (1386–8), was the father of the first queen of the house of Aviz and the grandfather of her brilliant progeny, and became a figure in the Portuguese tale of the *Twelve of England.* Earlier in the fourteenth century the English earls of Derby and Salisbury took part in the siege of Algeciras (1343),[1] at which the Knight of the *Prologue*[2] served with more persistence. Indeed, in the year 1343 or thereabout Castile was swarming with Englishmen and even with Englishwomen, who were attracted by the wars of the south and by the pilgrimages of the north of the Peninsula, so that for a poet of that time Jew and Gentile, Greek and Barbarian, native and foreigner, can be perfectly expressed by Castilian and English.[3] All these, and the Douglas who fought in Valencia, are potential conductors of Arthurian stories, quite apart from the uninterrupted and unmeasured stream of direct French influence that has always flowed across the Pyrenees. Picturesque enthusiasts for chivalrous ideals are but too embarrassingly common in the Spain of the fourteenth century, and it is similar in the thirteenth. We then have Edward Longshanks,[4]

[1] The Earl of Derby is mentioned in *Cronica de Alfonso XI.*, cap. ccxcii., and *Poema de Alfonso XI.*, coplas 2240 and 2272–81.

[2] The Knight continued to fight at sea.

> "In Gernade at the sege eek hadde he be
> Of Algezir, and riden in Belmarye." *Prol.* 56–7.

[3] Juan Ruiz, *Libro de Buen Amor*, copla 1224:

> "Matando e degollando e desollando reses,
> Dando a cuantos venían, castellanos e ingleses."

The Wife of Bath had been "in Galice at Seint Jame" (*Prol.* 466); and other instances may be found in A. Farinelli, *Viajes en España*. For the Douglas see Froissart (Globe Ed.), p. 27.

[4] For Edward see López Ferreira, *Historia . . . de Santiago de Compostela*, t. v. p. 76; Muntaner, capp. 71–92; Desclot, capp. 100, 104–5. For Sancho see Menéndez Pidal, *Poema de Mio Cid* (1911), t. iii. p. 640.

who accepted his wife and his spurs from Alfonso the Wise at Burgos in 1254, and whose visit was repaid by Sancho in the year following. Sancho, at least, had some cultural value, seeing that he first offered to English eyes the spectacle of a man walking on tapestry or carpets, and so caused no little scandal. Edward is likewise the villain of a chivalresque episode in the chronicles of Desclot and Muntaner, for he failed to clear the lists at Bordeaux when the King of Aragon wanted to fight the King of France; and his connection with the compilation of Rustician of Pisa makes him an object of interest for the Spanish *Tristan*. Another figure of this century is that of Affonso, count of Boulogne, who ascended the Portuguese throne in 1248.

> Seeing that the French redactions are dated, the first between 1210 and 1220, and the second 1230, it is by no means impossible that the count of Boulogne and those who were with him in France—at latest, from 1238 to 1245—should have caught the fashion there, not merely for pastorals and ballets, but also for the latest prose novelties on the *matière de Bretagne*—a predilection which spread and must sooner or later, I believe in the early years of D. Denis, lead to the nationalisation of the French texts.[1]

No one, so far as we are aware, has ventured to go back as far as the twelfth century nor to name a lady; and yet in that sex and century we may find a person who can be, almost evidentially, connected

[1] C. Michaëlis de Vasconcellos, *Lais de Bretanha*, in *Revista Lusitana*, t. vi. p. 27: "E como as redacções francesas datam, a primeira de 1210 a 20, e a segunda de 1230, não seria de modo algum impossivel que o Bolonhês e os que com elle assistiram em França—a mais tardar de 1238 a 1245—ahi se afeiçoassem, não só ao genero das pastorelas e balletas, mas tambem ás últimas novidades em prosa sobre matière de Bretagne—predilecção que, propagando-se, devia mais tarde ou mais cedo, creio que na mocidade de D. Denis, conduzir á nacionalização dos textos franceses."

with the first stirrings of the Arthurian spirit in Spain.[1] Eleanor or Leonor, daughter of Henry II. of England, was a very considerable person both in her native land of Gascony and in her adopted home in Spain. In the former she was the daughter of that Eleanor of Aquitaine who was the grand patroness of the troubadours, and to whom such works as the *Roman de Troye* were respectfully dedicated. Much of the poem of Kiot, which later became the *Parzival* of Wolfram von Eschenbach, was devoted to the illustration of her Angevin antecessors. Her father had received the dedication of the third edition (1154) of Geoffrey's *Historia Regum Britonum*, had discovered the tomb of Arthur in the Abbey of Glastonbury, was the patron of Map, whether he be real or a fiction, and received the genuine or spurious dedications of so many of the Arthurian novelists of his own age and of the next. Leonor herself brought her husband within the inner circle of European politics and maintained with regard to him a position of at least equality; for if we know the Angevins, we may be reasonably sure that she was not the pale, injured figure imagined by the various dramatists for the story of *La Judía de Toledo* or *Raquel*. Her son set a precedent for the name of Henry in Spanish royalty, she founded the monastery of Las Huelgas, and she conducted a war against John of England in respect of her claims on Gascony. This war almost cost England the pos-

[1] I refer the reader who desires a more technical statement to my article on *Geoffrey of Monmouth and Spanish Literature* in the *Modern Language Review*, vol. xvii. pp. 381–391. Thanks to the notice of the *Cronica de* 1404, which I owe to the scholarship and kindness of Miss Janet Perry of King's College, London, the present chapter can press the conclusions of that article yet further.

session of that mediæval dependency, and it might well have altered the course of history. It was prosecuted with decreasing vigour, and was terminated by the marriage of Edward Longshanks with another Leonor of Castile in 1254. With Richard she lived on terms of friendship. Besides being the most famous commander and military engineer of the age, he was, like herself, an Aquitanian by preference; and he is remembered in Arthurian circles as the patron of that Bernard de Ventadorn who first names Tristan, and (vicariously) as the purveyor into Germany of the original of Ulrich von Zatzikhoven's *Lanzelet*. He was the close friend of Alfonso II. of Aragon, who did not lack acquaintance with Arthur and the Arthurians.[1] Leonor, too, with her husband, was a patroness of letters, in touch with such poets as Bertran de Born and Ramón Vidal de Bezaudú; and she was quite capable of apprcciating an Arthurian allusion.[2]

[1] Alfonso II., as a patron of troubadours, would at least know the satire of Guiraut de Cabrera. Of his son Pedro II. it is said:

> "E ditz cel que las a rimadas
> Que anc lo reis Artus non vi
> Mas contar tot plan e auzi
> En la cort del plus honrat rei
> Que anc fos de neguna lei:
> Aço es lo rei d'Aragon
> Peire de pretz e fillz de don," etc.

Cf. Milá, *De los Trobadores en España* (1889), t. ii. of *Obras*, p. 151 n.

[2] For these points see Milá, *op. cit.*, pp. 117, 133 n. and 123. Bertran de Born hopes that Alfonso VIII. will interfere in the war of Richard Cœur de Lion and Philippe Auguste (1196–1199). Ramón Vidal de Bezaudú describes a literary event at the court of Alfonso VIII.:

> "E cant la cort complida fo
> Venc la reyn' Elionors
> Et anc negus no vi son cors.
> Estrecha venc en un mantel
> D'un drap de seda bon e bel
> Que hom apela sisclato

To sum up. If we are given a lady of fair character and literary propensities, and a book dedicated to her father is found to have been used in the court of her son in a document which is devoted chiefly to the affairs of her own reign, then it is reasonable to suppose that she, her entourage and her trousseau are the probable link between the original and the copy. If we also find that further references to this book are made by her great-grandson and his great-grandson, we may presume that it is a case of transmission through her family. And if we find that early knowledge of the whole Arthurian legend can be related to her descendants and their immediate dependants, to her great-grandson, his grandson and his great-grandson—all persons of literary eminence—we are almost compelled to assume for the earlier stages of Arthurian manuscripts in the vernacular the same or part of the same history of family transmission.

A contemporary of this Queen Leonor entered the first Castilian allusion to the Arthurian novels in a line of the *Anales Toledanos Primeros* [1] under the

Vermelhs ab lista d'argent fo
E y hac un levon d'aur devis.
Al rey soplega, pueis s'assis
Ad una part, lonhet de lui."

Guiraut de Calansó in an elegy on D. Fernando of Castile (1211) says:

"Qu'en lui era tot lo pretz restauratz
Del rey Artus qu'om sol dir e retraire,
On trobavan cosselh tug bezonhos."

[1] *España Sagrada*, t. xxiii. p. 381. In the *Modern Language Review*, xvii. (1922) p. 383, the present writer, following Milá and Menéndez y Pelayo, read: "Lidio el rey Citus con Mordret en Camlenc. Era MLXXX.," and argued that this figure was read in error for DLXXX. DLXXX. is given by both the British Museum copies of *España Sagrada*, and is correctly reported by Dr. H. Thomas in his *Spanish and Portuguese Romances of Chivalry*, chap. i.

year 542 A.D. (Julian era 580): "Lidio el Rey Zitus con Mordret su sobrino en Camblenc, Era DLXXX." The same date is given by the Conde Dom Pedro de Barcellos [1] in the second title of his *Livro das Linhagens* or *Nobiliario*, in a passage that summarises the *Historia Regum Britonum* of Geoffrey of Monmouth; and as dates are most fallible and perishable, and as this one was lost to the Arthurian Legend as early as the *Brut* of Wace, it is clear that the scribe of the Toledan Annals must have had in front of him a copy of the *Historia* itself. His work closes with the year 1219. These lists of dates were liable to frequent transcription and revision, but there is nothing in so meagre a statement that suggests an earlier knowledge of the *Historia*; its introduction into the Spanish Peninsula, therefore, we cannot define more precisely than as lying between the year of Queen Leonor's marriage and that of the *Anales Toledanos Primeros*, that is, between 1170 and 1219.

The copy which stood on the royal bookshelves was the source of the many references made by the Wise Alfonso to Geoffrey's work in the course of the vast compilation known as the *Grande et General Estoria*,[2] of which there is an authorised or "Chamber" edition dated 1280, a work not incommensurate with the encyclopædic Cambridge Histories. Its core is a translation of the whole Bible, supplemented, how-

[1] *Hist. Reg. Brit.*, lib. xi. cap. ii.: "Anno ab incarnatione dominica quingentesimo quadragesimo secundo." So *Nobiliario*, tit. ii.: "Esta batalha foy na era de quinhemtos e oytenta annos." On the other hand, *Brut*: "Sis cens et quarante deus ans"; and *Annales Cambriæ*: "537. Gueith Camlann in qua Arthur et Medraut corruerunt."

[2] For information concerning the *Grande et General Estoria* I am indebted to the courtesy of Don A. G. Solalinde, who permitted me to use the materials he has collected towards an edition of the work.

ever, by an inspiration of fine impartiality, from the Koran and other religious sources; parallel to, and interrupting, these translations is a history of the world due chiefly to Petrus Comestor. From the remotest fables of Ovid (moralised by John the Englishman) the narrative continues through the *Æneid* of Virgil and various historical sources up to the birth of Christ, and there the profane account has been broken off, though the Scriptural narrative continues into the unfinished *Quinta Parte.* Æneas naturally suggested the name of his grandson Brutus; and as Geoffrey had given his fictions probability by a liberal use of Biblical chronology, the royal compiler had only to mark his place at a convenient reference and return to his central translation. Thus we find scattered over the second, third and fourth parts of this Universal History a full and literal translation of the Bishop of St. Asaph's work, which Alfonso calls the *Estoria de las Bretannas,* from the third chapter of the first book until the eighth of the third. The passages omitted are the verses of the oracle (for which a blank space is allowed in the manuscript, and a prose paraphrase appended), the various dedications, and the chapter in praise of Britain. Declining the decadent gesticulations of the Welshman's Latinity as being unsuited to the modesty of a young idiom, and falling into occasional confusions when compelled to recapitulate, Alfonso is generally direct, adequate and uniform, though not eminently personal in his style. He breaks off the story of Brennus and Belinus in order to shape its conclusion according to the orthodox Livian narrative preserved by Godfrey of

Viterbo's *Pantheon*; so that, apart from what we know of the traditions of his family and successors, we cannot conjecture how he might have treated King Arthur. In his earlier *Primera Cronica General* or *Estoria de Espanna* (*c.* 1268) he happened to be following different originals, and his editorship so resembles that of a pair of scissors that he made no reference to Geoffrey for Arthur, nor even for Gratian Municeps, Constantine and Helena, or the fabulous settlement of Ireland by the Barclenses of Spain.

The tradition of royal authorship is continued in D. Pedro de Barcellos (*d.* 1350), Alfonso's great-grandson, the reputed and probable author of the greatest part of the *Nobiliario* or Book of Lineages (*Livro das Linhagens*).[1] This is the first important effort of Portuguese prose, and in this manner occupies a position analogous to that of Alfonso X.'s compilations, to several of which it is indebted. The first and second *Livros das Linhagens* were dry annotations of small interest, but the later versions have been remodelled on a wider plan, more broadly based in history and fable, employing a style that is brief, naïve and frequently graceful, admirably adapted to story-telling. It is less easy to assign a date to the work, represented as it is by a sixteenth-century manuscript and entered up to the date of Pedro the Cruel's death (1369), and a dozen other authors have added their labours to those of the Count of Barcellos; but it seems reasonable to assign the bulk of the work to the first third of the four-

[1] *Portugaliæ Monumenta Historica—Scriptores*, i. pp. 236–245. Titulo ii. is omitted in the Roman edition of 1640, by Estevam Paolino, as irrelevant to the interest of the work.

teenth century, and to credit the plan to D. Pedro himself. Into the plan, forming the genealogical chain between the Iberian monarchs and nobility and the most respectable antiquity, enters this Titulo Segundo of the Kings of Troy, and how they come from the lineage of Dardanus who first peopled Troy; of the Kings of Rome and of Julius Cæsar [and] Augustus; and of Brutus who peopled Britain, and of Constantine, of King Arthur, etc. The chapter contains a very brief summary of the whole *Historia Regum Britonum*, ending with the return of Ivor and Ini to Britain, where the author concludes—a little incoherently: "So far comes the direct lineage of the Kings of Troy and of Dardanus. Dardanus who peopled it first; and King Priam and his sons. And Brutus peopled Britain; and Utherpadragon and King Arthur of Britain. Constantine who preceded Arthur by a long time; and from Cadwalech to Cauadres. Here ends this genealogy of the Kings of Britain; henceforward the land was in the power of other kings who were lords of Britain, which we call England." The author's purpose is genealogy, and he omits the prophecies of Merlin and all his personal history, as well as the "praises" and "wonders" of Britain, and the names both of the author and of the work. For a few brief lines he allows himself to expand in an account of King Lear, which is justly remembered in Portugal; this allows us to note that he, like Alfonso, was following a manuscript of the Bishop of St. Asaph no whit different from the vulgate of 1154.[1]

[1] For the editions of Geoffrey, *cf.* Dr. S. Evan's Appendix to his translation of Geoffrey (Dent, "Temple Classics").

D. Pedro gives two dates: that of the Battle of Camlan as already cited, and that of Cadwallader's demise, 699 A.D.[1] His summary is marked to an unusual degree by palæographical decay; so that we get, for example, Socrim for Locrinus, Torineus for Corineus, Ieyr for Leil, Lucius Liber for Lucius Hiber, Rinal for Rival, Rey de Tostia for Rey d'Escocia. These errors are as old as the writer, for they often embarrass him. He is compelled to explain the derivation of Cornwall from his Torineus, thus: "And he gave one portion of the land to Torineus, and he was *afterwards called Corinus*, Corinea, and the name was afterwards corrupted and called Cornwall." He shows, too, a marked preference for Romance over Latin forms of the proper names; so that whereas his great-grandfather usually ends them in *-o* (representing *-us*), he gives such forms as Socrim, Ebrat, Juliam d'Euras, Dom Valo, Brene, Belim. Clearly his original was not a Latin text but a manuscript in some Romance speech, and yet, as we have observed above, it must have been immediately derived from Geoffrey. One error has the virtue of advising us as to the precise language of his original. Among the misreadings of the original it had chosen to corrupt Humbert to Imbereth: but it is necessary to derive the name of the River Humber (Hombre) from the King Humbert who

[1] *Cf.* Geoffrey's *Hist. Reg. Brit.*, xii. cap. xviii. By substituting *dia* for *anno* D. Pedro falls into a moment's confusion, as the correct calculation is 700—1 year=699. He reads: "Ante as calendas mayas, e esto foy em abril. Esto foy a cabo de seteçentos annos meos um dia da encarnaçam de Jesuchristo." Wace also translates Kalends into our reckoning: "Al disesetisme jor d'avril"; but his date is wrong:

> "Sis cens ans puis que Jhesu Crist
> En sainte Marie car prist."

died there, and as Imbereth had destroyed the etymon, the writer resorted to a popular explanation. He says it was called Hombre from the man who died there.[1] But this is as manifest nonsense in Portuguese as in English, nor can it be rationalised save by the Castilian *hombre* (man). D. Pedro, then, followed a Castilian abstract of the *Historia Regum Britonum*; and, all things considered, where would he obtain such a document so easily as from the court of the Alfonsos?

But the most remarkable feature of the second title of the *Nobiliario* and of its Castilian original is presented by the three paragraphs relating King Arthur's death.[2] The work follows Geoffrey's narra-

[1] P. 237: "E por aquelle homem que hi morreo ouue nome Agua-homem." The usual spelling in Castilian MSS. of the period is (*h*)*omne* or (*h*)*ome*, as also *nomne* and *nome*. (*H*)*omne* and *nomne* are probably cultisms preserved from the liturgy or from deeds which begin: *In Dei nomine*, etc. (*H*)*ome* and *nome* were pronunciations that aimed at culture but avoided the group *m'n*; but the popular speech no doubt always held to *hombre*, *nombre* (thus, *e.g.*, in the *Poema de Yuçuf*), as in all primary or secondary groups of *m'n*—*fembra*, *fanbre*, *miembrat*, etc.

[2] "*De rrey Artur filho de Vterpamdragom e das côrtes que fez, e aqueeçeo aa rrainha sua molher com seu sobrino Mordrech a que leixou a terra passamdo em Bretanha.*

"Morreo Vterpamdragom e rreynou seu filho rrey Artur de Bretanha, e foy boo rrey e leal e comquereo todolos seus emmiigos, e passou por muytas auemtuyras e fez muitas bomdades que todollos tempos do mundo fallarom dello. Este rrey Artur fez um dia em Chegerliom sa çidade côrtes. E estas côrtes foram muy boas e mui altas. A estas côrtes veerom doze caualleiros messegeiros que lhe emuiaua Luçius Liber que era emperador de Roma que se fezesse seu vassalho rrey Artur, e que teuesse aquella terra de sua maão. E se este nom fezesse que lhe mandaria tolher a terra per força e que faria justiça de seu corpo. Quamdo esto ouuio rrey Artur foy muito irado e mandou chamar toda sa gente que armas podiam leuar. E quando foy a Sam Miguel em monte Gargano combateosse com o gigante que era argulhoso e vemçeo e matouo. Lucius Liber quando soube que rrey Artur hia sobrelle chamou sa oste e toda sa gente e sayolhe ao caminho. E lidiarom ambos e vençeo elrrey Artur, e foy arrancado ho emperador. E elrrey Artur quando moueo de Bretanha por hir a esta guerra leixou a ssa terra a huum seo sobrinho que avia nome Mordrech.

"*De Mordrech sobrino delrrey Artur.*

"Este Mordrech que auia a terra em guarda de rrey Artur e a molher,

tive up to and after the Battle of Camlan; but in the course of that expedition we hear of Lancelot and Gannes and Avalon, which are all wanting to the Welshman. D. Pedro is not using the other Peninsular account of these events, for he does not know King Mark of Cornwall who is the concluding character of the *Merlin y Demanda*; nor is he following the more generally diffused French story in which King Arthur contemptuously refuses to confer with the traitor Mordred. In allowing this interview and in deducing the battle from the misinterpretation of a gesture among the personal retinue of the

quando elrrey foy fóra da terra alçousse com ella e quislhe jazer com a molher. E elrrey quando o soube tornousse com sa oste e veo sobre Mordrech. E Mordrech quando o soube filhou toda sa companha e sayo a elle sa batalha. E elles tiinham as aazes paradas pera lidar no monte de Camblet, e acordousse Mordrech que avia feito gramde traiçom e se emtrasse na batalha que seria vençido. E emuiou a elrrey que saysse a departe e falaria com elle, e elrrey assy o fez. E elles que estavam assy em esta falla sayo huuma gram serpente do freo a elrrey Artur, e quando a vyo meteo maão á espada e começeo a emcalçalla e Mordrech outrossi. E as gentes que estauam longe viram que hia huum após ho outro, e foromsse a ferir huumas aazes com as outras e foy grande a batalha, e morreo Galuam o filho de rrey Artur de huuma espadada que tragia sobresaada, que lha dera Lamçarote de Lago quando emtrara em réto ante a çidade de Ganes. Aqui morreo Mordrech e todollos boos caualleiros de huma parte e da outra. Elrrey Artur teue o campo e foy mall ferido de tres lamçadas e de huuma espadada que lhe deu Mordrech, e fezesse leuar a Islaualom por saar. Daqui adiante nom fallemos del se he viuo se he morto, nem Merlim nom disse del mais, nem eu nom sey ende mais. Os bretoões dizem que ainda he vivo. Esta batalha foy na era de quinhemtos e oytenta annos.

"*Da rrainha molher delrrey Artur e dous rrex que depois delrrei Artur ouue em Bretanha e como perdeo o seu nome de Bretanha e poseromlhe nome Ingraterra.*

"A rrainha sa molher de rrey Artur meteosse monja em huuma abadia e a pouco tempo morreo alli. E no rreyno de Bretanha ouue depois de rrey Artur dous rreys, e huuma parte ouve Loth de Leonis e a outra partida ouue Constantim o filho de Candor o duc de Cornualha. Depois da morte de rrey Loth de Leonis ouue hi outros dous rreys em Bretanha que forom do linhagem de rrey Artur e ouuerom gramdes batalhas sobre a terra, e emtanto veo Gormon que conquereo a terra e deitou todollos christaãos á perdiçom. E por esto perdeo Bretanha seu nome e poseromlhe nome Inglaterra."

monarchs, Barcellos stands close to the account given by our own Malory (Book xxi.), both depending on the lost original which Sommer has called the *Suite du Lancelot*. As that work extended, at all events, from the embassy of Lucius Hiber to the coronation of Constantine, son of Cador, it was easy to combine with Geoffrey. D. Pedro probably adheres to the *Historia* except in the first and second chapters of the eleventh book, and even in this case he copies Geoffrey's date as rendered in Julian eras (580). There are some differences of detail, certain of them due to the compression or carelessness of the Peninsular version, between Malory and the *Nobiliario*. The battles of Dover [1] and Baramdowne are omitted; Gawain's death is misplaced, he is wrongly termed the son of Arthur; Arthur has no dream nor sends an embassy to Mordred; he himself and not his knights gave the signal for battle, etc. We learn from D. Pedro, what we are not told by Malory, that this account rests on the authority of Merlin.

It is this same abstract, so far as we can judge, of the *Historia Regum Britonum*, modified in the same manner by the same extract from the *Suite du Lancelot*, that supplies the groundwork of the long Arthurian narrative inserted in the compila-

[1] The Viscount of Roda, En Ramón Perellós, saw Gawain's head at Dover in 1397 or 1398. Alfonso X., in the *Cantigas de Santa Maria*, No. 35, says:

"Et apareceu-lles Doura
A que pobrou rey Artur."

But how does he know this? Not from Geoffrey, nor the Vulgate *Lancelot*, nor any of the Spanish Arthurian types, nor from history, since the statement is wrong! Did it come from the *Suite du Lancelot*? It is not in Malory, but Malory follows that original chiefly in its last pages, and Dover is also mentioned with some frequency in the course of Arthur's early campaigns (*cf.* Sommer's *Vulgate*, t. ii., where it is written *Dovre*, *Doure*).

tion known as the *Cronica General de* 1404.[1] This *Cronica* has been fully discussed by D. Ramón Menéndez Pidal from a fifteenth-century manuscript in the possession of the antiquarian bookseller Vindel, comparison being also made with a manuscript in the library of the Escorial. The author is a Portuguese, though his sources are Castilian. He completed his work in the year 1404, fourteen years after having collected the materials; and his language

[1] R. Menéndez Pidal, *La Crónica General de* 1404, in *Revista de Archivos, Bibliotecas y Museos, 3a época, año vii,* 1903, 2, pp. 34–55, esp. 37–39. The passage lasts from fol. 20v to fol. 28v. It commences: "Aqui fala de Eneas que salio de Troya e dize por que llamaron Bretaña, . . ." etc. Fol. 21v: "Commo Balduc, rey de Inglaterra, quiso bolar et morio. . . ." Fol. 23r: "Del rey Algar . . . Del rey Elidur . . . Del rey Groboydam. . . ." Fol. 25r : "Dize la Estoria del Sancto Grayal, . . ." etc. Fol. 25v : "Morio Vterpadragon e regno su fijo Artur en Bretaña. . . ." Fol. 26: "Como Inglaterra fue convertida dos vezes. . . ." Fol. 28v: "Del malo enperador Juliano que fue falso hermitaño."

The extract from the *Suite du Lancelot* offers several *variæ lectiones* to the *Nobiliario's* text:

"E regno su fijo Artur *en* Bretaña—[omit] e foy boo . . . dello [but here Menéndez Pidal indicates his omission by suspensory points] —Este *buen* rey Artur fiez cortes vn dia en *Camalot* su çibdat—moy alta e *moy grand* e moy bueña—Lucius Yber—que se *tornase* su vasallo —[omits] e que teuesse . . . leuar [suspensory points indicate omission by transcriber]—[adds] E fue para lidar con este enperador—*en* San Miguell *del* Monte Gargano—muy orgulloso e *muy fero*—[adds] e desi fue lidar con aquel enperador—[omits] Lucius Liber . . . a molher [suspensory points]—[omits] fóra da terra—[adds] este su sobriño oyo dizer que su tio era muerto—*tomar* la mugier como *traydor*—sobre *su sobriño Mordarechque a Bretaña—con quantos puedo auer,* salio a el a la batalla—en Monte Tanblle [vl.: en el monte Tabellio]—envio *su mandado* a rey Artur—[omits] a departe—[adds] Desçendieron del mont a vn llano que dezian Salabres—[omits] do freo a elrrey Artur —enpeço de *yr en pus della*—otrosi *tanbien*—E as sus gentes, que estauan açierca, quando esto viron, pensaron que el vño queria ferir al otro que ellos non vian la serpente que ellos vian—e morieron ay de vña parte e de la otra los mas—[omits] e morreo Galuam . . . Ganes —[omits] e de huuma espadada que lhe deu Mordrech—[adds] et fiezosse leuar a sus caualleros pocos que con el ficaran viuos, por tal se podria guaresçier [omitting *Islaualom*]—non *sabemos* del—[omits] Esta batalha foy na era de quinhemtos e oytenta annos [also omits rubric]—E a rayña su mugier *vio que avia fecho grand mal*; e fiez se monja *en Corberque* en vna mongia, e a poco tienpo morio [vl.: en Çoberque]."

is at first a debased Castilian until, after the 58th folio, he breaks frankly into Portuguese. At a later date the work was made wholly Castilian. The nationality of the author might raise a presumption that he drew his information from one or other of the numerous redactions of Barcellos' work; but his treatment of the proper names is quite independent of that authority, he omits some phrases of the narrative, but, on the other hand, uses others which cannot be derived from the Portuguese text. We are left, therefore, with the assurance that the compiler of the *Cronica de* 1404 and he of the *Nobiliario* find their point of contact not directly between themselves, but in the same original, a summary of the *Historia* modified by the *Lancelot*, somewhat longer than either text, badly written by a peccant scribe, and composed, as we have seen, in the Castilian tongue. This original did not contain, however, a long extract from the *Baladro del Sabio Merlin*,[1]

[1] Fol. 25r: "Dize la *Estoria del Sancto Grayal et de rrey Artur* que este Aurelius avia nombre Vter et el otro Padragon: e diz que morio Vter, et que Padragon que tomo el nonbre del yrmano para con el suyo et se llamo Vterpadragon. Mas non fue ansi; que estos dos yrmanos el vno ouo nombre Aurelius et el otro Vterpadragon, et esta es la verdat.

"*De las prophecias del Merlin.*

"En este tenpo prophetizaua Merlin en Inglaterra et dezia las cosas que aviam de venir, et dixo a Vitiger que se non podria gardar de los fijos del rrey Costançio que ellos lle darian mala fim. Quien esto bien quisiere saber leya *el libro del Valadro de Merlim* [vl.: lea el libro debla obra de Merlin]. Et este Merlin dixo que Aurelius seria el primero rey esfuerçado et que el destroyria todos malquerientes. Et ansi fue. Vieno Aurelio yrmano mayor et paso el mar a la Grand Bretana et acogeronse a el todos los christianos que eran en la tierra et fizieronlo rey; et despues lydo con Vitiger et vençiolo et matolo et tomo la tierra que era suya. Despues conquisto mucha otra tierra et fue moy buen rey. Mas ençima morio con peçoña; que sus enemigos sabian vna fuente en que el bebia et poçoyaronla; e el vebiendo, morio. Quando rrey Aurelius fue muerto, alçaron sus vasallos por rey a su yrmano Huterpadragon."

which is peculiar to the chronicler of 1404. He shows in these excerpts his knowledge of chapters 52–180 of the *Baladro* as preserved to us; he cites it as part of the *La Estoria del Sancto Grayal et del rrey Artur*; and he seems to have read also the first part, or *Joseph Abaramatia.* Though not here used by D. Pedro, the *Baladro* was known to the chancellor Estevam da Guarda,[1] and was probably quoted by Barcellos himself in superscribing the second lyric of the *Cancioneiro Colocci-Brancutti*, so that the *Cronica de* 1404 cannot be regarded as our first knowledge of the existence of these translations. We merely remark that the *Suite du Lancelot* and the Boron-*Grail*-trilogy became successively connected with the *Historia Regum Britonum*, which they

Fol. 25v: "*Del rey Vterpadiagon, del qual se conta vn mal enxenplo e eneste capitulo fabla del rey Artur el qual dizen que es muerto e otros tienen aavn oje en dia es viuo.*

"Un dia fez este rrey cortes e fueron hy muchos rricos onbres e grandes senores e troxeron todos sus mugieres; e vieno ay vn duque de Cornualla, que troxo y su muger que auia nonbre Yguerna. Et esta dueña era mucho fermosa et vieno mucho afechada et muy ricamente garnida. Et en quanto seyan comiendo a la mesa viola el rey tan fermosa, et namorosse della tanto, que non ponia el ojo senon en ella. A dezia en su coraçion que se la non oviese, que seria muerto. Mas su marido el duque bien paro mientes en como el rrey cataua su mugier et acogiose con ella a vn su castiello que dezian Quenteol [vl.: Quinteol]. Et quando lo el rey sopo que el duque era ansi ydo, ayunto luego su hueste et çierco el duque en aquel castiello. Et envio luego por Merlin; e con su ayuda tanto fiez, que fue muerto el duque. E el rey tomo Yguerna por mugier et ovo della vn fijo a que dixeron Artur. Este fue el buen rey Artur de que todos fablan que fue tan buen rey, como podedes ver por su libro, se lo leyerdes. Despues ouo este rey, de Yguerna, vna fija que ouo nombre Elena; esta fue mogier de rey Loth. Deste Loth e de su mugier vieno Galuan e Garet et Agrauayn et Mordereque [vl.: Agrauayn e Morderique]."

Cf. also fol. 26: "Como Inglaterra fue conuertida dos vezes a la fe: *la vna por Josephas, fijo de Joseph de Varametia* e la otra por sant Agostin."

The second conversion is the only one recorded by the *Nobiliario* and Geoffrey of Monmouth.

[1] *Cancioneiro da Vaticana*, No. 930.

tended to obscure; and we can sum up the earlier history of Geoffrey's Spanish career, which is also to some extent a history of the introduction of the Arthurian literature, in a diagram:

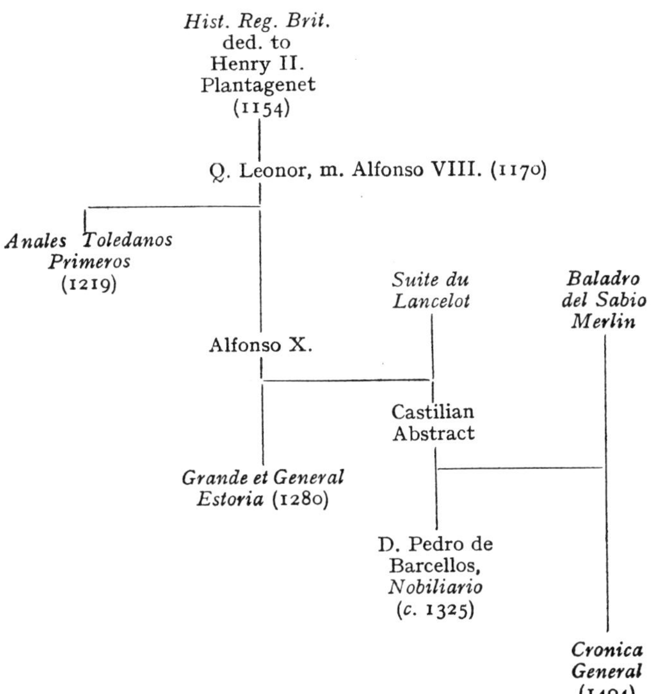

In the case of one portion of Arthurian literature, and that chronologically the earliest, our diagram seems to instruct us that Queen Leonor Plantagenet was its introducer in the Spanish Peninsula and Alfonso the Wise its disseminator; and a similar conclusion arises out of the consideration of allusions in the early Castilian and Portuguese works. Alfonso, of course, is somewhat of a portmanteau name in this era, covering all the yet undiscriminated literary activity of the Toledan rulers from the time of St. Fernando to Alfonso XI. and D. Juan Manuel: everywhere his energy is at work, his schemes are in progress, his policy of the absorption of foreign thought is continued, his withdrawal is felt in a perceptible diminution of literary vitality, but we know as yet too little to be able to specify his personal intervention in this or that detail. There were numberless collaborators in the Toledan school, some of whose names have been preserved; and after the Wise Alfonso there were other princely editors, Sancho IV., Alfonso XI., D. Juan Manuel. The mere citation of chivalresque figures, too, raises no presumption of their existence in either vernacular; though some romances, whether native or foreign, must be postulated as the basis of allusion, for one cannot allude *in vacuo*. Notwithstanding these reservations, however, it does seem possible to assert the personal interest of Alfonso X. in the *matière de Bretagne*, seeing that the *Cancioneiros* show him as quoting Brutus, Arthur, Merlin and Tristan. In these *Cancioneiros* he stands at the head of a new movement of Galician poetry, a gesture of impatience in face of the vague and distant Provençalism of Bonaval and other poets; for he aimed at reproducing not merely the forms, but also the spirit and sentiments of the Provençal troubadours, and among the new materials for poetry we find him using the Breton allusions.[1] Alfonso found a supporter in

[1] For the Arthurian allusions of the Galician *Cancioneiros, vide supra*. For Alfonso's Provençalism consult G. Bertoni, *Alfonso X. di Castiglia*

Gonçal' Eannes do Vinhal[1] (*d.* 1280; in Castilian, Gonzalo Ibáñez de Aguilar), a Portuguese by birth, but a vassal and favourite of Alfonso and his brethren, and enfeoffed in the territory of Seville, being created lord of Aguilar. As Guiraut de Cabrera had referred to the *temperadura de Breton*, so Gonçal' Eannes speaks of the *cantares de Cornoalha*. D. Diniz, Alfonso's grandson, was another partisan of his poetical school;[2] so, too, was the chancellor Estevam da Guarda and Pedro de Barcellos, Diniz' son: and the sum of the Arthurians of the *Cancioneiros* is completed by the soldier or jogral Fernand' Esquio[3] who, being promised a horse by one of the king's sons and not receiving it, humorously compares the animal to the Blatant Beast. Such men as Nun' Alvares Pereira, López de Ayala and Fernam Lopes are equally examples of this dynastic and courtly transmission of the Legend; Rodrigo Yáñez is the laureate of the eleventh Alfonso; D. Juan Manuel is the Wise Alfonso's nephew, the executor of some of his labours, and the finished exponent

ed il Provenzalismo della prima lirica portoghese, in *Archivum Romanicum*, vii. (1923), pp. 171–175, who comments on *Canc. Vat.*, No. 70 (to Pero da Ponte):

> "Vos non trobades come proençal
> Mais come Bernaldo de Bonaval,"

thus: "Dai pochi nomi dei trovatori qui ricordati si capisci già subito quale fosse l'imitazione provenzale che Alfonso X. amava e voleva: quella, cioè, ligia ai migliori trovatori e ai motivi più caratteristici della poesia occitanica, non quella indeterminata, vaga, indistinta, secondo la maniera del Bonaval e dai poeti della stessa generazione, che non penetrarono nel cuore della lirica dei trovatori, ma ne colsero sopra tutti gli elementi esteriori."—P. 174.

[1] *Canc. Vat.*, No. 1007. See his life by C. Michaëlis de Vasconcellos in *Canc. da Ajuda*, ii., or *Revista Lusitana*, vi. p. 30.

[2] *Canc. Vat.*, No. 132:

> "Quero eu en maneyra de proençal
> Fazer agora hun cantar d'amor."

[3] *Canc. Vat.*, No. 1140.

of his prose, and of his two falcons (Lanzarote and Galvan) one had belonged to D. Enrique, the king's brother. Almost the only mention of the Legend during the fourteenth century which cannot be attached to a court is the citation of *Tristan* by the Archpriest of Hita. Finally, we find in the Alfonsine circle some indications of Arthurian texts. Estevam da Guarda fully relates the final incident of the second book of the Boron-*Grail*; a paragraph from a *Lancelot* is in the hands of D. Pedro de Barcellos; D. Manuel, father of D. Juan Manuel and brother of Alfonso, is mentioned among the early prophecies of Merlin attached to the *Baladro*, and the king himself, the first to cite *Tristan*, is known to have been in touch with possessors of the version that came to be current in Spain, namely, Edward I. of England, the patron of Rustician's compilation, and Brunetto Latini who cites a portion of the same *Tristan* in his *Rhétorique*.[1]

[1] C. M. de Vasconcellos places Alfonso X.'s *Canc. Vat.*, No. 458, as early as 1260, which is the year when Brunetto Latini visited him on a mission from the Guelfs of Florence. We cite the *Rhétorique* later. Latini has left the following eulogy of the Castilian monarch (*Il Tesoretto*, ii. lines 129–134):

"Che già sotto la luna
Non si truova persona
Che per gentil legnagio,
Nè per alto barnagio
Tanto degno ne fosse
Com'esto Re Nanfosse."

Edward was at Burgos in 1254, *cf. España Sagrada*, xxvi. p. 319, and the references already given. The return visit of Sancho to London in 1255, and the continual relations through Eleanor of Castile, Edward's wife, represent yet more channels for literary intercourse between the Plantagenet and the Castilian.

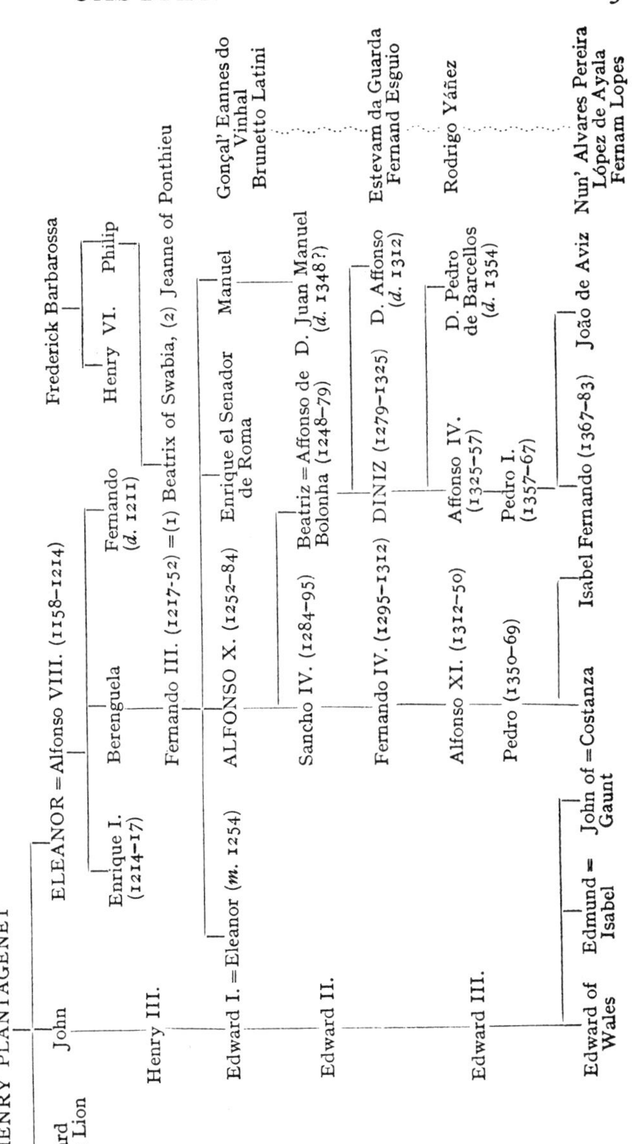
HENRY PLANTAGENET
Richard Cœur de Lion
John
ELEANOR = Alfonso VIII. (1158–1214)
Frederick Barbarossa
Henry III.
Enrique I. (1214–17)
Berenguela
Fernando (d. 1211)
Henry VI.
Philip
Fernando III. (1217-52) = (1) Beatrix of Swabia, (2) Jeanne of Ponthieu
Edward I. = Eleanor (m. 1254)
ALFONSO X. (1252–84)
Enrique el Senador de Roma
Manuel
Gonçal' Eannes do Vinhal
Brunetto Latini
Edward II.
Sancho IV. (1284–95)
Beatriz = Affonso de Bolonha (1248–79)
D. Juan Manuel (d. 1348?)
Fernando IV. (1295–1312)
DINIZ (1279–1325)
D. Affonso (d. 1312)
Estevam da Guarda
Fernand Esguio
Edward III.
Alfonso XI. (1312–50)
Affonso IV. (1325–57)
D. Pedro de Barcellos (d. 1354)
Rodrigo Yáñez
Pedro (1350–69)
Pedro I. (1357–67)
Edward of Wales
Edmund = Isabel
John of = Costanza Gaunt
Isabel
Fernando (1367–83)
João de Aviz
Nun' Alvares Pereira
López de Ayala
Fernam Lopes

ELEANOR PLANTAGENET AND THE ARTHURIAN LEGEND IN SPAIN

A. (1) Henry Plantagenet, titular patron of Arthurian Legend.

(2) Richard Cœur de Lion, friend of Alfonso II. of Aragon, patron of Bernard de Ventadorn and other troubadours, source of original of Ulrich von Zatzikhoven's *Lanzelet.*

(3) Eleanor, wife of Alfonso VIII., patron of letters. At court of Enrique I. *Anales Toledanos Primeros* redacted. Arthur and Fernando compared in 1211.

(4) Edward I., at Burgos with Alfonso X. in 1254, source of original of Rustician de Pisa's compilation.

(5) Emperor Henry VI., patron of Abbot Joachim and of Godfrey of Viterbo.

B. (6) Alfonso X., translated Geoffrey of Monmouth, and probably possessed abstract of same, first to allude to Tristan, patron of Gonçal' Eannes do Vinhal and of Brunetto Latini. Falcons Lançarote and Galvan named by D. Juan Manuel, the latter having pertained to Enrique el Senador de Roma. D. Manuel cited in *Baladro del Sabio Merlin.*

(7) Sancho IV., Alfonso XI., continued undertakings of Alfonso X. Round Table cited in *Gran Conquista de Ultramar.* Merlin and Tristan in *Poema de Alfonso XI.* (Rodrigo Yáñez). Merlin in *Cronica de Don Pedro* (Ayala).

C. (8) Affonso III., came from Boulogne to Portugal in 1248.

(9) Diniz, continued Alfonso X.'s poetical theories, alluded to Tristan and Iseult, patron of Estevam da Guarda (allusion to *Baladro* in *Canc. Vat.* 930). His brother's name was connected with the *Joseph* (1313) and *Amadis.*

(10) D. Pedro de Barcellos, editor of *Cancioneiros* and perhaps of *Lais de Bretanha.* Used various works of Alfonso X. for his *Nobiliario,* and Castilian conflation of Geoffrey of Monmouth and *Lancelot* for ***Titulo II.***

(11) Edward of Wales, Edmund, John of Gaunt, present in Spain or Portugal (1366–7, 1381, 1386–8, respectively).

(12) Tristan elements in love story of Pedro I. of Portugal. At court of Fernando, Galahad was model of Nun' Alvares Pereira. João I., patron of Fernam Lopes.

Before taking our leave of Geoffrey of Monmouth, it would be well to consider the vicissitudes of his Spanish career. His reputation was, perhaps, at its height, or already declining, when D. Pedro de Barcellos wrote the second title of his *Nobiliario*, for the vast Arthurian literature silted over the work of its only begetter. King Arthur eked out a precarious existence, apart from the romances, on processional banners,[1] in tableaux,[2] in allusions, and as one of the Nine Worthies,[3] until he was finally dismissed by Cervantes as no more than a crow![4] The original prophecies of Merlin (*Historia Regum Britonum*, lib. vii.) possibly did not reach Spain during the Middle Ages; nor can we be certain that the versions of Abbot Joachim and Alain de Lille, now in Madrid and Toledo respectively, were mediæval importations into the Peninsula. The notice of his life in the 104th chapter of the *Mar de Historias*[5] depends on a foreign source and seems to arise out of the French *Merlins*; while it was almost certainly Boron's *Merlin* that D. Juan I. of Aragon demanded from his archivist on the 24th November, 1391, and which was catalogued in the library of his successor. While yet crown prince, or, according to the Catalan formula, duke *primogenitus*, he had named three mastiffs Amadis, Ogier and Merlin,[6] in sign of his

[1] Rubió y Lluch, *Documents per l'Historia de la Cultura Catalana Mig-Eval*, i. p. 141 and ii. p. 104.
[2] Martorell, *Tirant lo Blanch*, cap. clxxvi., ed. Aguiló.
[3] *Cronica llamada: el triunpho de los nueve preciados de la fama* (Lisbon, Germão Galharde, 1530), etc.
[4] In a Cornish legend King Arthur was metamorphosed into a chough. *Cf.* J. D. Bruce, *The Evolution of Arthurian Romance*, i. p. 34 n., 74.
[5] Fernán Pérez de Guzmán, *Mar de Historias*, cap. ciiii.
[6] Rubió y Lluch, *op. cit.*, ii. p. 327.

devotion to the cavaliers of France, Britain and Spain. But Merlin continued to be Geoffrey's most successful fiction, and when detached from his context, he lived a vigorous life as the Zadkiel or Old Moore[1] of the Spanish Middle Ages, rising on two occasions—in López de Ayala[2] and in Cervantes—into literature. The former invented a vaticination which was all too applicable to the misfortunes of Pedro the Cruel. The text of the Moor Benihatin's riddle precedes the inevitable catastrophe of the tyrant, and the sevenfold exegesis reads as his knell. This passage, in which the chronicler's hate pursues his master—benefactor, perchance—through Death to the Judgment, is elaborately wrought and fashioned into a climax for the whole history; the almost painful sobriety of the general narrative is here only relaxed for a torrent of blistering damnation, and if the whole episode strikes our taste as prosaic, incongruous and somewhat of an anti-climax, we can profitably remember that it has been admired by the catholic and informed judgment of Menéndez y Pelayo,[3] the

[1] Merlin is a miracle-worker rather than a prophet in Alfonso X.'s *Cantigas de Santa Maria*, No. 108: "Como Santa Maria fez que nacesse o fillo do iudeu o rostro atras como ll'o Merlin rogara."

[2] *Cronica del Rey D. Pedro*, año xviii. cap 22; año xx. cap. 3: "En las partidas de occidente entre los montes y la mar nascera una ave negra, comedora e robadora, e tal que todos los panares del mundo queria acoger en si, e todo el oro del mundo querra poner en su estomago; e despues gormarlo ha, e tornara atras, e non perescera luego por esta dolencia. E dice mas, caersela han las alas, e secarsele han las plumas al sol, e andara de puerta en puerta, e ninguno la querra acoger, e encerrarse ha en selva, e morira y dos veces, una al mundo, y otra ante Dios, e desta guisa acabara."

[3] *Origenes de la Novela*, i. p. clxxviii: "Cuánto crece en la fantasía el prestigio pavoroso de la catástrofe de Montiel, con aquella especie de fatalidad trágica que se cierne sobre la cabeza de D. Pedro hasta mostrar cumplida en su persona la terrible profecía 'que fué fallada entre los libros e profecías que dicen que fizo Merlin' y sometida por el rey a la interpretación del sabio moro!"

prince of the critics of Spain. The gift or trick of prophecy was rife everywhere in the fourteenth and fifteenth centuries. In Aragon, vaticinations turned on the fortunes of the dynasty, the personal interests of princes, and the prospects of the Great Schism; they were fabricated by priests, gentlemen, and princes; and they received the anxious attention of the highest persons of the state.[1] In Portugal prophecy has always been current and applauded; and the same mania in Castile drew a quaintly-reasoned protest from the author of the *Vitorial*:[2]

> Beware of believing false prophecies [he writes] and trust them not, such as those of Merlin and other sayings: for I tell you sooth, that these things were devised and drawn of subtle men, cavillers, to win privity and to gain kings and great lords. . . . And if thou consider it well, *they make a new Merlin for a new king*: they do declare that that king must cross the sea, and destroy all the Moors, and win the Holy Places, and be Emperor; but thereafter we see it hap as God pleaseth. . . . Merlin was a good man of much wisdom. He was not a son of the Devil as some declare: for the Devil, being a spirit, may not beget children; he may provoke to sinful deed, which is his office. He is a disembodied substance, he cannot engender bodily things. But Merlin, by the great wisdom that he learned, would fain know more than behoved him and was deceived of the Devil, and he showed him many things to say; some whereof came true: for such is the manner of the Devil, and eke of whosoever knoweth the art to deceive, to place first some true thing to win credence thereby. . . . And so in that part of England he did say some things in which they found some truth; but in many more he did err; and they that now would utter certain matters, they compose them and say that Merlin discovered them.

The greater number of these prophecies are found attached to the *Baladro del Sabio Merlin*[3] in several

[1] Rubió y Lluch, *op. cit.*, i. No. 304 n., 423 and n., ii. p. xxv and No. 230.

[2] Gutierre Diez de Games, *El Vitorial*, ed. Llaguno y Amírola, pp. 29–30.

[3] *Baladro del Sabio Merlin*, ed. Bonilla, capp. 24 *ff.*, 137–42, 341, etc., and pp. 19–22, 155–162.

strata of interpolations; and if we hesitate over them, it is not for their intrinsic interest, which is slight, but because the eccentricities of the prophetic style are such that intelligible allusions are almost inevitably contemporary references. In all versions of Merlin's legend he makes prophecies before Vortiger, and the Peninsular novels are further enriched with his remarks to Utherpendragon, though these have been misplaced. In these prophecies the allusions are either to the subject-matter of the novel itself, or, at all events, to Arthurian interests; and they contain nothing more Spanish than a vague notice of the Arab Conquest. But the conclusion of the *Baladro* is occupied by a ὕστερα πρότερα of pronouncements, in which neither date nor order can be trusted, nor are contemporary circumstances clear. There is, however, a line of evident division between those utterances made by Merlin in London "one day" and those which he delivered "in that time" to Maestre Antonio. The former are lucid, anti-dynastic, fully developed; the latter are obscure, dynastic, and developed by means of a menagerie of "great lions," "cub lions," "angry lions," "wolf lions," etc., among whom D. Pedro the Cruel appears as "the ass of wickedness." The former are concerned with the wise foolishness of Alfonso X., the unfilial conduct of Sancho IV., the doom of Fernando IV., and thus cover the years 1283–1312; and we collect this note in connection with the earlier date, "the which sentence, thus given, was straightway revealed to an Augustinian friar of Molina who was studying in his cell for the morrow's sermon. And this friar told it forthwith to Prince Manuel," etc. Now, hostility to the dynasty was precisely the policy of D. Manuel, who intervened hypocritically in the struggles of father and son in the hope that both would be damaged, and it was continued into the reigns of Sancho IV., Fernando IV. and Alfonso XI. by his famous son D. Juan Manuel; but the same sentiments also served the turn of the Trastamaran adherents who were pleased to vilify all the antecedents of Pedro the Cruel, to whose death there is an undoubted reference. There are some good stories of a late complexion in these paragraphs and also a date, 1467. We are left, therefore, with an unfortunate ambiguity: either the whole passage was composed by a Trastamaran adherent (in 1467?) with a noticeably antiquarian taste for scandal, or (as we think more probable) there is a substratum of pamphleteering by a dependant of D. Juan Manuel and a later Trastamaran gloss.

Less difficulty attaches to those revelations introduced by the words "in that time Maestre Antonio,[1] being deeply versed in the Holy Catholic Faith and a great lover of God, learned that Merlin was in Great Britain, and he spake concerning the things that were to come," etc. This occurred, we are told, in the year 305 A.D. Merlin opened his harangue with a short geography of Spain, attributing the principality to Castile, and worked his way deviously from Don Rodrigo (with an allusion to the ballad)

[1] Don Anton or Maestre Antonio is, of course, a pseudonym, and it comes from the French original of the *Baladro del Sabio Merlin*, in which, as in the Parma MS. of Merlin's Prophecies and the Venetian edition of 1480, certain prophecies were delivered to *Maistre Anthoine*. *Cf.* Miss L. A. Paton, *Notes on the Manuscripts of the Prophécies de Merlin*, in *Publications of the Modern Language Association of America*, xxviii. (1913), p. 131.

through the primitive monarchs of Leon down to St. Fernando; and then, more expansively, from Alfonso XI. to the year 1488. It is evident that we have in this series more than one author. All references previous to Alfonso XI. are, however, jejune and distant, and so must be discarded. The so-called chapter 341 of the text is manifestly concerned with the minority of Alfonso XI. and the regency of Queen Maria; and though the zoological manner is firmly maintained throughout—especially in reference to Enrique III., Juan II., and later—the name of Maestre Antonio is not actually cited later than the "crowned lion of Spain" who was the great-great-grandson of Fernando III. Don Antón and the "crowned lion" reappear in the *Poema de Alfonso Onceno* of Rodrigo Yáñez, a work that breaks off in the year 1344, and his business is to decorate the victory of Río Salado (1340) with appropriate oracles. The style is no more than an amplification of the corresponding passages in the *Baladro*; the *maestro's* expedition to Britain is related in similar terms, and the tense of reference is past.[1] Don Antón's work, an

[1] *Poema de Alfonso Onceno*, "Expedition of Don Antón to Britain" (coplas 1808–1811):

"Merlin fablo d'Espanna
E dixo esta profeçia,
Estando en la Bretanna,
A vn maestro que y auia.
Don Anton era llamado
Este maestro que vos digo,
Sabidor e letrado,
De Don Merlin mucho amigo.
Este maestro sabidor
Asi le fue preguntar:
Don Merlin, por el mi amor,
Sepadesme declarar
La profeçia d'Espanna,
Que yo queria saber
Por vos alguna fasanna
De lo que se ha de faser."

interpolation on the *Baladro* and (as we opine) not the first interpolation, is thus bounded by the years 1312–1340.

After 1350 other prophets intervened, whom it is not possible to distinguish save by internal evidence. One probably wrote under the reign of the "sickly lion" (*leon doliente*), or Enrique III. (*d.* 1406), and to him we should be inclined to ascribe the diatribe against Pedro the Cruel; others refer to still later Trastamaran monarchs and even to the first rulers of united Spain, and the burden of their vaticinations is precisely what Gutierre Diez de Games has led us to expect—victory, the extension of Christendom, empire, and the reunion of the Church. In the whole range of these oracles there is not the least indication of Portuguese feeling; the temper is entirely Castilian or perhaps Leonese. We cannot, of course, declare peremptorily that prophecies were to be found attached to all editions of the *Baladro del Sabio Merlin* after the early fourteenth century, but it is clear that the poets of the *Cancionero de Baena* (before 1445) handled a volume of much the same

For the style of the prophecy:

1812–13: "Acabados los annos mil, E los tresientos de la Encarnacion, Cinquenta e neuve compliran. . . ." 1815: "Reynara vn leon coronado. . . ." 1817: "Vn leon dormiente. . . ." 1819: "puerco espin. . . ." 1820: "bestias brauas. . . ." 1822: "El dragon de la grand fromera. . . ." 1828: "En las couas de Ercoles Abran fuerte lid enplasada," etc. The same style is maintained in Yáñez's earlier prophecy: "En Toro cumplio su fin," etc.

Finally:

"La profeçia conte
Y torne en desir llano,
Yo Rodrigo Yannes la note
En lenguage castellano.
Copras de muy bien fablar,
Segunt dixo Merlin."
1841–2.

contents as that extant. Several rhymesters essay the rôle of a "new Merlin": Gonçalo Martínez de Medina is content with a vaguely prophetic manner;[1] Alfonso Álvarez de Villasandino (1350?–1428?) attributes a witticism of his own to the innocent British wizard. But Villasandino had already prophesied the conquest of Islam and the reunion of Christendom, using the menagerie of Maestre Antonio, and citing in support both Merlin and Fray Juan.[2] Fray Juan, however, can be no other than the translator of the Boron-trilogy, whose name occurs nowhere in the *Baladro*, but only in the *Demanda del Sancto Grial*; thus furnishing a convincing proof of the coherence of the *Baladro*, *Profecias* and *Demanda* in the first quarter of the fifteenth century.

In the sixteenth and seventeenth centuries Merlin was still a figure that could be brought forward in

[1] *Canc. Baena*, No. 332, Gonçalo Martínez prophesies: "por manera de pregunta escura"; No. 209, Villasandino says:

"pues Merlin
Propuso, muy secretado,
Un dicho ya declarado
Qu'el tomado
Es tornado
Tomador, e grant dalfyn
Espantable palançin."

[2] No. 199, Villasandino says:

"Del fuerte leon suso contenido
Dise el Merlin, concuerda Fray Juan."

Cf. Demanda, ed. Bonilla, cap. 52: "Ni yo Joannes Bivas no vos dire ende mas de lo que vos el dize, ca so frayle, e no quiero mentir."

K. Pietsch, in *Modern Philology*, xviii. (1920–1), p. 596, interprets this as an allusion to Jean de la Roche-Taillée, who is bracketed with Merlin elsewhere in the *Cancionero de Baena*:

"Cesaran muchos profetas
De Merlin et Rocaçisa."

He has, however, discovered the name of Juan Bivas in the text of the *Liuro de Josep Abaramatia*, which is dated 1313.

popular representations. The name only has survived of *Los Encantos de Merlin* [1] (Merlin's Enchantments) by one of the veterans of Lepanto, Rey de Artieda; and a manuscript in the Madrid National Library contains the *mojiganga* or burlesque of *Merlin y los animales* [2] by Juan Francisco de Tejera. From among the "properties" of the theatre or from the novel of *Tablante de Ricamonte* Cervantes resurrected the magician to perform a considerable part in the second part of *Don Quixote*.[3] He is the inventor of Clavileño; the duke's subtle steward masquerades as Merlin in order to distribute blows to Sancho and his master. Merlin is the arch-enchanter of the Cave of Montesinos (another figure from *Tablante*, but more famous in the Carolingian ballads), where Don Quixote sees in a jumble the main characters of Romance. What the Knight of La Mancha saw in the Cave of Montesinos does not correspond with any of the Arthurian novels of Spain or Portugal, nor is it easy to follow a recent American critic [4] into identifying it with one of the Grailbergs, so popular in Germany. The parallels quoted are not convincing, nor is their connection with Cervantes' library indicated; and if Cervantes knew any Grailberg or Sibyl's Paradise, he would obtain such indications not from Arthurian literature, but from the Castilian translation of *Guarino el Mezquino*,[5] which

[1] Rojas Villandrando, *Viaje Entretenido* (1603).
[2] Paz y Melia, *Biblioteca Nacional, MSS.—Catálogo I.—Teatro*, p. 617.
[3] Cervantes, *Don Quixote*, II. chaps. xl., xxv.–xxxvi., xxiii.
[4] P. S. Barto, *The Subterranean Grail Paradise of Cervantes*, in *Publications of the Modern Language Association of America*, xxxviii. 2, June 1923.
[5] *Cf.* Bonilla y San Martín, *Las Leyendas de Wagner*, 1913, pp. 17–28 ("Tannhäuser").

he had read, or from indigenous tales of the Cave of Salamanca.

Brutus of all Geoffrey's creatures departed least from his maker's image. He intervened, along with Brennus and Belinus, in the *Cronica de los Conquiridores* by the humanist Juan Fernández de Heredia (1310–96), whose mention of Godfrey of Viterbo's *Pantheon* warns us to look to the *Grande et General Estoria* for his inspiration.[1] But Geoffrey's narrative was completely rewritten in some unknown French *Brut*; it forms the basis of a long episode of the *Vitorial*, which treats with charming naïveté of the marriage of Brutus to Dorothea, Menelaus' daughter, and of her virtue; of the settlement of Britain, and the wars against the Giants or Saxons; of the colonisation of Brittany, the Marvels of England, the loss of the sovereignty by the Britons, and the commencement of the wars in Guienne.

Some credit was restored to Geoffrey by the Latin Renascence of the sixteenth century. He was read and condemned by Juan Luis Vives.[2] By way of Trevisa's version of Higden's *Polychronicon* the whole procession of puppets—Brutus, Madan, Guendolen, Lud, Lear, Cordelia, Constantine, Vortigern, Arthur, Mordred—pass into the *Fructo de los Tiempos* (1509) of Rodrigo Cuero,[3] who taught English history

[1] J. Domínguez Bordona, *La primera parte de la Crónica de los Conquiridores de Fernández de Heredia*, in *Revista de Filología Española*, x. (1923), pp. 380–388:
Libro iii.: "Aqui comiença el libro de Bruto de Bretaña" (3 rubrics); libro vi.: "Aqui comiença la estoria de Belyn e Breno" (15 rubrics).

[2] Vives, *Opera*, vi. p. 398: "Fabulosa sunt magis quæ de Britanniæ originibus quidam est commentus, a Bruto illos Trojano deducens, qui nullus unquam fuit."

[3] Rodrigo Cuero, *Historia de Inglaterra llamada Fructo de los Tiempos*, 1509 (Esc. MS., X. ii. 20, fols. 14 to about 38).

to three of our rulers—to Catherine of Aragon, Mary I. and Philip her consort. Through Polydore Virgil and other Italians, the same narrative occupies chapters 3–8 of a curious compendium of English and Scottish history as far as the accession of Mary of Scots, which is preserved in the National Library at Madrid.[1] This work shares with Alfonso's *Estoria de las Bretannas* the peculiarity of citing not Geoffrey, but Gildas. To the bibliophiles perhaps, and not to the Middle Ages, we are indebted for the existence in Spain of the commentaries of Abbot Joachim[2] and of Alain de Lille,[3] and of the *Liber Bruti et prophetæ Merlini*,[4] whose last English possessor was a Thomas Norton and the first Spanish mark is the stamp of Philip V.

[1] *Chronica que en breve compendioso estilo trata de todos los reyes que ha auido en Ynglaterra y esquosia y sus subcesos y guerras hasta nuestros tiempos con la discripçion de la isla sacada de varios autores nuevamente* (Bibl. Nac. MS. 1455=i. 144). It belonged in the sixteenth century to a Spanish gentleman whose name is illegible.

[2] Bibl. Nac. Madrid, MS. 59=B 70.

[3] *Prophetia Anglicana, hoc est Merlini Ambrosii Britanni . . . a Galfredo Monumentense latine conscripta, una cum septem libris explanationum . . . Alani de Insulis germani* (Toledo Cathedral, MS. seventeenth century, formerly belonged to Cardinal Zelada).

[4] Bibl. Nac. Madrid, MS. 6319=F 147. The manuscript is of the fourteenth century, vellum, by various hands, 74 folios. The Columbine Library at Seville formerly possessed a copy of Wace's *Brut*, written by an Italian in the fifteenth century, purchased at Milan in 1521 (*cf.* H. Harrisse, *Grandeza y decadencia de la Colombina*, Seville, 1886).

IV

THE BRETON LAYS: "CIFAR"

The *Historia Regum Britonum* took precedence above the other members of the Arthurian body in Spain, both by the antiquity of its composition and because the tongue in which it was expressed was more reverently received by librarians and bibliophiles; in the French romances a later distinction which can be made between prose and verse forms invests with especial interest any vestiges or survivors of the poetical state which can be discerned in the Peninsular literatures. Incidental lyrics can be found imbedded in *Amadis de Gaula* and in *Don Tristan de Leonis*, and the latter, though perhaps ancient, call for no comment here; but we are concerned to investigate reminiscences of the Breton lays as interpreted by the five *lais de Bretanha* of the *Cancioneiro Colocci-Brancutti* and in the fashioning of the novel of *El Cavallero Cifar.*

The former have been interpreted by the brilliant scholarship of Snra. D. Carolina Michaëlis de Vasconcellos, the greatest name in Portuguese criticism.[1] These five brief lyrics, which stand at the head of the *Cancioneiro Colocci-Brancutti*, one of three principal repositories of the Galaeco-Portuguese lyric of the fourteenth century, are singularly colourless little

[1] C. M. de Vasconcellos, *Lais de Bretanha*, in *Revista Lusitana*, vi. (1900), pp. 1 *ff.*; reprinted in *Cancioneiro da Ajuda* (Halle, 1904), ii. pp. 479–525; *Cancioneiro Colocci-Brancutti*, ed. Molteni, Nos. 1–5.

pieces. The first addresses Love personified, and praises the god for that culture and refinement which the sweet passion brings:

> Amor, des que m'a vos cheguei,
> Bem me posso de vos loar,
> Ca mui pouc', ant', a meu cuidar,
> Valia; mais, pois, enmendei. . . .[1]

This is a free translation of a lyric from *Tristan*:

> Amor, de vostre acointement
> Me lou ie molt, se dex mament!

It contains nothing more national or personal than the spontaneous *saudade* of the verse:

> Mui fremosa e de gran prez,
> *E que polo meu gran mal vi,*
> E de que sempre atendi
> Mal (ca ben nunca m'ela fez).[2]

The third and fourth are love-lyrics in absence, also drawn from the romance of *Tristan*:

> Mui gran temp' a, par Deus, que eu non vi
> Quen de beldade vence toda ren![3]

And:

> Don Amor, eu cant' e choro;
> E todo me ven d'ali:
> Da por que eu cant' e choro
> E por meu mal dia vi.[4]

They render:

> Grant temps a que ie ne vi cele
> Qui tote rienz vaint de biaute,

and:

> Damor vient mon chant et mon plor.

[1] "Love, after that I came to thee, I may well boast myself of thee, for very little, methinks, was I worth; but, thereafter, was I amended. . . ."

[2] "Most beautiful and great of price, and whom to my sore hurt I saw, from whom I aye awaited harm (for good she never did unto me)."

[3] "Long time, by God, is it since I have seen her who in loveliness excelleth all things."

[4] "Sir Love, I sing and weep, and all cometh to me from her for whom I sing and weep, and whom I saw in an evil hour."

The originals of the second and fifth *lais* have not been discovered. They are dancing songs or *bailadas* with refrains, sung by women, and of contrasted moods; for the first expresses hatred of Morhout, and the other praises Lancelot. The first terms itself a *bailada* or *cantiga* and claims to be a literal translation; the second is self-styled a *lais*.

O Marot haja mal-grado,
Porque nos aqui cantando
Andamos tan segurado,
A tan gran sabor andando!
  Mal-grad' aja! que cantamos
  E que tan en paz dançamos![1]

And:

Ledas sejamos orgemais!
E dancemos! Pois nos chegou
E o Deus con nosco juntou,
Cantemos-lhe aqueste lais!
  Ca este escudo e do melhor
  Omen que fez Nostro Senhor![2]

But though we cannot discover the original French lyrics, we can identify the prose form of the refrains;[3] for the first refers to a passage in the *Merlin* of the pseudo-Boron, where we read:

> Gauuain vient pres des damoyselles et escoute ce quelles dient. Et quant il la bien entendu, il demande a son cousin: "Entendes vous ceste chanson?" "Oil bien," fait il, "elles dient que mal gre en ait le Morholt."

The second is found in *Lancelot du Lac*:

> Et dirent que voirement estoit il li mieldres cheualiers del monde.

[1] "Evil befall the Morhout, forasmuch as we sing here and dance in such assurance, and move at our great pleasure! Evil befall him! Since we sing and dance so peaceably!"

[2] "Let us be blithe henceforth! and dance! Since he has come to us, and God has joined him to us, let us sing him this lay! For this shield belongeth to the best man our Lord hath made."

[3] We return to these lyrics in chaps. ix. and xi. *infra*; in the latter we also reconsider the three from *Tristan*.

Yet though these lays are colourless, they stand out none the less clearly from the other works in the Song-Books: they alone are attributed to foreign and fictitious authors; they alone are truly anonymous; they alone are *lais*; they alone translations; and they alone require prose commentaries. These are contained in the rubrics [1] and in old notes conserved by Colocci, and when confronted with the French *Tristan* they show a general conformity of subject, but considerable divergence of detail. On the hypothesis that these headings refer to one and the same work, Snra. de Vasconcellos [2] concludes:

> The few notices of the collector relative to Helys, Morhout, Lancelot and the daughter of King Pelles, diverge somewhat as I have shown from the narratives analysed by Löseth. The dilemma is: the redactor of the rubrics, whether he be (as I think) the translator of the lays himself, or the compiler of the *Cancioneiro*, condensed badly the complicated events which were described in

[1] "1. Este lais fez Elis o Baço que foi duc de Sansonha, quando passou aa gran Bretanha, que ora chaman Inglaterra. E passou la no tempo de Rei Artur, pora se combater con Tristan, porque lhe matara o padre en ũa batalha. E andando un dia en sa busca, foi pela Joyosa Guarda u era a Rainha Iseu de Cornoalha. E viu-a tan fremosa que adur lhe poderia omen no mundo achar par. Enamorouse enton d'ela e fez por ela este laix. Este lais posemos aa cima porque era o melhor que foi feito.

"2. Esta cantiga fezeron quatro donzelas a Marot d'Irlanda en tempo de Rei Artur, porque Marot filhava toda-las donzelas que achava en guarda dos cavaleiros, se as podia conquerer d'eles. E enviava-as pera Irlanda pera seeren sempre en servidon da terra. E esto fazia el porque fora morto seu padre por razon de ũa donzela que levava en guarda. [Colocci's note] Esta cantiga e a primeira que achamos que foi feita e fezeron-na quatro donzelas en el tempo del Rei Artur a Maraot d'Irlanda por la . . . tornada en lenguagem palavra por palavra e diz assi. . . .

"3. Don Tristan o Namorado fez esta cantiga.

"4. [Colocci] Don Tristan.

"5. Este laix fezeron donzelas a don Ançaroth quando estava na Insoa da Lidiça quando a Rainha Genevra o achou con a filha de rei Peles e lhi defendeo que non paresçesse ant'ela.

"[Colocci] Don Tristan per Genevra."

[2] C. M. de Vasconcellos, *Lais de Bretanha*, pp. 21 and 20.

the corresponding and lengthy chapters of the enormous romance, changing names and inventing facts; or else the text used really departed in a number of details from the stories we know:

1. Morhout was called Morhaut or Marhout, Marholt, whence on the one side Marout and Marôt, and on the other Marlot.
2. Morhout snatched all the damsels he could from the knights that escorted them, and sent them to Ireland as slaves.
3. The father of Morhout, who died on account of a beauty he was guarding, was mentioned.
4. Tristan's victory over Morhout was celebrated by various groups of damsels, freed when Morhout was taking them captive into Ireland.
5. The song and refrain they sang was noted as the first that was made.
6. Lançarote was called L'Ancelot or L'Ançaroth.
7. The *Isle de Joie* was the *Isle de Liesse*.
8. In this island the ladies of King Pelles' daughter celebrated with song and dance Lancelot's victory over Sir Albano or some other.
9. Tristan slew Helys I.
10. Helys II. was erroneously surnamed Le Brun.

The facts of agreement to which the rubrics allude, the fight with Morhout, the battle with Helys, the adventure with Galahad's mother, are so few that they do not lead to sure results concerning the originals. The existence of the five lays is, to my mind, not merely a strong, but an incontestable proof of the existence of the romances of *Tristan* and *Lancelot* in prose.

The last phrase is incontestable, though we may not slip into the assumption that these novels stood in Portuguese prose; for the same results would follow from the use of any other Iberian dialect. Galician was the agreed and conventional vehicle of the lyric, as Doric had been of the Greek ode, and was written by many others than inhabitants of Galicia or Portugal. The exposition of the rubrics, however, appears to be overloaded by the hypothesis which seems to refer all these to one composition, and that a *Tristan*. Arguments that begin in hypotheses should end either in known facts or in results that have a *prima facie* probability; and the emergence of so many unusual features warrants our reconsidering the initial assumption. The rubric of the second lay, the *bailada de escarnio*, has been shown to coincide with the details given in a passage relating to the contest of Bandemagus and Morhout in the *Baladro del Sabio Merlin*;[1] and we shall connect the poem itself with the opening of the triple adventure of Gawain, Ywain and Le Morholt. If it is the first that was made, we recollect that Bandemagus' exploits were the first after the commencement of the "Adventurous Times," and that these were begun about the time of the death of Balin le Savage, when Tristan was two or three years of age; it has, therefore, nothing to do with the battle of the Isle of Saint Sanson, nor was the latter accompanied by damsels whether as slaves or as songstresses. Similarly, despite Colocci's note, we ought to deduct the Lancelot *bailada* from *Tristan* and refer it to the third part of the romance of *Lanzarote de Lago*, though no longer extant in the surviving Spanish fragment.[2] Albano is not relevant to the passage, for he had been killed ten years previously, and Lancelot had done enough to prove his worth by defeating no less than two thousand knights in the Isle de Joie or de Liesse. These subtractions will explain Nos. 1, 2, 3, 5 (?), 7 (?) and 8 of Snra. de Vasconcellos'

[1] *Cf.* Bonilla, *Tristan* (1501), (1912), p. xxxiv and our chap. ix. Also *Baladro*, cap. 255, ed. Bonilla: "E Morloc embiaualas todas a Irlanda, e fazialas todas meter en vn castillo donde no podian salir despues; y esto hazia el por su padre e por dos sus hermanos, que eran buenos caualleros, que fueran muertos en vn torneo por juyzio de dueñas e donzellas que dieron en el reyno de Londres." And contrast *Tristan*, capp. 7–9.

[2] *Cf.* our chap. xi., *infra.*, and Sommer's *Vulgate Version of the Arthurian Legend*, v. pp. 379–403.

exposition, and we can by their help discard No. 4 and the latter part of 8; No. 6 (on the variant spelling L'Ancelot for Lancelot) is quite a normal feature of French Arthurian texts, though not elsewhere reproduced in Castilian or Portuguese romances; and the remaining points, Nos. 9 and 10, are quite normal within the prose *Tristan*, although not offered by the surviving Castilian *Don Tristan de Leonis*. The invasion of Logres by King Mark and the Saxons, their seizure of Yseult while Tristan lies ill in an abbey, and the announcement of these circumstances to Tristan, occupy three chapters of the *Demanda del Santo Grial*;[1] but we do not find there the song or its specific setting, the daughter of Brehus singing old lays of the lovers and the hero's rejoinder with the *Lai du Plours*, composed by him in Hantone Forest. The remaining songs are related to Helys,[2] father and son, in the first year of the Quest of the Holy Grail, when Tristan travelled *incognito* with a plain green shield and chanced on the younger Helys, son of the Saxon Helys whom he had killed in the Cornish invasion of the preceding year; after the battle of Saxony Tristan heard the song of birds in a forest, and his mind being flooded with thoughts of Yseut, he sang the third lay. The identification of the originals in the romance of *Tristan* certifies them as undoubtedly part of that novel in spite of their absence from the extant Spanish tale. But there is strong reason to believe in the existence at one time in the Spanish Peninsula of another, and wholly different,

[1] *Demanda del Santo Grial*, ed. Bonilla, capp. 210, 289–290.
[2] C. M. de Vasconcellos, *Lais de Bretanha*, commentary on lays 1 and 3.

Spanish or Portuguese *Libro de Tristan*,[1] attached to the *Lanzarote de Lago*, and into which, for chronological reasons, these lyrics might well enter.

In conclusion, we prefer to believe that the rubrics of the *lais de Bretanha* are not impeccable in their reference to Arthurian fact, but their inaccuracy does not amount to "changing names and inventing facts"; for that is only necessary if we adopt a hypothesis of unity to which we are by no circumstances compelled. The Morholt *bailada* is intelligible in the *Baladro del Sabio Merlin*, which we have good cause to believe was in circulation among the trovadores of D. Diniz' court. The Ançaroth *bailada* should be referred to the romance of *Lanzarote de Lago*; and the three love-lyrics are to be assigned to a book of *Tristan*, and quite probably (until we learn more than we now know) to that *Libro de Tristan* which was a limb of the Spanish Lancelot-cycle.

The matter of certain Breton lays and of novels pertaining to the Arthurian Legend is found influencing the *Historia del Cavallero de Dios que avia nombre Cifar*[2] *el qual por sus virtuosas obras et hazañosas cosas fue rey de Menton*, the oldest original Castilian fiction.[3] The prologue, which is omitted from the

[1] *Lanzarote de Lago*, fol. 355v: "Aqui se acaba el segundo y tercero libro de don lançarote y a se de començar el libro de don tristan, . . ." etc.

[2] G. Baist, *Grundriss der rom. Phil.*, II. ii. p. 439: "Die älteste selbständige kastilische Fiktion." *A propos* of Baist, if he is not cited as frequently as others in these notes, it is because the thesis we present has so much in common with his observations concerning the Arthurian romances in Spain. Our principal difference is that he dates the translations somewhat later than seems advisable, and that he is somewhat dogmatically Castilian. In this he is well supported by such evidence as we have, but it is desirable in theory to make a more liberal allowance for the different dialectal literatures at so early a period.

[3] Manuscripts in Madrid and Paris: ed. 1512, in the Bibliothèque National, Paris: ed. H. Michelant, Tübingen, 1872 (t. 112 of *Bibliothek*

printed edition of 1512, after mentioning the Jubilee of 1300, proceeds to describe the negotiations and acts connected with the sepulture of the Cardinal D. Gonzalo García Gudiel (*d.* 4th July, 1299), a ceremony which attracted considerable attention as it was the first interment of a cardinal in Spain; and among the distinguished persons that went out to meet the archdeacon Ferrand Martínez, the conductor of the *cortège* and presumptive writer of the prologue, were Fernando IV. (*d.* 1312) and his wife Da. Maria, the Archbishop of Toledo, and a bishop of Calahorra who is known to have died before 1305. The author of the prologue then introduces the history of Cifar, which he supposes to have been translated from Chaldean into Latin, and from Latin into Spanish. The *Historia del Cavallero de Dios*, in spite of its antiquity and the original merits of its composition, is not among the books most readily accessible to the student, but owes its currency still, in the main, to the analyses of C. P. Wagner, Menéndez y Pelayo and Dr. H. Thomas. It is no single work, but "a specimen of all the types of fiction and even of doctrinal literature which had till then been essayed in Europe." In its main outlines, however, it falls into three parts or books. The first recounts the adventures of Cifar himself, who, like so many heroes of Byzantine novels, and especially like St. Eustace or Placidas, became separated in strange wise from his wife and children, and after many days recovered them in a foreign land. This

des litterarischen Vereins von Stuttgart). C. P. Wagner, *Sources of El Cavallero Cifar*, in *Revue Hispanique*, x. pp. 5–104; Menéndez y Pelayo, *Origenes de la Novela*, i. pp. clxxxvi–cc ; H. Thomas, *Spanish and Portuguese Romances of Chivalry*, pp. 11–20.

first portion is but faintly tinged with military spirit or anything analogous to the Breton fictions. The second book is occupied by the counsel given by the knight to his sons Garfin and Roboan; it derives from the collection of maxims of Oriental origin known as the *Flores de la Filosofia*, and has much in common with the *Castigos y Documentos* which D. Sancho IV. directed to his son. In the third part the whole atmosphere is charged with fantasy, magic and chivalry. Roboan sets out on his travels a professed knight-errant. He displays his prowess in the kingdom of Pandulfa, the county of Turbia, and the empire of Tigrida, which he could not fail to obtain in due course along with the hand and heart of its empress Seringa. Still more marked is the colouring of an episode in which he visits the Fortunate Islands (*Islas Dotadas*) and is for a season the accepted husband of the lady Nobleza, until the devil tempts him by gifts to break the taboo in virtue of which he holds his bride. A very similar story had already figured in the first book; there the Cavallero Atrevido had dwelt with a mysterious Lady of the Lake until he, too, had transgressed the conditions of his stay.

When Grima, Cifar's wife, is wrongly suspected of adultery by her husband, the circumstantial evidence resembles that offered in the thirty-sixth tale of the *Libro de Patronio*,[1] but the sentence to the stake recalls

[1] *Libro de Patronio o del Conde Lucanor*, enxenplo 36: "De lo que contescio a un mercadero cuando fallo su mujer et su fijo durmiendo en uno."

For all parallels here cited, see C. P. Wagner, *loc. cit.* The death sentence for adultery is also found in the first pages of *Amadis de*

one of the perils of Queen Guenevere. Cifar is not altogether blameless at that season, for he possesses two wives; their meeting and the generous silence of the injured party provide a parallel to the *Lai d'Eliduc* of Marie de France. If Cifar captures a city under cover of simulated madness, so does Tristan in *La Folie Tristan*, but King David had long anticipated his use of lunacy as a military ruse; and if the Emperor of Tigrida neither laughs nor allows the inquisitive to retain their heads, he is probably a reminiscence of the *Lai de Tristan qui onques ne risi*. The episode of the Islas Dotadas recalls Geoffrey's *Insulæ Fortunatæ* and is already sufficiently Breton in tone, apart from the specific citation of the *Estoria de don Juan fijo del rrey Orian*, or Ywain, though the events alleged proceed from the *Lai de Lanval*. The fairy queen who cannot refuse her hero anything, the taboos, the demon tumbling in the water, the magic boat that moves without oars, the white boar, the damsels meeting Roboan at the postern, are all so many reflections of the lays of *Lanval*, *Graelent* and *Guigemar*; and the citation of Arthur's fight with the Cat Paus (*Cath Palug*) in chapter 105 of the first part indicates some variant of the *Livre d'Artus*. The third section of *El Cavallero Cifar* is thus found to be a liberal adaptation of various Arthurian motives, which begin to influence also the narrative of the first book. They

Gaula, where it is unjustly attributed to the Scottish code. Thence the libel proceeded to *Orlando Furioso*, iv. 59:

> "L'aspra legge di Scozia, empia e severa,
> Vuol ch'ogni donna e di ciascuna sorte,
> Ch'ad uom si giunga e non gli sia mogliera,
> S'accusata ne viene, abbia la morte."

derive both from romances and from lays, which the author presumably read in their French form, seeing that his Arthurianism stands apart from the general movement of translation in the Spanish Peninsula.

But its principal merit does not consist of this, nor in having incorporated into our literature a great number of foreign elements, but in the creation of a very original type whose practical philosophy in the form of incessant maxims derives not from books, but from the proverbial or *paroemiologic* philosophy of our people. The Ribaldo, a figure wholly foreign to previous chivalresque literature, represents the invasion of Spanish realism into the type of fiction most apparently opposed to its nature, and the importance of such a creation is not small when one considers that the Ribaldo is the only known predecessor of Sancho Panza.[1]

[1] Menéndez y Pelayo, *Orígenes de la Novela*, i. pp. cxcvii–cxcviii. The Ribaldo is the acute and sententious squire of Cifar, who follows his fortunes loyally though he considers him "desventurado e de poco recabdo."

V

THE ARTHURIAN NOVELS IN CATALONIA

In respect of the introduction and diffusion of the *matière de Bretagne* the county of Barcelona and the kingdoms of Valencia and the Baleares appear to have followed an impulse different to that of the central and western portions of the Iberian Peninsula. Here the novels were known earlier and translated later than elsewhere; here they derive from the court of Pedro IV. (1336–87); elsewhere from that of Alfonso X. (1252–84). Despite many moments of approximation, consequent on the dictation of their respective originals, there is no demonstrable relationship between the Catalan and Castilian-Portuguese cycles. For these circumstances there is no need to allege any ethnic dislike among the Catalans for the fancies of chivalry or love: we know not what we are, and our race is what we deem it. To describe the temper of a nation in a formula has tempted many a critic since Juvenal and Tacitus, but these definitions are honeycombed with exceptions and have little utility as practical guides. Whatever element of Celtic mythology or of irrationality may have been found in its distant origins, the Arthurian Legend approached Catalan literature, even as it entered the Castilian and Portuguese, only when the process of Gallicisation was complete, and when the new inspiration had become the code of European society.

But the literatures of the centre and west are discriminated from that of the east by the fundamental sundering of language, which Holy Writ has rightly judged to be the principal source of division among the human species. In a wide semicircle from Lisbon to the Ebro the dialects of Iberian Romance shade imperceptibly into one another, and the language of Zaragoza is not unintelligible by the estuary of the Tagus. These dialects, previous to the emergence of the two literary speeches—Portuguese, Galician, Leonese of various shades, Castilian old and new, Asturian, Navarrese, Aragonese—might be legitimately employed in the composition of prose or poetry, or be specialised to the expression of particular inspirations. Galician, for example, was the tongue not only of the native, but also of the Spanish stranger or even foreigner who felt the lyrical impulse; but the vast epics and *débats* of the *mester de clerecía* are impartially sprinkled over the dialects of mediæval Spain, though the *mester de juglaría* was concentrated in Old Castile. Iberian Romance was still fluid when the Breton fictions began to circulate in the central plateau and the western declivities, and it is only with the *Libro de Patronio* of D. Juan Manuel and the *Nobiliario* of D. Pedro that we perceive the established antithesis of two literary tongues. To the incoming *matière de Bretagne* Iberian Romance still presented a linguistic unity, reflected in a cultural oneness that overrode local distinctions and depended for inspiration on the thought of Northern France. Only in the case of the lyric was it induced to borrow from Provence; nor is it desirable to interpose that language, though philologically intermediate between

French and the Iberian tongues and actually rooted in a portion of the Peninsula, between the Spanish vernaculars and their sources. Spanish and Portuguese literature is deeply in the debt of France, somewhat of Provence, and hardly conscious of Catalan.

At the eastern terminus of the Iberian segment, the Aragonese dialects strip themselves of their distinguishing marks over a broad band of fifty miles in depth; but though the variations are gradual, their total product is a new speech-group evidently distinguished from the tongues of the centre and west, and as manifestly akin to the dialects of Provence. Provençal of the west or *lemosí* was, in fact, the language of literature in Catalonia during the twelfth and thirteenth centuries; and if the fourteenth established *pla catalanesch* in prose, *lemosí* continued to characterise the diction of the poets Torroella and Metge. The gradual establishment of the national speech may be followed in the archives of that era. "From 1300 to 1350 we find some thirty-two documents in Catalan as against 180 in Latin. From 1350 to 1400 the proportion is totally inverse: 385 documents of the first class as against 180 of the second. It is during the last quarter of the century that Catalan documents chiefly predominate, and in Martin I.'s reign there are redacted in Latin only the most bureaucratic sections of the Chancery."[1] From these conditions it follows that the Catalans of the thirteenth and fourteenth centuries could enjoy the Arthurian fictions on exactly the same

[1] Rubió y Lluch, *Documents per l'Historia de la Cultura Catalana Mig-Eval*, ii. p. lxxii.

terms as their co-linguists of Southern France; that translation could not be made before the literary language existed; and that, in fact, Catalonia has never been more under the necessity of translating from French than we of translating Burns or Henryson. No more than a glossary has even been needful, for educated Catalonia is bilingual and even trilingual. Northern French is appreciated without impediment, read with avidity, and employed at the writer's option.[1] The national dialect depends on the eager receptivity of the Catalan mind, which has produced a literature of translation from all languages that is probably without a peer, on local patriotism, and on an ineradicable love of the maternal cadences of *lo pus bell catalanesch del mon*. Thus, *a priori*, the Breton romances would early enter Catalonia through the linguistic affinity, and for the same reason be translated late: in Ibero-Romance penetration would be retarded by language and translation be an early necessity: but each group of dialects had independent recourse to the French originals, without the officious mediation of a second strange tongue. The *matière de Bretagne* of the Spanish Peninsula, therefore, is divided into two independent bodies of translations—those of the centre and west and those of the east.

Our earliest notice of the romances within Catalan

[1] The option is thus expressed in the fourteenth-century poem of *Frère-de-Joie et Sœur-de-plaisir* (*Romania*, xiii. p. 275):

"Sitot frances sa bel lengatge,
Nom pac en re de son linatge,
Car son erguylos ses merce,
Ez erguyll ab mi nos conve,
Car entrels francs humils ay apres,
Per qu'eu no vull parlar frances."

territory dates back to the reign of Alfonso II. (1162–1196), a troubadour and patron of troubadours, friend of Cœur-de-Lion, and sovereign of that Guiraut de Cabrera (*c.* 1170) whose extensive acquaintance with the *temperadura de Breton* we have already noticed.[1] Pedro II. (1196–1213), the loser of the battle of Muret, merited comparison with King Arthur; and to Jaime el Conquistador (1213–1276) the secondary Arthurian *Roman de Jaufre* was dedicated.[2] In the son of the Conqueror, Pedro the Great (1276–1283), we find the finished type of a knight-errant, whose exploit of holding the lists at Bordeaux, despite the manifest or covert disloyalty of the sovereigns of France and England, fills many of the most brilliant pages of Muntaner.[3] The later Catalan troubadours continue to point their verses with Arthurian names. Guillem de Cervera [4] says:

> Sa muller fets Tristayns morir, car noy jasia,
> Que de als tot son coman e son voler fasia;

and Severí de Gerona (*c.* 1270) names among womankind's victims:

> David e Salamo,
> E Lot, el fort Samso,
> Tristany, e d autres mouts;

[1] *Cf.* chap. ii., and Milá, *De los Trobadores en España* (1889), p. 273; Milá, *op. cit.*, p. 151 n.

[2] *Grundriss der rom. Phil.*, II. ii. p. 8: "Der Dichter giebt vor, dass er die Erzählung von einem Ritter am Hofe des Königs von Aragon vernommen habe. Aus den weiteren Angaben, die er über letzteren macht, scheint hervorzugehen, dass Jacob I. (1213–76) gemeint ist, und dass die Entstehungszeit des Gedichtes etwa in die Jahre zwischen 1222 und 1232 zu setzen ist."

[3] Muntaner, *Cronica del rey En Pere*, capp. 71–92.

[4] *Cf.* Bonilla y San Martín, *Don Tristan de Leonis* (1501), 1912, pp. xxvi–xxx; Rubió y Lluch, *Noticia de dos manuscrits d'un Lançalot català*, in *Revista de Bibliografía Catalana*, iii. pp. 5 *ff.*

and later names

> Lansalot e Tristany,
> Persaual e Juani,
> Rotlan e Oliuer,
> Berart de Monleyder,
> E l Xarles qui conques.

The same interest in the Breton fictions persisted in the national period of Catalan literature, and finds its most striking expression in the *Faula* of Guillem de Torrella or Torroella.[1] In a long poem of some 1250 lines, written in a Provençal that struggles with Catalan varied by speeches in a Majorcan French, Torroella gives us the narrative of an Arthurian dream. On a midsummer morn he was whisked away on the back of a whale from Soller, Majorca, to a far eastern land. A serpent, in a French that pleased the poet's ear, declared that this was the island of Morgane la Fée and of Arthur:

> Qu'enysi tu poires aperceuoir
> Que tu es en l'ilh' anquantea
> On repaira Morgan la fea
> E missire lo reys Artus.

Shortly after he saw a palfrey, richly caparisoned

> A la manera de Peris,

whose harness was adorned with many a story of love—of Floris and Blancheflor, of Iseut la Blonde and Tristan who in love so loved each other, and of other distinguished folk; and we are further notified

[1] Milá, *Poëtes Catalans* (Paris, 1876), or Denk, *Geschichte des altcatalanischen Litteratur* (1893), pp. 222–228. We have not been able to meet with the *Estudi històric i literari* (Barcelona, 1907) of G. Llabrès, cited in Crescini e Todesco's *Inchiesta del San Graal*, Intro. Note.

that as the palfrey moved, the silver bells hanging from his poitrail tinkled out one of Tristan's lays:

> Notant vn lay de Tristany,
> Qui molt es plasent de ausir.

Having mounted the horse, Torroella approached a palace, where he was welcomed by a pleasant and pretty girl of sixteen, who proved to be Morgane herself. Entering together, Torroella noted the beauty of the walls, which were hung with rich devices of chivalry. There you could recognise in the distinguished concourse,[1] Lancelot, Tristan, Palomides,

[1] "Hon yeu regardey pres e lung
Les voltes e'ls entelhamens
Els vayrols que subtilemens
Eron obrats de mantes guises.
D'aur e d'azur hi ac diuises
Junctes, batalhas e torneigs,
Amors, jauzimens e domneigs,
Certs [?] hi ha pleyts d'homes presans
E d'altres fayts richs, ben stants,
Qui donen prets segons valor.
De Tristany lo fin aymador
Virets lay pinxes les amors,
Les proesas e la valors
Perquen son temps laus e prets hac;
E del prous Lancelot del Lac
Pogrets vezer lay examen
Lo sen, la força, l'ardimen
Ab que mantench caualeria.
Lay pogretz vesser la folhia
De Pelomidas lo fortiu
Queb son coratge sobraltiu
Manech a ffi mant rich assay.
D'Ivan lo cortes virets lay
Les proeses e les cortesies
E d'Arech les caualeries
E de Galuany les aventuras.
Las batalhas forts e duras
De Baorç e de Perçaual
Que'en la gesta del Sant Graal
Fforen ensems ab Galeas
Quez hanc per armes no fo laç,
Ne per trebalh que sofferis.
De Galeot, celh que hom dis
Lo filh de la bella Ganyanda,
Viretz lay com ac amor granda

Iwain, Erec, Gawain, the three Grail-Questers, Gallehault, Blioberis, Leonel, Keu, Dinadan, Garieth, Sagramor, and many others. But Torroella complained that he did not see the king. Through a small ring, which Morgane by way of answer held to his eye, he discerned a bed: on the bed lay a young man, at the foot stood two noble matrons robed in black. Morgane named the company—Arthur, Valour, Love,—and the youthful invalid delivered a pessimistic address in corroboration to his sword Excalibur. At length he noticed the Majorcan, and on inquiry learned from Morgane that he had been brought of set purpose to communicate between Arthur and the world. Scientifically sceptical, the Catalan was prompted to ask if the king were really Arthur:

> Siets vos, Senyor, lo rei Artus,
> Celh qui attendon li Breto?

Arthur assented with some impatience; but Torroella

> Vas Lancelot per cuy morich,
> Car stet lonch temps que nol vich,
> Nen poch sauber cert nouell;
> De Blio e de Leyonell
> Com foren prous e assaians;
> De Quochs e Dinadans
> Los folhs gabs que saubion dir.
> Encara hi pogues pausar
> Los fayts d'armes e lur afar
> De Siuarlot e de Brunor,
> De Garryet e de Sagramor
> E cascuns del fis amadors
> Qui trebalharen per amors
> En bades ses nulh altre pro.
> Estor de Mares hi fo
> E Dodinell lo salvatge
> E d'Iuany maint rich vaselhatge
> E de molts altres hi fou la vida
> Asaut poxan [?] e diuissida."
>
> MILÁ, *Poëtes Catalans*, pp. 16–17.

remarked that the *Mort d'Arthur* had recounted his death. (Some details are given in the manuscript, though not reproduced by Milá. This account of the battle of Camlan, however,

> Segons que recompta la gesta,

is the only indication within our reach of the contents of the Catalan *Mort d'Arthur.*) The king's life, it was explained, had been preserved by the care of Morgane and the virtue of the Tigris; his youth was refreshed annually by the visits of the Holy Grail. But his melancholy was occasioned by what he saw in his sword, and in that blade Torroella found allegorically represented the truism that the mean-spirited prosper and the worthy are so tied that they can effect nothing. To preach the obvious Morgane sent back to Majorca the poet-squire.

The *Faula* is imitated in certain details by the *Libre de Fortuna e Prudencia* of Bernat Metge (1381), and at about the same time (1398) the author of the *Cobles de la Divisio del Regno de Mallorca* mentions "lo rei Artus." Two *testaments*, that of En Bernat Serradell de Vich (1419) and the *Testament d'Amor*, allude to Tristan, Lancelot, Gouvernal, and "lo castell de la Perillosa Guarda." The poetic dynasty of March [1] was familiar with the British fictions; as may be indicated by Jacme March's composition dated 31st August, 1370, from "La Joyosa Garda," by Arnau's mention of Tristan, Lancelot, Gallehault, Palomides, Brunehort [2] and Agravain in his *Canço*

[1] In addition to the authorities quoted, *cf.* A. Pagès, *Auzias March et ses prédécesseurs* (Paris, 1912), pp. 181–3, 143, 424, 175, 230 (*Bibliothèque des Hautes Etudes*, fasc. 194).

[2] From the Round Table romance of *Claris et Laris.*

d'Amor Tençonada, by Auzias' citation of Lancelot,[1] and by his disciple, Juan de Rocafort's,[2] song:

> Enamorat no fou mes d'Isolda
> Aquell gentil e valeros Tristany.

But the indebtedness of Auzias March was more subtle, for he relied principally on Arthurian chivalry for his casuistry of love, less by direct reference than through the *De Arte Honeste Amandi* of André le Chapelain, which afforded him a systematic exposition of the *amour courtois* as conceived by the writers of romance.[3] The *De Arte Amandi* was partly translated in the *Retgles d'Amor* of Domingo Mascó,[4] a servitor of Juan I. and Martin I. of Aragon; and under the latter's pious reign amorous sophistry was reprimanded by Fr. Antoni Canals,[5] the translator of the *Modus bene vivendi*, who advises one of that monarch's chamberlains to read only approved books, not frivolous books like the fables of Lancelot and Tristan, nor the *Roman de Reynard*, nor books provocative of concupiscence, such as books of love or books on the art of love, the *De Vetula* of (Pseudo-) Ovid, or useless books like books of tales and snatches, but rather devout books, books of Christian faith; such a book is the one he now dedicates to the ladies, and more especially to the maidens, of the court, for therein they will find matter full of all pure

[1] *Obres*, No. xv., ed. Amadeu Pagès (Barcelona, 1912). This is his only direct mention of the Arthurian characters.

[2] Denk, *Geschichte der altcatalanischen Litteratur*, p. 331.

[3] A. Pagès, *Auzias March et ses prédécesseurs*, p. 230; *cf.* pp. 317–18, 342, etc.

[4] MS. No. 2-Ll-i (fol. 46), Biblioteca Particular de Su Majestad, Madrid.

[5] A. Pagès, *op. cit.*, p. 175, citing *Docs. Inéd. del Archivo General de Aragón*, t. xiii. p. 420.

honesty. The novels of the fifteenth century are still marked, as we might expect, by Arthurian references. A passage of *Curial y Guelfa*,[1] often cited, indicates that the work of translation was not yet completed; and *Tirant lo Blanch*,[2] adducing the whole range of Arthurian heroes, seems to feel that their code of ideas and motives is not compatible with the more practical and cynical mind of his own age.

Valuable information concerning the quality and effect of the Arthurian idea upon the Catalan mind may thus be derived from the allusions and citations of general literature, but they leave us still without guidance as to the types of books and stories current, the progress and time of translation. The bilingual constitution of the public has obscured the last point to such an extent that the documents add but one fact to the knowledge of texts extant in the vernacular. It is not always possible to restrict any particular allusion to a specific book; but a clear light on the Arthurian types in circulation is shed by the great collection of documents wherewith A. Rubió y Lluch has illustrated his country's culture and his own. There must have been something peculiarly intimate and, as it were, patriarchal in the bonds uniting the princes of Aragon to their kingdom, with its three parliaments and two languages, governed by a varying title and different interests, for many of their sovereigns are distin-

[1] *Curial y Guelfa*, ed. Rubió y Lluch (Barcelona, 1901), p. 124: "Empero yo vull seguir la manera daquells cathalans qui trasladaren los libres de Tristany e de Lançalot, e tornaren los de lengua francesa en lengua catalana."

[2] Martorell, *Tirant lo Blanch*, ed. Aguiló, capp. 37, 103, 173, 174, etc.: Joseph Abaramatia, Lançalot del Lach, Boors, Perseualt, Galeas, lo Sant Greal, Tristany, Isolda, Ginebra, Artus, Morgana.

guished less by number than by sobriquet—the Battler, the Conqueror, the Great, the Ceremonious or he of the Dagger, the Ecclesiastic—and the archives of Aragon are stamped, to an extent without parallel in Europe, with the impress of the total activity of the monarchs and their families, the moulds of their dispositions, and the fluctuations of their passions and sentiments.[1] Where else will a king preen his verses, or a crown-prince ask in candid vanity the effect his compositions have had upon his nearest kin; or leave deposited a letter to his wife of which the sole end is to record his impressions under the song of a nightingale? Orders are given for exotic writings, and a sovereign finds time to laud the servant of his forebears; another drops an allusion to the *Divina Commedia* and bursts into a heartfelt eulogy upon learning,—

> quoniam sola scientia dicitur summa nobilitas in hac vita,—

and registers the *Gloria del Principat de Catalunya*, an eloquent oration before parliament rising even in the exordium from earth to a heavenly country as he quotes: *Gloriosa dicta sunt de te, Cathalonia!* In the period which these documents embrace the varying characters of the correspondents stand out in clearest relief: Jaime II., a decided if unscrupulous patron of letters, the initiator of patriotic eloquence, and the first to introduce culture to its archives; the colourless and troubled Alfonso III.; Pedro IV., a figure of restless activity whose influence is felt

[1] A. Rubió y Lluch, *Documents per l'Historia de la Cultura Catalana Mig-Eval*, 2 vols. (Barcelona, Institut d'Estudis Catalans, 1908–21). The student should read the whole of his introductions, to which I have endeavoured to approximate these paragraphs in phrase as in subject.

intimately in all departments and every detail, historian, orator, poet, and jurisconsult; Juan I., humanist and Hellenist, a *dilettante* whose eager curiosity for letters breaks into the archives long before his accession; Martin I., silent as a prince, sincerely attached to science, solitary and contemplative, whom even his spiritual guides are compelled to readdress to the business of government. And so, too, we get to know the queens: Da. Leonor, Pedro's wife, with her passion for French tapestries; Da. Violante de Bar, the reader of the latest French verses and admirer of the *Heroïdes*; Da. Maria de Luna, as much piety's slave as is her husband, Martin I. The correspondence is, of course, merely royal; but from what we have observed it differs from the efforts of private persons or religious communities only in scale. There is, perhaps, an emphasis on *belles lettres* rather than erudition; but the national dynasty, becoming more and more Catalanised, participates more and more in the life and aspirations of the community, opening the roads by which its culture was to advance. From patrons of troubadours they make themselves troubadours, historians, orators, musicians, artists; they speak a language still understood by their countrymen, and after six centuries have rolled by, their profoundly Catalan voice and mind find echoes of love and patriotic yearning.[1]

Into these archives enter many of the most famous names of Catalan literature, Lull, Arnau de Vilanova, Fernández de Heredia, Muntaner, Descoll, Metge and Eximeniç; and of foreign origin Rubió y Lluch's documents present more than two hundred titles of

[1] Rubió y Lluch, *op. cit.*, ii. pp. x–xiii.

books, proceeding from languages as far flung as Castilian, Provençal, French, Italian, Latin, Greek, Arabic and Hebrew. Among these, perhaps, the Arthurian Legend fills no very great space; yet to it some of the writers return with significant iteration. Pedro the Ceremonious is particularly urgent; and in general the documents present a clearer statement of the state of these interests in the fourteenth century in the county of Barcelona than can be given for Castile and Portugal.

I. On the 3rd July, 1385, the Infante D. Juan borrows the *Croniques d'Anglaterra* from Mossen Ramon Alemany de Cervelló, and in 1392 he refuses to send the *Llibre del Conestable* to his cousin, unless in exchange for the *Croniques de Bretanya* held by Mossen Guerau de Cervelló.[1] We have no clue as to the contents or language of these works. The Nine Worthies included the name of Arthur of Britain, and we find Pedro IV. purchasing tapestries from France, which depict them or their history, as early as 1347 and 1351.[2] King Arthur enjoyed the honour of a cloth entirely devoted to himself, bought and paid for in Paris on the 2nd September, 1368, on behalf of Pedro's queen, Da. Leonor.[3] He, at least, would be present in those books of the *Tabula Rotonda* or *Taula Redona* [4] (the latter, we observe, is a Catalan title inserted in a Latin context) copied for Pedro IV. in 1349 by Ramon d'Oliver of Perpignan, and in 1356 by Bernat Valls. The same ground was covered

[1] *Documents*, i. Nos. 366 and 419.
[2] *Ibid.*, i. Nos. 135 and 157.
[3] *Ibid.*, ii. p. 104 n. 1: ".i. drap frances de la istoria del rey Artus, lo qual es lonc de .iiii. alnes."
[4] *Ibid.*, i. Nos. 144, 171, 172.

pictorially in the French figured cloth of thirty-six palms in length in which was illustrated the *Istoria Militum Mense Rotunde*, one of ten similar tapestries or "draps istoriats" which cost Queen Leonor of Sicilia 32 florins 9 grossi in March 1356. The documents do not indicate what was the content of these books of the Round Table, though they do seem to suggest a Catalan translation between the years 1349 and 1356. The inference is precarious and unconfirmed. These works above named concerned Arthur and probably Brutus, but cannot otherwise be classified.

II. Of the various novels relating to Tristan, the *Meliadux*,[1] in French, was purchased by Pedro IV. on the 27th March, 1339; and the entire series, also in French, bound in two volumes—*Meliadux*[2] with *Guiron le Courtois*, making the romance of *Palamedes*, and *Tristan de Leonis*—are offered by the duke primogenitus to his wife in 1383. In Martin's reign Tristan was popular enough to appear at public festivities, seeing that he was depicted on the trappings of horses at the state entry of the king into Valencia in 1402,[3] along with Iseut, Lancelot, Guenevere, and also Aristotle, Virgil, Jason, Semiramis, Solomon, the Count of Barcelona, Empress, Pope and Saladin. The novel of *Tristan* in French

[1] *Documents*, i. No. 101.

[2] *Ibid.*, i. No. 344: "Nos hir, cercans nostres libres, ne trobam dos entre los altres, scrits abdos en ffrances: la un es del rey Meliadux e del bon caveller sene pahor, e de Gurm lo cortes, e de Donahi lo Ros ab d altres cavallers molts, l altre es de Tristany, ystoriat."

[3] *Cf.* Bonilla, *Tristan* (1501), 1912, who quotes: "Item, donj an bernat godal per xv paraments de caual que auia pintat e donat son or e argent e altres colors, ço es, lo parament d aristotil e d virgili, e d tristany e d jsolda, e de jason e d eropra, e d etnas e d semjramis, e d lançalot e d ginebre, e d salomo e del conte de barcelona, e de la imperadriu e del papa, e los de saladrjn. . . ." (From the account of the expenses of King Martin's entry into Valencia in 1402.)

appeared in the inventory of the library of the unfortunate Prince of Viana, who perished in 1461; but for an assurance of a Catalan version we have nothing to allege except the passage already quoted from *Curial y Guelfa*.

III. The cycle of the Holy Grail also appears in these documents. Vespasian was commemorated on two of the tapestries of Queen Leonor: the one, in gold and velvet, depicted Titus and his father; the other, purchased at Montpellier in December 1368, contained the history of the destruction of Jerusalem.[1] In Castile and Portugal this novel was slightly adapted to serve as a general introduction for the cycle of the Holy Grail: in Catalan it is likewise still extant, and has been published by the Llibrería de l'Avenç as *La Destrucció de Jerusalem*.[2] The *Joseph of Arimathia* or *Estoire del Saint Graal* is not found among our sources, unless it entered into one of the unclassified compilations above described, but it seems that the *Livre de Merlin*, presumably according to the variant of the Pseudo-Robert de Boron, is to be understood from the *Profacies de Merlí en frances* of D. Martin's library, which Juan I. had handled in 1391.[3] While still

[1] *Documents*, i. No. 209, ii. p. 104 n. 1: "Un drap de lana françes, a obs de paret, de diverses colors, en lo qual es la istoria del rey Vespesia que pren la ciutat de Jherusalem."

[2] *Destrucció de Jerusalem*, Barcelona, Llibrería de l'Avenç (*Histories d'altres temps*, No. 8, ed. Miquel y Planas).

[3] *Documents*, ii. p. 327 n. 1, and No. 338: "Item un altre libre appellat *Profacies de Merli* en frances scrit en pergamins ab post de fust cubert de cuyrs vermell ab .v. claus petits a cada post et ab dos tancadors de parxa groch e vermell, lo qual comença: 'Cien droyt,' e faneix: 'Explicit les profacies.' El manuscrit de la llibrería del rey Martí comença igual que 'l Merlí de Robert de Boron publicat per G. Paris y J. Ulrich (Paris, 1886), encara que aquesta coincidencia, en mots tan típichs, no significa res."

prince, the Infante D. Juan had named one of his hounds Merlin (1372) in token of his respect for Arthurian knight-errantry, and he read with diligence those prophecies of contemporary Merlins which promised that one of his lineage should be crowned emperor.[1] The third part of the trilogy, the *Quest of the Holy Grail* according to the version ascribed to Walter Map, was current in Catalan, and is guaranteed by the text which Crescini and Todesco have edited for the Institute of Catalan Studies. A French manuscript of this romance was in the library of the Prince of Viana; and it is one of the books and other valuables concerning which Pedro IV. wrote to Pedro Zapata on behalf of the princesses Blanca and Maria in 1342.[2] The document is in Latin, the inventory in Aragonese; it is therefore possible that the work may have to be referred to the Castilian-Portuguese group of translations, which would be generally those current in Aragon, and this further raises the doubt as to whether it was a Map- or a Boron-*Quest*, seeing that both versions were known in Castile.[3]

IV. It is with reference to the *Lancelot* that we are best guided. A copy was bequeathed by Jaime II., whose collection came largely from the spoil of

[1] *Documents*, i. No. 299: "Entes havem per vostre nebot Galceran de Margarola que vos d aquestes dies trametets al senyor rey .i. libre en lo qual fa mencio, entra altres cosas, de la contesa d aquests papas, e que .i. de la casa d Arago devie esser coronat per emperador."

[2] *Ibid.*, ii. No. 68.

[3] The Kingdom of Navarre presents another instance of bilingualism in Spain. At one time part of the royalty of France, at another ruled by such kings as Thibaut of Champagne, the French novels must have circulated freely in certain social classes. In the library of Carlos III. were found: *Un Romans de Lancelot. Item un Romanz Pampeluno vieio de Lanzelot et Bors su Compaynero*. Navarrese, as a dialect, differs by but a shade from Aragonese.

the Templars, to his son Raimundo Berenguer on the 6th August, 1319.[1] His chaplain, Domingo Gil d'Arenós, began to transcribe this romance in 1336 and completed it for Pedro IV. in 1339;[2] and yet another copy was executed by Jaume Capcir, chaplain of the church of St. John at Perpignan--the *entrepôt* of Franco-Catalan culture—in 1346. The Infante Juan sent a copy of the novel in 1374 to Abram de Carcassonne,[3] a Jewish bookbinder, and five years later communicates under his privy seal with the Viscount of Roda,[4] En Ramon Perellós, saying that he has borrowed a French *Lancelot* in admiration of its beauty. But the letters of principal interest to us are those in which Pedro IV. requires Pedro Palau to return to him the book of *Lançalot en catalá* which the duke primogenitus had been reading. They are dated respectively 17th February[5]

[1] *Documents*, ii. No. 40: "Item dicto infanti Raimundo Berengarii unum librum cohopertum de partge viridi et cum platonibus qui incipit: 'apres ce che maestres Gauters,' et finit in ultima linea: 'lo fasca e digats tuyt amen,' et videtur liber de Lançalot."

[2] *Ibid.*, ii. No. 59 and n.; i. Nos. 105 and 127.

[3] *Ibid.*, ii. No. 182.

[4] *Ibid.*, i. No. 301, an unusually charming letter:

"Lo PRIMOGENIT D ARAGO,

"Veçcomte: nos aci estants sabem que vos hic haviets en la vostra casa .i. bell libre de Lançalot en frances; e quan l aguem vist per sa bellesa havem lo ns pres e retengut, volents e pregants vos que, tota vegada que avinent ho haiats, nos certiffiquets ab vostres letres que tots los novells e ardits que sapiats. e fer nos n ets agradable servey, dada en Perpenya, sots nostre segell secret, a .xx. dies de juny de l any .mccclxxix.

"PRIMOGENITUS.

"Fuit directa viçecomiti de Roda."

[5] *Ibid.*, i. No. 204:

"Lo REY,

"Manam vos que, vista la present, per persona certa nos trametats aci a la ciutat de Valencia lo libre de Lançalot qui es escrit en lengua catalana e en pergami, e lo qual lo duch primogenit tenie l altre die en Barchinona. e aço no laquiets. dada en Valencia, sots nostre segell secret, a .xvii. dies de ffebrer de l any .mccclxii.

"Fuit directa Petro Palau."

and 16th March, 1362,[1] and as the prince was then eleven years of age, we can probably deduce both the *terminus ad quem* of the translation and its didactic purpose. We are strangely drawn to a king wise enough to know that *Lancelot du Lac* is incomparably the best of books for boys, who considered archbishops the fit porters of such a treasure, and whose librarians had the good taste to retain it for a whole month after his peremptory demand! It is probably part of this *Lançalot en catalá*[2] which

[1] *Documents*, i. No. 205:

"Lo rey,

"Manam vos que de continent, vista la present, nos enviets per l arquebisbe de Caller o per altra persona, lo libre de Lançalot, de pergami, escrit en cathala, en lo qual legia nostre fill lo duch quan erem a Barchinona. e maravellam nos molt com no l nos havets ja trames, maiorment com altra vegada vos hajam escrit d aquesta raho matexa. dada en Valencia sots nostre segell secret, a .xvi. dies de març en l any de la nativitat de Nostre Senyor .mccclxii.

"Rex Petrus.

"Fuit directa Petro Palau, tenenti claves archivi domini regis Barchinone.

"Dominus rex mandavit mihi Jacobo de Castilione."

We cannot, of course, absolutely conclude that there was no Catalan translation previous to this date, but only that we have no trace of one such. In a similar case the documents begin to mention Perellós' translation of the *Purgatorium Sti. Patricii* only in 1386 (*Documents*, i. No. 382 and n.), which is the basis of later versions by Montalbán, Lope de Vega, and Calderón. Yet the same work had already been translated by Ramon Ros de Tárrega (ed. R. Miquel y Planas, *Llegendes de l altra vida*). The same history is possible for the *Lancelot*, but we have no evidence in its support.

[2] I transcribe the following paragraph, of which I can give no account, from Gayangos, *Libros de Caballerías* (*Biblioteca de Autores Españoles*, No. 40), pp. x–xi, n. 9: "Mi amigo, el señor don Mariano Aguiló, bibliotecario segundo de Barcelona, me ha comunicado últimamente, entre otras noticias curiosas relativas a este ramo de bibliografía, la de una novela en prosa catalana sobre este mismo asunto de Lanzarote del Lago, intitulada: *Tragedia ordenada per Mossen Gras, la qual es part de la gran obra dels actes del famos caualler Lançalot del Lac, en la qual se mostra clarament quant les solacies en las cosas de amor danyen: et com als qui verdaderament amen, ninguna cosa les desobliga. Endereçada al egregi compte de Iscla.* Por estar falto al fin el ejemplar de este libro, que parece impreso a fines del siglo xv o principios del xvi, no se puede calcular cuál sería su extensión."

survives in the fragment found at Campos in Majorca, and transcribed by En Mateu Obrador.

V. In semi-dependence on the legends of the British court of Camalot the old Provençal *Roman de Jaufre*[1] had been connected with the name of Jaime I. and circulated among his successors, the lessons of the *amour courtois* were transcribed by Domingo Mascó in the *Retgles d'Amor* and were combated by Fray Antoni Canals' *Modus Bene Vivendi* in the court of Martin I.[2]

VI. Finally, the self-standing Spanish novels, which arose in free imitation of the *matière de Bretagne*, were appreciated by the princes of Aragon. A certain Eximeno de Monreal, an Aragonese, offered to transcribe the *Historia del Cavallero Cifar*[3] in 1361; and Pedro IV. insisted somewhat testily on the fulfilment of this promise, *cum autem dictus liber sit nobis multipliciter opportunus*. *Amadis de Gaula* was remembered in the name of one of the Infante D. Juan's hounds in the year 1372, along with Merlin from the Grail story, and Ogier from the *Romancero*.[4]

The royal correspondence gives us a systematic review of the Catalan interest in Breton fictions during the middle and later years of the fourteenth century, though it is less satisfactory as an account of the labour of translation. That there was much activity is evident; but of its whole product but two fragments have been recovered and presented to our perusal by the industry of scholars. A single folio,

[1] The *Istoria de Jaufre* was painted on the walls of the Moorish room in the Aljafería of Zaragoza (*Documents*, i. No. 160, of date 23rd February, 1352. A letter in Aragonese).

[2] *Ut supra*.

[3] *Documents*, i. No. 199.

[4] *Ibid.*, ii. p. 327, n. 1.

numbered clxxxvij, was discovered in the archives of the parish of Campos in Majorca, and has been illustrated by Rubió y Lluch and copied by M. Obrador.[1] It is part of an account of the great fight between Sir Lancelot and the felon knight Sir Carados.[2] The battle is already raging in the plain, but Lancelot's strength tells; the combatants enter Carados' castle locked in a deadly embrace; Carados breaks free and tries to mount a stair, and Lancelot has the misfortune to shatter his sword on a step. But a damsel gives him a blade from the knight's armoury and shuts the door on that traitor; his right arm is severed by Lancelot, and he recognises in the sword a prophecy that he would be slain by his own blade and by what he loved best. Carados leaps into a fosse that leads to Gawain's prison—and so the fragment breaks off. Its collation with the corresponding portion of the Castilian *Lanzarote de Lago* demonstrates an identity of story without correspondence of words. The sword which Lancelot breaks, for example, is in Catalan "the good sword of King Arthur which he carried, which was one of the good swords in the world"; but in Castilian it is the sword received that is "one of the fair swords in the world." A second comparison falls to be made. The two narratives are of approximately the same length, but the Catalan is the more closely written and crowds into a single folio, numbered 187, the matter of the Spanish folios 88r–90r.[3] The latter is

[1] *Revista de Bibliografía Catalana*, iii. (1903), pp. 5 *ff*.

[2] P. Paris, *Romans de la Table Ronde*, iv. (*Lancelot du Lac*), laisse lxxxiv.

[3] Rubió y Lluch, in *Revista de Bibliografía Catalana*, iii. pp. 5 *ff*., and Obrador's transcription.

numbered from the commencement of the second book of *Lancelot*; it follows, evidently, that the Catalan folio is torn from a romance embracing both books—unless we choose the improbable alternative that it was originally a mere fragment bound up and numbered with other manuscripts. This folio belongs to the late fourteenth century, and may have been the subject of an allusion in Majorca in 1441; and though this first part is lost, it is possible that we still have its French original, for the manuscript numbered 485 in the National Library at Madrid, named by Gallardo[1] *Libro de Caballerías* and by O. Klob[2] *Artus*, is in fact a first book of *Lancelot du Lac*, extending from the hero's birth to the great gathering at the Roche aux Saisnes.[3] At this point an *explicit* is begun, but is scratched out; a new hand continues the narrative, but soon tails off into a series of scribbles. The last page has been torn in half and mended with a strip of paper, and the badness of the writing, together with much thumbing, impairs its legibility. But at least two notes as to ownership can be made out:

> Al molt alt e molt poderos seyor Infan . . . mo bur . . . comte dampuries,

and

> Senyor jac Roy d' payllas.

The fly-leaf assigns the work to the printed library of D. Gaspar Galcerán de Gurrea y Aragon, Count

[1] Gallardo, *Ensayo de una Biblioteca Española*, ii. app.

[2] O. Klob, in *Zeitschrift für rom. Phil.*, xxvi. p. 177 n.

[3] Bibl. Nac. Madrid, MS. No. 485=B. 14, French, paper, fifteenth century, 284 fols., initials illuminated, no titles: on back, *Flos Mundi*: fols. 26–35 bound after 36–48, and fol. 241 after 246. Between 228 and 229 is a leaf dated 1536, inscribed with three lines from the *Magnificat*.

of Guimerá, etc.; and the scribe's trick of confusing unaccented *e* and *a* might suggest that he also was a Catalan. The manuscript was evidently one of the French novels which circulated among princely readers in Catalonia during the fifteenth century, and was probably a copy of another belonging to the previous century, and of the same type and use.

A more considerable production, though still a fragment, is the version of the *Quest* mentioned by Varnhagen, and edited by Crescini and Todesco for the Institute of Catalan Studies.[1] The original manuscript contains 137 folios, of which the first 130 are occupied by this text. An *ex libris* announces that it was at one time possessed by Jo: Vinc. Pinelli, and an annotation by that bibliophile runs: *La quarta parte del terzo volume di Lancelot du Lach in lingua catalana scritta l'anno* 1380. *La quale risponde allo stampato in lengua francese per Gioan Petit in foglio, Parisi*, 1533, *à ch.* 65 *et finisce a ch.* 116. *Vita miracoli e morte di S. Bernardo in versi antichi in calce.* The date of the transcription is given in a short note of ownership by the transcriber, G. Rexach, dated 16th May, 1380;[2] and it would appear that his surname, and his affection for the vowel *a*, both characterise him as a Majorcan. The narrative opens with precipitation on the *recto* of the first folio: "And at that time the story says that, at the Feast of Pentecost, the companions of the Round Table . . ." The fair damsel duly arrives on horseback to announce the

[1] V. Crescini and V. Todesco, *La Versione Catalana dell' Inchiesta del San Graal secondo il codice dell' Ambrosiana di Milano*, 179 *sup.* (Barcelona, Institut d'Estudis Catalans, 1917). The story is studied sufficiently in Crescini's introduction, which we follow.

[2] "Aquast lebre es den .G. Rexach / lo qual la escrit hi acabat dimecras / a xvi yõrs de mayg de. lãy .m / ccc lxxx."

coming of Galahad; and after the achievement of the adventures of the Siege Perilous and the Sword, the whole court breaks up in the Quest of the Holy Grail, which is humiliating to the greater number. The narrator takes his reader unsparingly through all the intricate adventures of the questers and all the tautological admonitions of the priests, until at length the Holy Vessel is discovered, and Sir Galahad dies in bliss; and so little does he vary from the traditional exposition of his subject that the English reader can become possessed of his whole matter in the more graceful prose of Sir Thomas Malory (Books xiii.–xvii.). Galahad dead, Percival in a hermitage, and Bors at Camalot once more, the book is hurriedly concluded by an acknowledgment of that Mestre Galter who made the book of the High Quest of the Holy Grail for love of King Henry.

The characteristic marks of this work are studied by Crescini in a prologue to his edition, and it is only incumbent on us to recapitulate the chief of his points. He has compared it scrupulously with H. O. Sommer's *Vulgate Version of the Arthurian Romances*, with the Spanish and Portuguese novels as edited by Bonilla and Reinhardstoettner, and with the *Libro terzo de' gran fatti del valeroso Lancilotto del Lago*, printed at Venice in 1569, by Michele Tramezzino. The translation stands apart from the Castilian-Portuguese romance, but close to the Vulgate, by describing that type of *Quest* which is connected with the name of Walter Map.[1] We should

[1] Fol. 130v: "E lo Rey Artus tramas per tots sos clergas de sa cort, aquals qui les aventuras matian en ascrit ni les aventuras qui eran avangudes als caveles de layns, e si comta Baorts les avantures del Sant Grasal axi con el las avie vistas e foran mases an escrit ab los

add that even when the Castilian *Demanda del Sancto Grial* breaks away from the pseudo-Boron to follow Map (capp. 373–390), the Catalan continues to present differences of phrase;[1] so that the striking alteration made by the Castilian redactor is not to be attributed to the influence of the Catalan. Among the variant readings of the Vulgate the *Inchiesta* is found agreeing chiefly with those denoted *M*;[2] but as this concordance is not regular and continuous, it is clear that the translator handled not *M*, but another manuscript of *M*'s family. He misunderstands, omits, and blurs his original, though some of his faults are to be debited to his copyist; and his method of translation is the most literal that can be imagined.[3]

altres libras don mestre Galter fan al libre del Sant Grasal per amor del Rey Anrich son senyor, qal fan traledar de lati an romans e si as afinat lo libre abtant que pus non parle de las avantures del Sant Grasal en ast libre ni en altre, e si era nagu qui mas na dixes non fase a craure.

"Aqui fanax la storia del Sant Grasal.

"Finito libro sit laus gloria x̄p̄ō."

[1] *Cf.*, v. gr., *Demanda*, cap. 389: "Estuuo assi Perseual en la mongia siruiendo a Jesu Christo vn año y vn mes, y a cabo deste tienpo passose deste siglo; y los monjes lo enterraron en el palacio spiritual cerca de su hermana e cerca del buen rey Galaz, ca assi auia el mandado."

And *Inchiesta*, fol. 130r: "E si vische Perseval .j. any e puyxs traspasa dest segle e sen puya fer compaya a Galeas sus alt el sel e sil fan Baorts soterar apres de sa sor e apres de Galeas al Palau Asparital."

[2] Bibl. Nat. Paris, MS., fonds fr., 342.

[3] *Cf. Vulgate*: "Lors fu galaas apeles & il vint auant si saienoilla deuant les sains & iura comme loiax cheualiers que' (il) ceste queste maintenroit vn an & .j. ior & plus encore sil le couenoit faire. ne iamais a cort ne reuenra deuant quil saura la uerite del saint graal sil le puet trouer ne sauoir en nule maniere."

And *Inchiesta*: "Lavos fo apelat Galeas e el vanch evant e sagonola devant los sans e iura can a leal caveler qual aqasta questa mantandra .j. any e .j. yorn hi mes ancara quel yames a cort no tornara tro qua el sapia la veritat del sant grasal, si el ho pot saber en naguna manera."

Agreement of *Inchiesta* with *Vulgate*, pp. xiv–xxvii; with *M*, pp. xxviii–xxix; disagreement with *M*, p. xxx; errors of translator, pp. xxxi–xxxv; errors of copyist, pp. xxxv–xxxviii; occasional independence of *Inchiesta*, pp. xxxix–xliii. All references are to Crescini's Introduction.

Some of the version's mistakes or the hesitations between different renderings of the same idea belong indubitably to the translator, whose name is not to be discovered; but palæographical blunders (such as "Reus lo senascal" for "Kex li senescaus" of the French, "los yorns del Fas" for "los yorns del flos," "ancare tamudas" for "an car tanudas") are found, without implying a long tradition for the manuscript, and must be referred to Rexach. Rexach brings his work to a close with the achievement of the Quest, and he probably copied no more than this narrative. The dimensions of the original translation may have been more considerable, and in its primitive form it embraced, no doubt, the complete novel of *Lancelot du Lac.* Whether the Ambrosian fragment be related to the folio of Campos is not determined; and the date of translation from the French, which must have been previous to 1380, may be provisionally connected with the first allusion to *Lançalot en catalá*, namely the 17th February, 1362. It is, however, clear that neither the one nor the other Lancelot fragment influenced or was affected by the extant texts of the central and western translations.

VI

THE ARTHURIAN NOVELS IN CASTILE AND PORTUGAL: "TRISTAN"[1]

We may thus, after a long preamble, approach the individual romances of the Castilian-Portuguese group. The novels extant in either of these literatures, which may proceed from a greater number of dialects, are found to fall within a restricted number of types, and exist either in interrelated versions on both sides of the border, or where one element is lacking, are still insufficiently explained without the evidence of both literatures. On the one hand, the intricate mazes of the trilogy of the Holy Grail cover both cultures;

[1] Texts. Manuscripts: *Tristan*, fragt., 1 folio, fourteenth century, Bibl. Nac., Madrid; *Cuento de Tristan*, fragt., fourteenth or fifteenth century, Vatican, No. 6428.

Early Editions: *Libro del esforzado cavallero Don Tristan de Leonis*, Valladolid, Juan de Burgos, 1501; Seville, Juan Varela, 1520 (F. Columbus, *Registrum*, No. 4008); Seville, Juan Cromberger, 1528; Seville, Juan Cromberger, 1533 (perhaps a misprint for 1528); *Coronica nuevamente emendada y añadida del buen cauallero Don Tristan de Leonis y del rey Don Tristan de Leonis el joven, su hijo*, Seville, Dominico de Robertis, 1534.

Reprints: Bonilla, *Anales de la Literatura Española*, 1904 (Fragt. Bibl. Nac., also in Bonilla, *Tristan* (1501)); Monaci, *Facsimili di antichi manoscritti*, Rome, Martelli, No. 6, and *Tristan de Leonis*, ed. Bonilla, 1921 (Fragt. Vatican); *Tristan de Leonis*, ed. Bonilla, Madrid, 1912 (ed. of 1501); *Libros de Caballerias*, i. pp. 339–457, ed. Bonilla, Madrid, 1907 (ed. of 1528).

Criticism: Bonilla y San Martín, *Tristan de Leonis*, Madrid, 1912, Intro.; *id.*, *Anales de la Literatura Española*, 1904; *id.*, *Leyendas de Wagner*, Madrid, 1913; G. T. Northup, *The Italian Origin of the Spanish Prose Tristram Versions*, in *Romanic Review*, iii., 1912, pp. 194–222; and in *Modern Philology*, xi., 1913, pp. 259–265; *id.*, in *Modern Language Notes*, xxviii. 1913, pp. 30–31; C. M. de Vasconcellos, *Lais de Bretanha*, in *Revista Lusitana*, vi., 1900, or in *Cancioneiro da Ajuda*, ii.

on the other hand, the texts relating to Tristan and Lancelot have survived only in Castilian, but their traces are also seen in the West. The present state of the romances is modern, belonging to their decadence, and it will be necessary to require of each one singly the circumstances of its origin and the language or dialect of its first form; such particulars are difficult to seek, and are in certain instances inaccessible; but what evidence of their history remains within our comprehension appears to refer them to one initial impulse, to an influence radiating from the court of the Spanish monarchs at Toledo into the subcourt of the kings of Portugal. Other novels may have existed which did not show these international features; but on such, in their absence as bodies or even as traditions, we can pass no judgment. On the other hand, the same Arthurian complex may have extended into the Catalan province through the dialect of Aragon; but once more, as we have shown, there is no certain evidence of such intercourse, and some probable cause to deny it. The documents of the house of Aragon, as well as the existing Catalan texts, point to an independent motive and a later date for the process of translation.

The criteria of politics or language do not assist us to assign the romances separately to either the Castilian or the Portuguese literature, because they belong to that period of uniform experience and local divergence which the Castilian rulers indicated as the "Empire of the Spains," but our exposition can follow the earlier discrimination of the novels themselves. The story of Tristan stands aloof from the whole court of King Arthur, where he is a late and infrequent visitor, and it is developed in another world amid the narrow seas of Cornwall, Ireland and Brittany. Even when the powerful influence of Sir Lancelot admitted Tristan to the companionship of the Round Table and conventionalised his character, the Cornish cavalier remained almost entirely strange to the greatest achievement of that body, the Quest of the Holy Grail. For these reasons it is convenient to treat first of *Don Tristan de Leonis*; then to cut a way through the tangle of Grail romances, the *Historia de Vespasiano o de la Destruccion de Jerusalem*, the *Joseph Abaramatia*, the *Baladro del Sabio Merlin con sus Profecias*, and the *Demanda del Sancto Grial*; and by so doing we shall have disentangled the romance of *Lanzarote de Lago*, whose protagonist is also deuteragonist of every other Arthurian history, and who was liable to cancellation by his apparent coincidence with other narratives. Further, the Castilian book of Lancelot is a mere fragment in our hands, though from the Grail complex we can comb out other episodes of his history. Whether these *membra disjecta* may lawfully be ascribed to a great cyclic romance of the hero, such as, it is to be presumed, was attempted by the first translator, is not clear; but the necessity for their collection gives priority in our exposition to the *Merlin y Demanda* over the *Lanzarote*. The order we propose to adopt, therefore, is not chronological but latitudinal, conditioned by the readiness with which each part may be detached from the general mass; and we begin with Tristan.

Tristan's adventures in the Spanish versions pertain to two distinct phases of his character and two different stages of his legend, according as they are intended to illustrate his passion for Queen Iseut or to equate him in prowess to Lancelot. The latter occupy the middle part of the novel, and give a setting to three great battles between the paladins and one between Tristan and Galahad, Lancelot's *alter ego*. In these his character is reduced to the conventions of knighthood and closely modelled on that of his rival; while Lancelot, Guenevere, and the peevish Arthur are drawn into a resemblance to the Cornish "triangle." Those passages which concern Tristan and Iseut are of a more ancient and essential character.[1] King Mark's baseness is powerfully illustrated in the opening chapter by a timid compliance with Le Morholt's demands and the dastardly murder of a brother. Then we hear of the birth and early troubles of Tristan, his perils from the unrequited passion of Belisenda, his deliverance of Cornwall from the Irish tribute imposed by Le Morholt, who deals him a traitorous blow. Morholt perishes in Ireland, whither after two years Tristan follows. Cured by Iseut, he becomes a noted jouster; but as the notch in his sword is found to tally with a fragment left in Le Morholt's skull, he falls into danger of his life and is banished. Mark, being worsted in a love affair by his nephew, revengefully orders him to fetch Iseut from Ireland to become Queen of Cornwall; which errand Tristan is enabled to accomplish safely as by chance he meets with an occasion of aiding the King of Ireland against an accuser. Through the mistake of Brangwain, however, Tristan and Iseut

[1] Capp. 1–42, 48, 53, 55–56, 65–66, 80–83. I quote from *Tristan* (1501), ed. Bonilla, 1912.

drank the *lovedranc* intended for Iseut and King Mark, and their destiny was fixed. They turned aside from their voyage to stay for a time in the Giant's Isle; and on reaching Tintagel they contrived to hoodwink the suspicious bridegroom. For some time they had to fight against the plots of Lamorad, Aldaret and a jealous damsel, being at length taken, condemned, and freed from an ignominious death only by the friendly offices of Sagramor. Escaping to the House of the Wise Damsel, they are again surprised by Mark; while Tristan lies wounded by a poisoned arrow, Iseut is swept away to strict confinement at Tintagel. Unable to see his lady, Tristan took his way to Brittany, to be cured of his sufferings by Iseut Blanche-Mains, whom, after an expedition against a count of Egipta, he marries in the hope of forgetting the other. But the marriage is not consummated; memories of the Cornish Iseut restrain him, and her jealous epistle stings him into a return to England (capp. 1–41). Tristan and Mark are reconciled (48); but the lovers flee from the scandal-mongers of the court (53), and are welcomed by Lancelot and Guenevere at Joyosa Guarda (55–6). Another reconciliation is effected by King Arthur, who shows them to Mark sleeping in one bed, but divided by a naked sword (65–6). The conclusion (80–3) concerns the death of Tristan: how he was mortally wounded by his uncle, and of his sad farewells; how Iseut visited him, and how they perished in a last embrace. No vengeance is taken on King Mark except by his conscience; but the volume is eloquently closed by Tristan's own account of the features and beauty of Iseut.

Such is the main thread of the narrative as it was known in Spain. The translator dealt skilfully with his original, and though his manner is paratactic, it is rarely amorphous. The first forty chapters are rapid and active; the last three slower, but eloquent and rising to a much-admired climax in the description of Iseut.[1] It is possible, however, that not all of these excellences were coeval with the work itself, for the style bears a certain family resemblance to that of the *Baladro del Sabio Merlin* of 1498, both books being issued by Juan de Burgos. Something of the gift of phrase is lacking, perhaps, in the inserted adventures,[2] which at all events inflict an irreparable wound on the unity of the composition. The voyage from Brittany to Tintagel was interrupted in order to allow Tristan to display to Kahedin (Quedin) the adventures of the Gasta Floresta, where Arthur was entrapped (capp. 42–7). No sooner was Tristan back at court than he spent five precious chapters in the defence of the Passage of Tintagel—a feat more worthy of Suero de Quiñones than of the Cornish lover—and in his first battle with Sir Lancelot (48–52). The escape from the courtiers' sneers leads to three tournaments[3] and another skirmish with Lancelot (54); and by transferring the lovers from a forest *mise-en-scène*, it destroys the credibility of the drawn sword as evidence of their continence. Thirteen chapters are miscellaneous (67-79): Tristan

[1] See Bonilla's note, *Tristan* (1501), pp. 382–4.

[2] Combining the events of cap. 75 and those of 25, Garci-Ordóñez de Montalvo (*Amadis*, iv. cap. 48, dedication 1492, first known ed. 1508) cites *El libro de don Tristan e de Lanzarote*, an appropriate title. *Cf.* Bonilla's note, *op. cit.*, p. 331.

[3] Iseut's ardour has also cooled, so that she can say: "No vine con vos sino por ver vuestras cauallerias" (cap. 58).

fights Palomades, and later Lancelot at the *Perron Merlin*; he takes Morholt's seat at the Round Table; he is defeated by the ancient knight of Uther's court, Branor le Brun; Morgane la Fée vainly tries to seduce him, as she had assaulted Lancelot; he has a drawn battle with Sir Galahad. If any retrenchments have been made in the novel, it is probably in this section that we should expect them; nor would any blame attach to the abbreviator, except that he would not have been sufficiently drastic.

The Spanish story of Tristan is contained in a number of texts which are closely interrelated. The first printed edition, which is also the earliest complete document, was executed at Valladolid by Juan de Burgos in 1501, and may now be seen at the British Museum. The first three folios have been damaged, but probably contained the *Prohemio*, or Prologue, addressed by Felipe Camus to the Lord of Chimay, which was certainly found in the second edition, published at Seville in 1520 by Juan Varela, and can still be read in Cromberger's reprint and in that of Dominico de Robertis. There is an Epilogue addressed to a "muy virtuoso señor," which, despite some flagrant modernisms of style, may have been ancient in the main. Juan de Burgos, who seems to have had a weakness for prefaces, fitted to this a *Prohemio* lifted bodily out of his manuscript of the *Historia de los nobles caualleros Oliueros de Castilla y Artus dalgarbe*, which he published in 1499 after the second French edition of *Listoire de Oliuier de Castille et de son loyal compaignon Artus Dalgarbe* (Geneva, Maistre Loys Garbin, *c.* 1492). A second edition of this work was in the press at the same time as the *Tristan*,

1501. It is possible that his fraud has cancelled some preface of real historical value; at all events, having neither prologue nor epilogue to which we can safely refer, our resources for divining the history of the translation are severely circumscribed. A great advance was made by Sr. Bonilla's discovery of a single folio, numbered ccxxxvii (cancelled) and ccxxiii, of this same translation in the fourteenth century. The sheet is illustrated with a group representing the ancient knight, Branor or Brauor el Brun, in conversation with a lady and followed by her daughter, all three figures being horsed. Compared with the edition of 1501, this fragment shows only slight variations: omissions of single phrases (MS.: *nin de mejor consejo; mas el cauallero non fue / y con ellos/*), unimportant additions (MS.: *hedat de çiento annos;/*—ed. 1501: *hedad de mas de cient años*), changes of words (MS.: *la mayor marauilla / en armas*—ed. 1501: *la mayor caualleria en armas*—MS.: *comido*—ed. 1501: *cenado*), and modernisations of vocabulary or morphology (MS.: *auedes*, *sepades*—ed. 1501: *aueys*, *quexeys*, etc.). The same processes are continued in the edition of 1528 (1528: *alferez*, *contado por pecado*—1501: *aferez*, *acaloñado pecado*), and still more liberally in the issue of 1534, in which the publisher prides himself on his alterations. We remain with the assurance that the whole romance can be referred back to the fourteenth century, though it is not possible to guarantee the integrity of single phrases, nor still less of the vocabulary.

In the fourteenth century it was probably a trifle longer than in its present form, seeing that by a theory of omission and contraction we can account for its principal points of divergence from the other variant of the same original translation, the *Cuento de Tristan*.[1] This is contained in a large fragment preserved in the library of the Vatican (No. 6428), which ascends to the fifteenth or the late fourteenth century, and so closely approaches the printed version as to postulate a common ancestor. The contents are almost identical, particularly in the highly characteristic ordering of the plots to betray the lovers; and the correspondence continues evenly through the whole course of the narrative from its abrupt opening at the stepmother's first attempt to poison Tristan to its close in the liberation of Arthur in the Gasta Floresta, or at the tourney of Louverzerp. But the most striking contrast arises out of the proper names,[2] which seem to imply a considerable period of separation between the two traditions. They correspond in general to readings given by the *Tavola Ritonda* or the Riccardiano *Tristano*, with which these Castilian romances seem to form a sub-group of the Prose-*Tristan*. Vacilla-

[1] G. T. Northup, in *Romanic Review*, iii. p. 208, No. 21; p. 209, Nos. 29 and 31; p. 210, Nos. 1 and 5; p. 211, Nos. 7 and 9. I have not been able to see Bonilla's reprint of the *Cuento de Tristan*. He says it ends at p. 206, l. 20, of his *Tristan* (1501), but Northup ends it with Arthur and Lancelot's visit to Tristan at Louverzerp (*i.e.*, p. 275).

[2] Prof. Northup cites amongst others (giving the *Cuento* first): Egite, Agite, Egipte—Egypta; Languisin—Languines; Balisen, Belisen—Belisenda; Grata sangre—Gaturas; Briobris, Brioles de Gaunes, Blioberis—Brioberis, Blioberis de Gaones; Bordo, Bros, Bors, Boz, Bort, Borz, Bers, Brez—Bordon, Bores; Brunor—Brauor; Tarasyn—Cornezino; Castillo del Pero—Castillo del Ploto (for Ploro); Delizdra, Dulzdra—Edon; La dueña del Quarto Blanco de la Espina—La dueña del Lago de la Espina; Godino, Gudino—Echides, Aldaret; Goruanas, etc.—Gorualan; Estor de Mares, Astor, Eror—Estor de Mares; Yseo la Baça—Yseo la Brunda; Joyosa Guarda—Giosa Guarda; El Rrey Senescal—Queas; Godis—Quedin; Lambrosyn, Lanbron, Linbrosin—Lambagues, Lanbrojesin; Amorante, El Amorante, Lamorante, Amorat, Lamoratto de Gales—Lamorad de Ganoes, etc.

tion is most evident in the Vatican fragment; in the printed text there is a noticeable attempt at uniformity, which is probably not original but due to editing for the press. As we are ignorant of the manuscript tradition on either side, these divergences do not form a secure basis for deductions, nor can we safely venture to reconcile their discords. The Vatican fragment breaks off before those parts for which the Spanish *Tristan* is the sole evidence, but the conclusion of the narrative (capp. 80–3) is confirmed by one of the oldest of the Spanish ballads,[1] which some poet of great genius compounded, partly from phrases scattered about the prose of these chapters, and partly from the consecrated language of other ballads. The *romance* of

Herido esta don Tristan . . .

is further augmented by a suggestion drawn from folk-lore: the tears of the lovers watered that *mala yerba* (also found in the Portuguese ballads of *Dona Auzenda* and *Conde Ninho*) which has power to impregnate women. In a later and more lyrical stage, certain versions assert that a woman, who speaks in the first person, ate and so suffered, and, by a transition to the third person, we are brought by others

[1] See the versions and clever reconstruction of Bonilla, *Tristan* (1501), 1912, pp. 393–401 (App. iii.). Where the prose text does not contain a phrase, it should rather be explained as a loan from the ballad-maker's stock. So we would be inclined to invert some of Bonilla's last paragraph on the influence of this poem on others; *e.g.*, "de una mala lanzada . . . de fuera tiembla el asta . . ." comes from *Nuño Vero*, "cuanto una missa rezada . . ." from the *Infante Vengador*, but "juntanse boca con boca . . ." comes from the prose: "e estando abraçados boca con boca, le salio el anima del cuerpo." The special mark of the ballad is its extraordinary compression and poignancy of grief; that of the prose is its involution and luxury of grief.

to the absurd conclusion that Iseut ate and became pregnant from a flower that sprang from her grave.

The agreement of the two Castilian versions implies their common descent from a single original, either as two translations of the same foreign text, or as different copies of the same translation affected by different influences. In either case, they are versions of one foreign romance, whether that were expressed in the Portuguese language, in the Italian or in the French; and this source may be indicated by X. But X—the consensus of TL (*Don Tristan de Leonis*) and TV (*Cuento de Tristan*, Vatican)—may be further compared with the Riccardiano *Tristano* (RT)[1] and its congeners, and with *La Tavola Ritonda o l'Istoria di Tristano* (TR),[2] so as to produce a new series of romances marked by common characteristics, either as descending from a single original or as marked by the influence of a version which contrasts strongly with the novels analysed by Löseth.[3] The Italian romances differ considerably from the Castilian, and (according to Professor Northup) their divergences bring them much closer to the Vulgate French *Tristan*; they may have been compiled from a variety of sources, and their retention of Gallicisms indicates close contact with French manuscripts.[4] But however their composition be explained, the consensus of

[1] *Il Tristano Riccardiano*, ed. E. G. Parodi (Bologna, 1896, *Coll. de Opere inedite o rare*).

[2] *La Tavola Ritonda o l'Istoria di Tristano*, ed. F. L. Polidori (Bologna, 1896, same series).

[3] E. Löseth, *Le Roman en Prose de Tristan*, etc.

[4] For the classification of the Italian romances, the reader is referred to Professor E. G. Gardner's *Arthurian Legend in Italian Literature*, which this book is intended to accompany. The present writer intends to make no assertion concerning the Italian versions themselves, but only concerning their agreement with the Castilian.

X (or TL+TV) with RT and TR must be explained by reference to some other model Y, strikingly different from the commonalty of Prose-*Tristans*, and certainly written in French. If we postpone, therefore, the controversy as to the language of X, and the specific differences of the Italian novels, we should expect to find general approval for a genealogy of the Spanish-Italian group in this form:

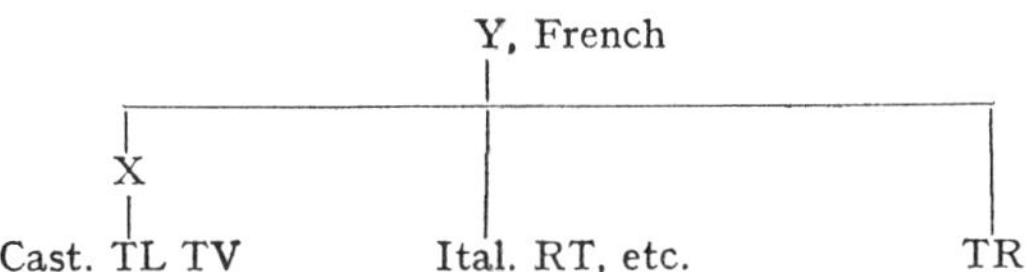

in which Y is an hypothetical manuscript in French differing from the ordinary Prose-*Tristan* in all the points of agreement between TL, TV, RT, TR.[1]

At a later period the romance known in Spain came again into contact with an Italian author, though he wrote in French. The 71–75th chapters of *Don Tristan de Leonis* are given over to the exploits of one of Uther Pendragon's contemporaries, the ancient knight Brauor el Brun,[2] and it is with this episode that the vast compilation of Rustician of Pisa opens. The incident belongs to the original tradition of the Spanish versions, for it is, happily, guaranteed by the fragment discovered by Bonilla, and the correspondence with Rustician is close, without identity.[3]

[1] TL, TV, RT, TR have been compared by Bonilla, *Tristan* (1501), 1912, Intro., and by Northup, *loc. cit.* RT ends abruptly in the forest of Darnantes (Gasta Floresta in the Spanish), and at the same point TR turns to other sources, including Thomas. The corresponding paragraphs of Löseth are Nos. 19–75a.

[2] Löseth, paras. 621–2. The πρέσβυς ἱππότης occurs also in mediæval Greek.

[3] For example, Lancelot jousts and is beaten in Rustician, but not in Castilian; nor are Arthur and the kings overthrown. Consult Bonilla's footnotes for other differences.

Not only are the names different and much corrupted, but sundry details have been altered. After the conclusion of this episode, which Rustician prefixed to his compilation merely because it was a record of Uther Pendragon's first Round Table, and which implies the admission of Tristan to the second, the writer alludes to that hero's desertion of Iseut of Brittany (cap. 42 of the Castilian), the adventures of the Gasta Floresta (42 *ff.*), and the battle at the *Perron Merlin* (67).[1] The Spanish chapters 76–7 correspond fairly to Rustician's next episodes,[2] but that which follows is not repeated south of the Pyrenees; [3] and there is but a momentary resemblance at the end of chapter 78. After an allusion to Guiron, Rustician plunged in his 65th folio into the greater part of the vast *Palamède*, which is anterior to the story of Tristan.[4] It is evident that Rustician's collection of ὕστερα πρότερα cannot be allowed for a fair copy of his original, least of all in respect of its order; he may be accepted in certain cases as evidence of the existence of certain episodes in his source, he is of no weight as a negation of others. The Castilian novel coincides partially with his matter in an adventure that is otherwise hard to come by, but not either with his phrasing, nor with his order. It does not, therefore, seem to be incumbent on us to suppose that the Spanish translator followed Rustician, whether at first or at second hand, whether in a French or in an Italian version, but that he used his original, and perhaps his immediate original.

Before proceeding to the discussion of the ulti-

[1] Löseth, para. 623.
[2] *Ibid.*, 624.
[3] *Ibid.*, 625.
[4] *Ibid.*, 629.

mate problem of these versions, it remains to notice or recall to mind the slight traces of the Portuguese romance. The *Livro de Tristam* of D. Duarte's library (*d.* 1437)[1] is not assigned to any special language, though we have no desire to refuse it to the Portuguese; but apart from that, the sole evidence of a Portuguese romance is that presented by the *lais de Bretanha*. Two of the quintet should be referred to other romances, and the remaining trio, though undoubtedly derived from a Prose-*Tristan*, find no place in *Don Tristan de Leonis*. It is possible, as has been said, that they may have formed part of the *Libro de Tristan* attached to *Lanzarote de Lago*; or they may have been dropped from the helter-skelter of episodes which occupy chapters 67–79 of the novel we are considering; or they may be the sole survivors of a third translation, perchance a Portuguese one; or they may have been taken from a foreign context, whose prose never was translated.

The five *lais de Bretanha* are no certain evidence of a Portuguese text, nor of any translation at all; they do not agree with the extant romance; and they are irrelevant as evidence of the language of X, the original from which both Spanish variants descend. We have already sufficiently discussed the *a priori* basis of the theory of Portuguese priority,[2] and in this case, as elsewhere, it fails for want of substance. An Italian theory has been championed by a distinguished American scholar; and the pains which Professor Northup has bestowed on his thesis have given, at least, a useful analysis and collation of the

[1] Erroneously stated by Graesse to have been Aragonese. *Cf.* Northup, in *Modern Language Notes*, xxviii. pp. 30–31.

[2] *Revista Lusitana*, vi. See our chap. iv.

Spanish-Italian group.[1] In a list of twenty-six points he finds the two Spanish manuscripts in agreement with the *Tristano Riccardiano* and the *Tavola Ritonda*, against the readings of Löseth's analysis. "They agree in disarrangements of the proper order; in a curious interchange of leading characters; in erroneous interpretations of proper names, in stupid perversions of the legend, and in other respects besides." These points, he holds, constitute our romances into an unorthodox sub-group of the Prose-*Tristan*. He then adduces thirty-two "instances where the Italian versions have remained more faithful to the original than the Spanish," and nine "instances where TV, TL, are nearer the French than the Italian versions or some one of them"; noting that "while the two Spanish versions are almost invariably in accord, the two principal Italian texts are more disposed to differ." These forty-one points would have indicated, we might suppose, the *differentia* in the sub-group measured by the standard of the Vulgate *Tristan*, and we might have suspected that the Italian divergences were due to contamination or other wilful change (as in the names of the *Tavola Ritonda*); but Professor Northup uses his ratio of thirty-two to nine to place the Italian versions "much closer to the French" than the Spanish. His "French" and "original" are, it would seem, the *Tristan* of Löseth's analysis; yet the common eccentricities of the two Italian romances, even apart from the Spanish consent, are sufficient to demand an "original" very different from that Vulgate form. To this unorthodox

[1] G. T. Northup, *The Italian Origin of the Spanish Prose Tristram Versions*, in the *Romanic Review*, iii., 1912, pp. 194–222, and in *Modern Philology*, xi. 1913, pp. 259–265.

original Y, which must assuredly have been written in French, all the agreements of the Spanish-Italian group refer: these concordances, therefore, do not advance at all the thesis that the immediate original of the Spanish texts, our X, was an Italian manuscript. The only admissible evidence of that would be incontrovertible Italianisms in the Spanish text. In the language I can discern no trace; among the proper names, the greater number of the cases of agreement cited by Professor Northup refer to Y, and in the few instances where a name presents some special feature of interest, we fail to see (especially considering our total ignorance of the manuscript tradition of these versions) that much is gained by the Italian thesis. They seem to be all capable of a purely Spanish explanation. Italian literature did powerfully affect that of the Spanish Peninsula towards the end of the fifteenth century, but there are serious objections to the notion that it was already producing effects in the thirteenth or early fourteenth.

The case for the Italian origin of the Spanish Prose-*Tristan* is founded upon the evidence of proper names, of which we do not know the original form nor the later manuscript tradition. It is also urged that the Italian novels stand closer to the Vulgate, but it is by that proportion likely that the Castilian conform more exactly to their own unorthodox source. If Gallicisms abound in the Riccardiano *Tristano* and the *Tavola Ritonda*, this is a sign not merely of translation, but also of a literary state in which French was the cultural medium of Italian writers. Rustician and Brunetto Latini belong to that epoch of Italian letters; but no such practice was established at any time in Spain or Portugal. Gallicisms (such as the word *aferez*) are not wholly wanting in the *Tristan de Leonis*, but succeeding editors during a couple of centuries gradually planed them away. There seems to us insufficient reason to make an exception for this novel from the general line of development followed by the *matière de Bretagne* in Spain, and Sr. Bonilla is almost certainly correct when he champions a French original (X). This original no longer exists, but we are not without reports of its contents. In relating Rustician's compilation to *Don Tristan de Leonis*, we have already seen cause to connect them through Rustician's model. The Castilian romances are undoubtedly a faithful translation, for free composition in Arthurian matters was unknown, if we deduct certain obvious cases, in the Castilian-Portuguese group, nor even practised in the Catalan; on the other hand, Rustician gives us to understand that he will operate with freedom and combine his sources. The preface of *maistre Rusticiens de Pise* declares that he "translated" or "compiled" his romance from the "Book of monseigneur Edward, King of England, when he passed beyond the sea in Our Lord's service to conquer the Holy Sepulchre," and the tone of his preamble prepares us for his singularly independent attitude towards the chronology of the romance.[1]

[1] *Cf.* H. L. D. Ward, *Catalogue of Romances in the British Museum*, i. p. 367. Also Löseth, *Roman en Prose de Tristan*, pp. 423–4: "Seigneurs empereurs et princes et ducs et contes et barons et chevaliers et vavasseurs et bourgois et tous les preudommes de cestui monde qui avez talent de vous delitez en rommans, si prenez cestui et le faites lire de chief en chief; si orrez toutes les grans avantures qui advindrent entre les chevaliers errans du temps au roy Uterpendragon jusques au temps

The *Livre monseigneur Edouart* contained the *Tristan* and the *Palamède*, and certainly held Rustician's opening adventure, that of Branor le Brun the ancient knight; but we may reasonably suppose that its development was more logical. Now, the owner of the manuscript was the brother-in-law of the King of Castile, whom he had visited in 1254, whose embassy he had received in 1255, and whom he might be more likely to oblige with a book or a transcript than a grammarian of Pisa. Alfonso X. began to quote *Tristan*[1] about the year 1260. In 1260 he was visited by Brunetto Latini, whom he entertained in a fashion that pleased that connoisseur of letters; and

au roy Artus, son fils, et des compaignons de la Table Reonde, et sachiez tout vraiement que cist livres fut translatez du livre monseigneur Edouart, le roi d'Engleterre, en cellui temps que il passa oultre la mer ou service nostre seigneur Dame Dieu pour conquester le saint sepulcre, et maistre Rusticiens de Pise, lequel est ymaginez yci dessus, compila ce rommant. Car il en translata toutes les merveilleuses nouvelles et aventures qu'il trouva en cellui livre et traita tout certainement de toutes les aventures du monde, et si sachiez qu'il traitera plus de monseigneur de Lancelot du lac et de monseign. Tristan, le filz au roy Meliadus de Loonois, que d'autres, pour ce qu'ilz furent sans faille les meilleurs chevaliers qui a ce temps furent en terre, et li maistres en dira de ces deux pluseurs choses et pluseurs nouvelles que furent entre eux que l'en trouvera escript en tous les autres libres. Et pour ce que le maistre les trouva escrips ou livre d'Engleterre, si metra une grant aventure tout premierement, qui advint a Kamalot en la court le roy Artus, le sire de Bretaingne.

"[Rubric] Ci commence le livre du roy Meliadus de Leonnois qui fu pere au bon chevalier Tristan, neveu au roy Marc de Cornouaille, et premierement de Brannor le Brun, qui avoit .vi. vins ans d'aage, et comment il vint a la court le roy Artus et amena une noble demoiselle avecques lui, et comment il abati de coup de lance .xii. roys et tous les chevaliers de la Tab.Re., ne oncques ne le porent remuer de selle. Et parole après du bon chevalier sans paour et de Guiron le courtoys et de Arioham de Soissoigne," etc.

[1] *Canc. da Vat.*, 468b:

> ". . . ca ia paris
> Damor non foi tam coitado
> Nen tristam nunca soffrerõ
> Tal affam. . . ."

For the date, *cf. Revista Lusitana*, vi. p. 24.

Brunetto, being detained in France from 1261 to 1269, inserted in his *Trésor*[1] a quotation highly characteristic of what was to be the Spanish tradition. The description of Iseut's loveliness[2] has been refashioned, perhaps, nearer to the heart's desire of the Spanish editor;[3] and the same process is evident in the variants of Latini's own manuscripts. But the order and most striking phrases have been retained and expanded (unless Latini abbreviated), and the eloquent sentiment of the passage makes it unforgettable even in a finely-perorated romance.

So much may be known or inferred concerning the French source of the Spanish *Tristan*, but we have still to determine the circumstances of the translation. 1254 and 1260 seem to be dates in the

[1] Brunetto Latini, *Li Livres dou Trésors*, ed. Chabaille (Paris, 1863), liv. iii. (Rhétorique), part i. chap. xiii.: "Autressi fist Tristans quant il devisa la biauté la roine Yseult. Si chevol, fist il, resplandissent comme fil d'or, ses frons sormonte la flor de lis, si noir sourcil sont ploié comme petit arconniau, une petite voie de lait les dessevre parmi la ligne dou neis, et est si par mesure que il n'i a ne plus ne mains, si oil, qui sormontent toutes esmeraudes, reluisent en son front comme .ij. estoïles; sa face ensuit la biauté dou matinet, car ele est de vermoil et de blanc ensemble, en tel maniere que l'un ne l'autre ne resplandit malement; la bouche petite et les levres auques espesses et ardans, de bele color, et les dens plus blanches que pelles, et sont establies par ordre et par mesure; mais ne pantere ne nule espice nule se puet comparer à sa très douce alaine; ses mentons est assez plus poliz que marbres; nus laiz ne donne color à son col, ne cristal ne resplendit à sa gorge. De ses droites espaules descendent .ij. braz grailles et lons, et blanches mains où la char est mole et tendre; les doiz granz, traitis et reonz; sor quoi reluist la biautez de ses ongles; ses très biaus piz est aornez de .ij. pomes de paradis, qui sont autressi comme une masse de noif. Et si est si graille par la ceinture que on la porroit porpendre dedanz ses mains. Mais je me tairai des autres parties dedanz, desqueles li corages parole miex que la langue."

There are numerous and instructive *variæ lectiones*.

[2] The passage is absent from all the Vulgate *Tristans* analysed by Löseth. It is absent from Rustician, but that is not sufficient to demonstrate its absence from the *Livre monseigneur Edouart*. Actually it exists only in B. Latini and *Don Tristan de Leonis*.

[3] One suspects *marfil* and *nieve*, for instance, in a Spanish text of the sixteenth century.

history of the introduction of the original;[1] and the mention of *doblas de oro*, a type of coinage issued first by Alfonso X. about the year 1262, fixes the earliest possible date for the Castilian version.[2] Rustician's compilation is dated 1271–2, but the date, as we have shown, is not to be judged relevant to that of the Spanish version, seeing that their relationship lies through their common source; but there seems little reason to place the translation earlier than the reign of D. Sancho IV. (1284–96). A concluding limit is found in the well-known allusion to *Cifar*, *Amadis* and *Tristan* by Juan García de Castrogeriz,[3] between 1345 and 1350. Some critics, in a conservative spirit, allow that the *Amadis* was in existence in 1345, and that the *Tristan* must be allowed some priority; conceding two years, we have 1343, when it is called a novelty by the picaresque Archpriest of Hita. But even conservatism has its perils. The *Amadis* is of a date, in all likelihood, considerably earlier than its first mention; and what was novel to Juan Ruiz may not have been novel to readers more happily circumstanced in regard to the translation. Instances of belated fame may be quoted from any literature. The fame of Milton seems to have been a novelty to the readers of the *Spectator* despite Dryden's admiration; ballads were a new interest for readers of Percy's *Reliques*. The archpriest has not explained

[1] Bonilla, *Tristan* (1501), pp. xlii–xliii, discusses the date and manner in which the legend entered Spain, and adumbrates a Catalan theory. But that is a different question to the determination of the circumstances of a particular manuscript.

[2] Bonilla, *Tristan* (1501), p. 164 and n., pp. xliii–xliv.

[3] Fouché-Delbosc, *La plus ancienne mention d'Amadis*, in *Revue Hispanique*, xv. p. 815.

his meaning in the use of the word *agora* (now).[1] There is no evidence or probability of his familiar acquaintance with knightly society,—save on an occasion when he figured as a culprit before an aristocrat of the Church!—and we may take it that he was not favourably placed for the acquisition of textbooks of chivalry and high courtly love. The student will, therefore, do well to retain a complete openness of mind, and to assume the liberty of the whole range of dates between 1262 and 1343.

It is still profitable, however, to consider the *Tristan* in relation to other romances of the Breton cycle in Spain, and especially as regards the *Baladro del Sabio Merlin*. In discussing the birth of Palomades, the edition of 1501 refers the reader to *El Libro de Merlin*; but the reference is spurious. The *Baladro* does not treat of the events there recorded, for they are related only in the first Prologue of the edition of 1498. That Prologue is an adaptation of the chapter in *Tristan* by the editor of both works, Juan de Burgos, and this allusion to the *Libro de Merlin* is an adroit puff. The two texts are, in their French state, wholly unrelated, and the *Tristan de Leonis*, unlike the ordinary *Tristans*, satisfies few of the allusions made by any part of the Boron-trilogy to this hero: yet *Don Tristan de Leonis* (cap. 70) is equipped with an almost certain allusion to the *Conte del Brait*, which it terms *La Coronica del Rey*

[1] Juan Ruiz, *Libro de Buen Amor*, copla 1703:

> "Ca nunca fue tan leal Blanca-flor a Frores,
> Nin es *agora* Tristan con todos sus amores."

Baist, *Grundriss der rom. Phil.*, II. ii. p. 438: "Für den Archipreste de Hita war der Prosa-Tristan ein neues Buch und zweifellos ein neues kastilisches." The deductions are too many for a not unambiguous text.

Artur.[1] When Tristan took his seat at the Round Table, he occupied the chair which had been used by Morholt. This Morholt of Ireland, says the translator of the Spanish text, was slain by Tristan, and the cause is given at full length in the *Coronica del Rey Artur.* It seems, then, that he was unable to identify him with the minotaur slain in the Isle of Saint Sanson, or, as his narrative expresses it, the Isla sin Ventura; and the impediment to the identification is the different cause assigned, or supposed to be assigned, for his death. If we look for a text which satisfies these requirements of the allusion, we shall not find it elsewhere than in the *Conte del Brait*, as that novel has been preserved in the *Baladro del Sabio Merlin*, of which the *Coronica del Rey Artur* seems to have been a second title. We have already recorded the opinion that the earliest additions to the *Baladro* were made shortly after the year 1312; and we shall proceed to show in another chapter that the work was first dedicated to Sancho IV. after he had surmounted the great crisis of D. Juan's insurrection, about the year 1291. The translator of the *Tristan* would seem to have worked in the

[1] The title *Coronica del Rey Artus* is implied in MS. 2–G–5 of the Bibl. Part. de S.M., Madrid: *La estoria de Merlin . . . y del rrey Artus* (fol. 282v), and by the *Cronica General de* 1404: *La Estoria del Sancto Grayal et de rrey Artur* (fol. 25). The reference is to *Baladro*, cap. 255, which belongs, as we shall show, not to Robert de Boron's *Merlin*, but to Hélye's *Conte del Brait.* In that passage Morholt's death is predicted, but his besetting sin is said to be enslaving damsels, and not, as in the *Tristan*, collecting tribute from Cornwall. The identification of the two is not made in the *Baladro*, but in the Pseudo-Boron's *Merlin* and in Malory, where the same account is given of Morholt, it is expressly said that he is the Morholt killed in the Island of Saint Sanson. The passage in *Tristan* reads (cap. 70, p. 298): "El matara a Morlot de Yrlanda; & la causa de donde esta auentura venia, en la coronica del rey Artur da dello mucha cuenta; quien lo quisiere ver por estenso, alli lo hallara, e porque no hazia a la ystoria, no se escruio aqui, saluo lo que a nuestro proposito haze."

same company as the translator of the *Baladro*, and had his eye either on the other Peninsular text or on its French original. Which?

There is an *a priori* case that the first text to be quoted, the *Tristan*, which is also considerably the most interesting and worthy, was also the first to be translated; and this prejudice is slightly confirmed by the manner in which the *Tristan*, notwithstanding the allusion just given, seems to ignore the special technique of the other translation. The principal Arthurian names are already fixed by custom,—Artus or Artur, Lanzarote, Ginebra, Tristan, Yseo, Joyosa Guarda, Camalote, Merlin, etc. The minor personalities are quoted with far less certainty or agreement between the two versions, and the vacillations of the Vatican manuscript or *Cuento de Tristan* are especially numerous; so that, although we are chary of drawing any conclusions from an orthography whose history is so little known, it certainly does seem that the translator of *Tristan* is the less supported by an established tradition. A divergence which deserves particular notice lies in the renderings of the name *Beste Glatissante.* The rendering *Bestia Ladrador*, chosen by the *Baladro*, became the standard of reference, and as such is used as early as the poem of Esquio in the *Cancioneiro da Vaticana* (No. 1140). But the *Tristan*, from an original *Grattasante* perhaps, offers *Bestia Grata Sangre* and *Bestia Gaturas* (cap. 42). Similarly, the word *Baladro*, which came to be the characteristic mark of the other translation, is nowhere mentioned in *Don Tristan de Leonis*; but on the other hand, it must be stated that this is in accordance with the practice of the *Merlin y Demanda* itself, which always means by *Cuento del Baladro* the *Conte del Brait*; and further, the title given in the passage already cited is justified by the *Cronica de* 1404 and by the fragmentary *Merlin* in the Palace Library. Still more conspicuous in the trilogy is the translation of *Quest* by the word *Demanda*, the same equivalent being adopted in 1313 by the translator of the *Joseph Abaramatia*, and it referred not merely to the third part, but also to the whole trilogy of the Holy Grail: in *Don Tristan de Leonis* the word is unknown. This novel has occasion (cap. 70) to refer to the opening incidents of the *Quest*, *i.e.* those which are common to both Map and the Pseudo-Boron and occupy the first forty-eight chapters of the Spanish version, and its reference is to the *Libro del Santo Grial*.[1] Elsewhere the word *Quest* is turned by *conquista*, with the verb *conquerir*, a usage entirely foreign to the *Baladro* and *Demanda*, though it occurs twice in cap. 341, which contains prophecies in the style of Maestre Antonio.[2] Citations of *El Libro de las Aventuras* are common to the *Tristan* (cap. 70), *Baladro* (cap. 240), and *Demanda* (cap. 344), and so must be written off as pre-Castilian. On the whole we are inclined to think that the translator of *Tristan* did not have the advantage of reading the translation of the *Merlin*, and that his work is to be placed some years earlier than the latter. That the two works should be found in contact might also have been presumed from external evidence, which tends

[1] As far as the "Aventura del Santo Escudo con la Cruz Vermeja" (*Demanda*, ed. Bonilla, capp. 46–8).

[2] *Tristan* (1501), ed. Bonilla, p. 346: "por conquerir la conquista." *Baladro*, ed. Bonilla, cap. 341: "la conquista del Santo Grial."

to show that the former was transmitted through Alfonso X., and the latter was translated for his son D. Sancho IV.

No hint survives of the name of the translator, nor of the patron for whom the translation was made. We endeavour to sum up the leading probabilities with regard to the Spanish *Tristan* in the following diagram:

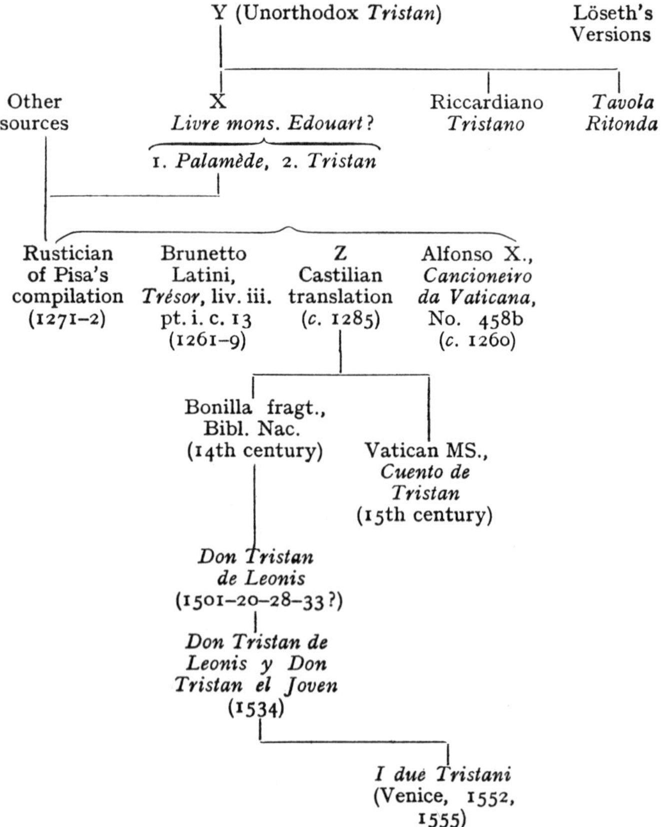

The vast *Roman de Palamède*, which serves as an introduction to Tristan's history, has left no trace in Spain or Portugal; and the continuation of his lineage in *Ysaie le Triste* is equally without fruit.[1] But the last Spanish redactor of *Don Tristan de Leonis* attached to the original novel a long continuation under the name of *Tristan el Joven*, his son.[2] Dominico de Robertis' edition was selected for translation into Italian, and appeared at Venice in 1552 and 1555 from the press of Michele Tramezzino under the title, *Le opere magnanime dei due Tristani, cavalieri della Tavola Ritonda*. Nothing is known of the author, beyond what may be deduced from his outrageous handling of the Portuguese nation; his method, like that of Lope de Vega in *La Hermosura de Angelica* and *La Jerusalen Conquistada*, is to divert a conspicuous foreign success into Spanish territory, and to lay a new veneer over the characters. He attributes to the Cornish lovers a son Tristan, who is directed by a dream to seek his fortune in the Peninsula, where he fights the Miramamolin (Amîr al-Mu'minîn) of Africa and accepts the hand of the Infanta Maria. The plot, as retailed by Gayangos,[3] runs in this manner:

The young Tristan received the order of knighthood in time to swear to the Quest of the Holy

[1] The *Historia de los Amores de Clareo y Florisea y de los Trabajos de Isea* (Venice, 1544), by Nuñez de Reinoso, is a sentimental and allegorical novel of peripaties on the Greek model. It is not a romance of chivalry, nor even a pastoral, though written on an *Insula Pastoril*. A free translation into Portuguese goes under the name *Historia dos Trabalhos da sem-ventura Iseo*. *Cf.* C. M. Vasconcellos, *Grundriss der rom. Phil.*, II. ii. p. 336.

[2] *Coronica nueuamente emendada y añadida del buen cauallero don Tristan de Leonis y del rey don Tristan de Leonis el Joven, su hijo*, Seville, Dominico de Robertis, 1534.

[3] Gayangos, *Libros de Caballerias*, pp. xiv–xv.

Grail. Queen Guenevere, still beautiful in spite of her years, became enamoured of the graces of the young knight, who, at the age of barely seventeen, conquered and slew in single combat Orribes, a powerful giant who had terrorised the entire kingdom by his feats of cruelty. But young Tristan displayed his qualities in the Peninsula, whither he was directed by a dream; for he thought he beheld a city bounded on the north by lofty mountains and on the south by spreading plains. In this city the King of Spain, a good-looking young man, abode with his only sister, a princess as lovely and radiant as the sun, who approached him, and by touching his left side drew forth his heart and went her way. Urged by the pleasing prospect, the knight set sail and landed in that part of Castile which borders on Navarre. Passing by Pamplona and Logroño, he jousted with certain knights who forbade his passage over a bridge: at Burgos he made the acquaintance of Palisendo, with whom he continued on to the court of King Juan, for so was the Castilian monarch named. Well received by the ruler, who conceded him the singular privilege of a present of his *chapeu*, and by the Infanta Maria, who, impressed with his gentle bearing, took him into her service, he earned his lodgings as one of her knights. At the court he conquered three French knights, and gained distinction in the jousts by his valour and dexterity, and in the *saraos* by his nobleness and address. In the end the enamoured princess confides her secret to Jeronima Torrente, her Aragonese lady-in-waiting. On the report that the Moors have invaded Spanish territory, three captains—Velasco, Guzmán and

Mendoza—led out a numerous host of warriors, accompanied by the foreign knight, who was soon the principal cause of the Moslem *débâcle*. Meanwhile the African Miramamolin, Amolihacen-quebir, being likewise an admirer of the Infanta Maria, crossed another sector of the Castilian frontier with the whole Moorish power, fully resolved on seizing the lady or perishing in the attempt. Taking Nájera, he made for Burgos by forced marches, and surprised the princess as she took her ease in the king's garden, half a league from the town, and conducted her a prisoner to his own domain. Tristan advanced to the attack, killed the pagan and ten of his stoutest knights, rescued the Infanta and restored her to her brother's arms, and effected an equal exchange of her hand for that of his own sister Iseo, whom the king had long admired. The matrimonial party took ship at La Coruña, and after celebrating the weddings in England, King Juan and Queen Iseo returned to their government. The tale gives itself out for a translation of a French version of an English original.

VII

THE ARTHURIAN NOVELS IN CASTILE AND PORTUGAL: "VESPASIAN"[1]

FROM the press of Castilian and Portuguese romances which relate to the Holy Grail it is possible to detach two for separate consideration, the *Vespasian* and the *Joseph*; the one because its relevance to the Arthurian cycle is only momentary, and its introduction probably late, and the other because the disruption of manuscripts has isolated those which remain.

The old French poem of *La Vengeance Nostre Seigneur*, composed in the late twelfth or early thirteenth century, embraced two apocryphal traditions which were originally distinct. The *Cura sanitatis Tiberii Cæsaris Augusti* told how the True Image of Christ was successfully applied by St. Veronica and St. Clement to the malady of the Emperor Tiberius. In the *Vindicta Salvatoris* a monkish imagination was exercised in revenging Our Lord's martyrdom on the people of Judea, and as He had been sold for thirty

[1] EARLY EDITIONS: *La Estoria del Noble Vespasiano*, Toledo, Juan Vázquez, *c.* 1486 or 1490; Seville, Pedro Brun, 1499; etc.; *Estoria do muy nobre Vespasiano, emperador de Roma*, Lisbon, Valentim de Moravia, 1496.

REPRINTS: F.-M. Esteves Pereira, *Historia de Vespasiano*, Lisbon, 1905 (ed. 1496); R. Fouché-Delbosc, in *Revue Hispanique*, xxi. (ed. of 1499); Bonilla, *Libros de Caballerías*, ii. An *Aucto de la destruicion de Jerusalen* is No. 30 of Rouanet's *Cólección de autos, etc., del siglo xvi.*, Madrid, 1901.

CRITICISM: K. Haebler, *Bibliografía Ibérica del siglo xv.*, i. p. 327; ii. p. 186; F.-M. Esteves Pereira, *op. cit.*, Intro.; *cf.* also W. Suchier, *Ueber das altfranzösische Gedicht von der Zerstörung Jerusalems*, in *Zeitschrift für rom. Phil.*, xxiv.

pence, so the Jews were sold thirty for a penny. By exchanging Tiberius for Vespasian, by causing the grateful emperor to desire baptism, and by inspiring him to demonstrate the sincerity of his conversion by a pogrom of the Jewish nation, we reach the single romance; and religious vindictiveness was glutted when the victims were said to have been disembowelled in the search for swallowed gold, and when Pilate, unable to rest in any prison, was overwhelmed in the depths of Hell.

This romance had some popularity in the England of the thirteenth and fourteenth centuries,[1] and found a home in the court of the Ceremonious Pedro and in the literature of Catalonia;[2] but in Spain and Portugal its history seems to fall within the era of the printing press. Nine French incunables under the title *Destruction de Jerusalem* or *Destruction de Jerusalem et la Mort de Pilate*, are enumerated by Brunet, and from one of these the Toledan printer Juan Vázquez, who is not known to have issued any books after 1490, translated *La Estoria del Noble Vespasiano*.[3] Translated again into Portuguese under the title *Estoria do muy nobre Vespasiano, emperador de Roma*, it was published in 1496 by Valentim de Moravia, as the second work to be printed in that kingdom. It may have been written for him by one of the friars of the convent of Xabregas, who had revised the *Vita Christi* (a book issued from the same fount of type) in 1495.[4] The language is archaic

[1] Schofield, *English Literature from the Norman Conquest to Chaucer* (London, 1906), p. 378.

[2] See our chap. v.

[3] K. Haebler, *op. cit.*

[4] The *Vita Christi* and *Vespasian* were issued in one volume at Rouen, 1488.

in certain respects, and agrees better with the style of the reign of João II. than with that of Manoel I.; and the text was reinforced by a number of striking woodcuts.[1] These illustrations, slightly modified, were adopted by the Sevillan printer Pedro Brun, who issued the second Castilian edition in 1499; and Snr. Esteves Pereira is of the opinion that he was so industrious as to retranslate this work from the Portuguese in place of merely copying its Castilian predecessor. Other editions of this arid chronicle saw the light, and in 1525, under the title *Destroyçam de Jerusalem*, it is found in the library of the Portuguese monarch. A modern reader may smile at the grotesque spite and mediæval remoteness of the narrative, but it seems to have had some value in the eyes of the Jew-haters of 1492 and 1496. Manoel I. sent a century of copies—to the praise of God and the exaltation of His holy Catholic Faith!—to his Christian brother of Abyssinia, Prester John; and the same topic was treated in *autos* before the populace of Castile.[2]

The connection with the Grail-story is of the slightest. The imprisonment and miraculous preservation of Joseph of Arimathia are described in the 23rd chapter, and we are assured that Jafel, his nephew, would speak more freely in the *Libro del Santo Grial.*[3] As regards the *Vespasiano* itself, it was written by Jafel under the orders of Joseph and of Jacob pater Mariæ Jacobi, who witnessed all those matters.

[1] Fouché-Delbosc reproduced fifteen woodcuts in his reprint of this edition. Esteves Pereira's text has none.

[2] C. M. de Vasconcellos, *Grundriss der rom. Phil.*, II. ii. p. 215; Rouanet, *Colección de Autos, etc.*, No. 30.

[3] Cap. 23: "Mas esto dexaron estar porque Jafel no lo porna en oluido, e fablara del en el libro del santo Greal."

VIII

THE ARTHURIAN NOVELS IN CASTILE AND PORTUGAL: THE "HOLY GRAIL"; "JOSEPH OF ARIMATHIA"[1]

THE first portion of the Grail-story was made accessible to Spanish and Portuguese readers by two manuscripts, the one in Portuguese and the other in a Castilian that is highly infected with Leonese or even Galician-Portuguese elements. The history of the former is romantic. Though mentioned by Varnhagen,

[1] MANUSCRIPTS: *Liuro de Josep Abaramatia* (Torre do Tombo, MS. Alcobaça, No. 643, sixteenth century, 311 fols., 250 × 190 mm.: "Liuro de josep abaramatia Intetulado aprimeira parte Da demãda do sãto grial ata aprese͂te idade nũca vista. treladado Do proprio original por ho doutor Manuel Alũez. Corregedor da Ilha desã miguel. Deregido ao muy alto e poderoso principe El Rei Dom João ho .zº. Deste nome Elrrey nosso Sñor"); *Libro de Josep Abarimatia* (Bibl. Particular de S.M., Madrid, MS. 2–G–5, parchment, 1469–70, by Pedro Ortiz, 302 fols., 240 × 140 mm.: (fols. 251–282) "Esta parte se llama el libro de iosep abarimatia e otrosi libro del sancto Grial que es el escodilla en que comeo Jesu Christo").

REPRINTS (selections): O. Klob, *Beiträge zur Span. und Port. Gral-Litteratur*, in *Zeitschrift für rom. Phil.*, xxvi. pp. 167–205 (Alc. 643 and 2–G–5); J. J. Nunes, *Uma Amostra do Livro de Josep ab Arimatia*, in *Revista Lusitana*, xi. pp. 223 *ff.* (Alc. 643, fols. 101–110: "De como ElRei Mordaim vio a nao em que ha dona que ha ele vyera amdava e do que come ela passou. Dos gramdes trabalhos que Mordaym na pena pasou e das temtaçoes que ho diabo lhe fez e do que lhe Deos dise.") The Arthurian portion of MS. 2–G–5 has been reprinted in full by K. Pietsch, *Spanish Grail Fragments*, i., Chicago, 1924 (*Modern Philology Monographs of the University of Chicago*).

CRITICISM: O. Klob, *op. cit.*; J. J. Nunes, *op. cit.*; C. M. de Vasconcellos in *Revista Lusitana*, vi.; K. Pietsch, *op. cit.*, Intro. *Cf.* also authorities cited under our chap. ix.

Before O. Klob's description the MS. Alc. 643 was mentioned by Varnhagen, *Cancioneirinho de Trovas Antigas*, p. 165; K. von Reinhardstoettner, *Demanda do Santo Graal*, Intro., pp. ix–x; M. Menéndez y Pelayo, *Origenes de la Novela*, i. p. clxxvi; C. M. de Vasconcellos, *Grundriss der rom. Phil.*, II. ii. p. 215. A. Morel-Fatio, in *Romania*, x. p. 300, O. Klob, *op. cit.*, and K. Pietsch, *The Madrid Manuscript of the Spanish Grail Fragments*, in *Modern Philology*, xviii. (1920–21), pp. 147–156, 591–596, describe MS. 2–G–5.

the *Liuro de Josep Abaramatia* was written down and lamented for lost until O. Klob found and described it in 1902. It is still without an edition or satisfactory treatment; but we can gain some approximate notion of its contents from the discoverer's account, and some knowledge of its language and style from Snr. J. J. Nunes. It is a manuscript of the sixteenth century, of 311 folios and 118 chapters, containing the first part of a Grail-trilogy which should have been entitled *A Demanda do Santo Grial*; and it is said to correspond to the *Estoire del Saint Graal* which is the first branch of H. O. Sommer's *Vulgate Version of the Arthurian Legend.* The opening chapters relate the heavenly vision accorded to the author and his reception of a booklet no bigger than a man's hand, and they relate how his spirit was taken away by an angel. In the fifteenth chapter the narrative commences, and it maintains its even tenour close to the common French story, varied by slight abbreviations, extensions and omissions, as well as some variations of the orthography of proper names; it finds its conclusion in the death of King Lancelot and in the marvels connected therewith, uttering the prophecy that the guardian lions of his tomb would be slain by Sir Lancelot du Lac. The spelling is generally that of the sixteenth century, but the language presents frequent points of contact with that of the *trovadores*; and the matter and phrasing are of an assured antiquity.[1]

[1] J. J. Nunes, *op. cit.*: "Uma leitura attenta faz-nos ver a grande semelhança que a sua lingua apresenta com a dos trovadores; a collocação das palavras, as formas d'estas e até alguns archaismos estão-nos a dizer que o copista do seculo xvi., embora procurasse pôr-lhe o estilo e dição ao corrente da epoca deixou vestigios bem visiveis do exemplar que tinha ante os olhos, quiça copia tambem de outro mais antigo."

Whatever may be said concerning the story contained in the manuscript of the Torre do Tombo, the circumstances alleged by its superscription, preamble and colophon are so numerous that they suggest an opportunity for infinite argument. According to the superscription, this book is the first part of the *Demanda do Santo Grial*, and had not been seen previously to its "translation" (meaning transference) from the original by Dr. Manuel Alvarez, corregidor of the Ilha de S. Miguel, who dedicates it to João III.[1] João III. reigned from 1521 to 1557; but it would appear that Dr. Alvarez's "original" or "translation" circulated among the poets of the *Cancioneiro de Resende* (published 1516), where it is cited.[2] The preamble declares the nature of the "original," the circumstances of the discovery, and the method of "translation." The "original" was an illuminated parchment[3] of some two hundred years of age, found at Riba d'Ancora, near the parish church, in the possession of a "very ancient old woman";[4] the time of his find is stated to have been when his father acted as the king's corregidor in Entre Douro e Minho. The "translation" amounted to no more than the alteration of unintelligible

[1] *Ut supra*, bibliographical note. In ascribing the dedication to João III. I follow the authorities for this MS., for whom ".z°." means "III." But may not the reading have been ".ij.°," and the dedication to João II. (*d.* 1495)? In that case the citation by the *Cancioneiro de Resende* is more intelligible.

[2] *Cancioneiro de Resende*, i. p. 278:

"cumprido mestreescola
Ou Josep Baramatya."

[3] "Spto em pergaminho e iluminado Eacaise De dozentos anños que foi spto."

[4] "Uma velha de muy antiga idade." In the margin: "tté huma Fraguezia."

words and the substitution of readings for what was illegible,[1] and Dr. Alvarez begs the king to appoint some competent person to rejuvenate the style; "for as I have said [he writes], I have changed only the unintelligible words, passing over those of that ancient time which can be understood." His work is, in fact, a transcription (*tresladação*), and he shows no consciousness of a foreign original.

It is possible, if we choose to be literal, to drive a wedge between the date given by Dr. Alvarez to his "original" (1521 less 200, *i.e.* 1321) and the year defined with five-fold precision by the colophon, or 1313. Here a Juan Sánchez (João Samchez), a schoolmaster in Astorga of Leon,[2] employing a rather lordly style, announces that he "caused the book to be made," five years after the establishment of the University of Coimbra, under the papacy of Pope Clement, who destroyed the Order of the Temple and convened the Council of Vienne, and laid an interdict on Castile; in the same year Queen Constance died and the Infante Felipe married D. Affonso's daughter in the year 1312 or 1313. The settlement of the University at Coimbra occurred in the year 1308; its fifth year was, therefore, 1312–13. Pope Clement V. reigned from 1305 to 1314, summoned the Council of Vienne which was sitting in the year 1311, and pronounced sentence on the

[1] "Não mudei señão hos vocabulos inẽteligiueis."

[2] "Este liuro mamdou fazer João samchez mestre escolla Dastorga no quimto ano que o estado de coimbra foy feito e no tempo Dopapa Clemente que destroio aordem Deltemple e fez O comcilio geral Em viana e posho entredito Em castela e neste ano se finou a Rainha dona Costamça em são fagumdo E casou o imfante Dom filipe coma filha De Dom aº. ano de 13 e XIII. anos." So O. Klob. Varnhagen read 1312; Nunes, seemingly, 1314. The last stroke is obscure; *estado* is an error for *estudo*.

Order of the Temple in the year 1312. He also directed the Spanish episcopate to institute proceedings against the Templars of their own country, and Alfonso, Bishop of Astorga (1301–14), was present at the convention of the province of Santiago de Compostela held in Salamanca in 1310 or 1311.[1] It is not stated whether he was supported on that occasion by his *mestreescola*; but among many intrigues that arose out of the peril of the Templars, the Infante Felipe (about the year 1307) made himself conspicuous by plotting with the Grand Master Rodrigo Yáñez to be trustee for their property, to the detriment of the Crown. An interdict[2] was laid by Clement V. on Castile in 1310 because Fernando IV. had diverted the tithes to his own pocket; it was raised towards the end of 1313 during the minority of Alfonso XI., whose guardian, Queen Maria de Molina, could not afford to lose the support of the Church. Some months previously to the repeal of the interdict, Queen Costanza of Castile, daughter of King Diniz of Portugal and wife of D. Fernando IV., had died at Sahagun;[3] and her demise had a considerable repercussion on politics, seeing that D. Juan Manuel, D. Juan el Tuerto, and other disaffected partisans were endeavouring to cover their pretensions to the guardianship of the infant king under her rights upon her son. Costanza dead, Alfonso XI. reverted to the care of his grandmother, the able Maria de Molina. Among the uncles of the late king, the ablest and youngest was the Infante

[1] *España Sagrada*, xvi. p. 251.

[2] *Cron. de D. Fernando IV.*, cap. xv. (1310), and *Cron. de D. Alfonso XI.*, cap. vi. (1313).

[3] *Cron. de Alfonso XI.*, cap. vi. (1313).

Felipe, who was not always disposed to act in concert with the queen-grandmother. He had no children;[1] but he was married before 1322 to a lady named Margarita.[2] Our text is the only authority we have been able to discover for the two statements, —that the marriage took place in 1313, and that Margarita was the daughter of D. Affonso. The only possible Affonso of these times (as it is certain that she was not the daughter of the crown prince of Portugal) was D. Affonso de Portugal, the second son of King Affonso III. of Portugal. He does not enjoy a separate article in the *Nobiliario* of D. Pedro de Barcellos, his nephew, probably because all his children were daughters: two are mentioned in that authority, Da. Isabel who married D. Juan el Tuerto, and Da. Maria who married D. Tello. To these our text seems to add Da. Margarita who married the Infante Felipe. It is quite likely that she possessed some affinity to D. Juan Manuel, as she was commissioned in 1322 to prepare his daughter Costanza for marriage with Alfonso XI. of Castile. D. Affonso's grand-daughter Da. Maria married the elder or the younger D. Juan Núñez. Returning to D. Affonso de Portugal himself, we know that he married Da. Violante Manuel, daughter of Alfonso X.'s brother D. Manuel and sister of the famous D. Juan Manuel, and that he transferred his allegiance to the Castilian Crown in 1304, dying in 1312. His name and his daughters' bind together almost every element of opposition to the regency of Queen Maria de Molina; so that the marriage of D. Felipe to Da.

[1] *Port. Mon. Hist.—Scriptores*, i. p. 277.
[2] *Cron. de Alfonso XI.*, cap. xlii. (1322).

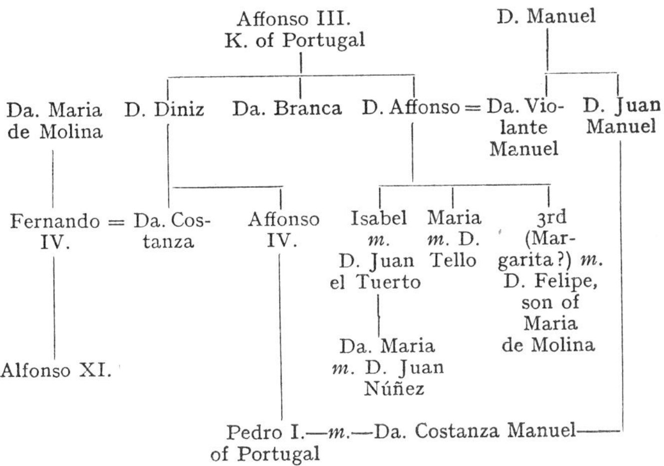

Margarita, if she were indeed his daughter, would be an important event in the politics of the regency. His connection with the translator of an Arthurian novel is indirectly supported by the view advanced by Snra. de Vasconcellos,[1] correctly (as we think), that he was the Infante Affonso de Portugal who interfered with the composition of the great derivative of the *matière de Bretagne*, the romance of *Amadis de Gaula*.[2]

Of the data offered by Juan Sánchez four can be verified from the chronicles, and the fifth has, at least, the merit of not being capable of fabrication from sources that are vulgarly accessible. It only remains for us to identify Juan Sánchez himself. The name Sánchez, however, is like the sands of the sea

[1] C. M. de Vasconcellos, *Lais de Bretanha, ad fin. Cf.* chap. xii.

[2] If it should be necessary to suppose an error in the text, an emendation of "r°" (*i.e. ruberto*) for "a°" would divert the allusion to the marriage of Philippe of Valois to Jeanne, daughter of Robert of Burgundy, which took place in 1313.

for multitude. At this period it was borne by a favourite, a Bishop of Ávila, two *caballeros* of Segovia, and all the bastards—a goodly throng—of King Diniz, including the celebrated D. Pedro Sanchez, Count of Barcellos, whom we have repeatedly mentioned.[1] Schoolmasters cut no very deep furrow in the world, and no information seems to be attainable concerning the incumbent of that office (doubtless a subordinate of the bishop) in the city of Astorga during the year 1313; so that the suggestions which we shall proceed to make, we advance less in the belief of their correctness than in the hope of stimulating further research into this point among students more happily circumstanced for its elucidation.

A schoolmaster of the Middle Ages who dates his literary work by the politics of both Church and State in two kingdoms, who seems to show a definite party bias, and who has books made to his order, is not likely to have been an inconsiderable figure; and we should probably do well to look for his name among that of the lesser nobility—the *caballeros*, and not the *ricos homes*, of the time. A certain *caballero*,[2] Sancho Sánchez de Velasco, enjoyed the favour of King Fernando IV., who granted him the office of *merino mayor* of Castile; but he was fiercely attacked by the Cortes of Valladolid in April, 1310, and had to surrender his *merindad* to Ferrand Ruiz de Saldaña, a partisan of D. Juan el Tuerto, the self-styled King of Leon. He had married a niece of the Bishop of

[1] A Juan Sánchez was *mayordomo* to D. Juan Manuel, but this employment prevents his identification with the schoolmaster.

[2] The passages referring to Sancho Sánchez de Velasco and Juan Sánchez de Velasco in the *Cron. de Fern. IV.* and *Cron. de Alfonso XI.* are to be found on pp. 131, 148, 150, 156, 158, 159, 175 of *Bibl. de Aut. Esp.*, No. 66.

Orense in Galicia, and in 1312, on information supplied by the latter, he seized the chance of defeating one of D. Juan el Tuerto's schemes with regard to the regency. To do so he had only to warn D. Juan Núñez of the plot, which was framed by the one partisan with a view to the exclusion of the other. But by this league with D. Juan Núñez, Sancho Sánchez entered one of the opposition parties arrayed against Maria de Molina's regency, and so became in a short time the ally, after an anarchical fashion, of D. Juan Manuel and even D. Juan el Tuerto, both of whom were powerfully established in the kingdom of Leon. His brother, Juan Sánchez de Velasco, is the only Sánchez of Christian name Juan who is thrown up by the chronicles and nobiliaries of the time. He was twice employed on embassies to prominent nobles (once to D. Juan el Tuerto in 1310) by King Fernando IV.; and he doubtless suffered from his brother's eclipse. The natural procedure for a favourite's brother in those times would be to attach to himself some minor clerical appointment, which would leave him with one leg in either world, and wait for sudden promotion in either Church or State.[1] His expectations may be measured by those of Gutierre Gómez, whose brother was also a favourite but managed to weather the storm of 1310, and who jumped, by royal favour, from a simple archdeaconry to the archbishopric of Toledo and primacy of Spain. But whoever the schoolmaster Sánchez may have been, there is no reason to doubt that his name in the colophon stands in entire good faith.

[1] According to *España Sagrada*, xvi. p. 252, the bishop of Astorga from 1315–26 was a Juan. That Juan's surname is not given, and his very tenure of office seems to be of the nature of an inference.

As much doubt rests upon the language of the first *Liuro de Josep Abaramatia*. Dr. Alvarez speaks of a transcription (*treladação*) and of the furbishing up of an antiquated text, but his language is not precise enough to exclude the notion of "translation." It is possible, too, to find a gap of eight years, according to his own evidence, between his "proper original" and that which the schoolmaster completed in 1313. It is not a simple question of deciding between the claims of Castilian and of Portuguese, seeing that an Astorgan of the fourteenth century might have employed the neighbouring Galician or Castilian, or might equally well have chosen to write in his own Astorgan *patois*. Whether an average bureaucrat of the sixteenth century could have classified correctly a piece of genuine dialect writing seems to me doubtful; but the speech of Astorga has the peculiarity of being now preserved only within the Portuguese territory. It is spoken to-day at Miranda on the Douro, the most westerly of the central dialects being still in use at the extreme south-west of the ancient diocese of Astorga. The same diocese can be used to account for the transmission of the manuscript; for, having passed from the capital to the extremity, it was an easy progress down the Douro to its mouth. The discovery of an Arthurian relic in the parish church of a village can be paralleled by the Lancelot-fragment which was recovered from the archives of the church at Campos in Majorca; and if the "old woman of very advanced age" seem somewhat novelistic, it was, and perhaps still is, in such circumstances that the collector may look for finds in the lands of the river Lethe.

The *Liuro de Josep Abaramatia* occupies a situation of some loneliness in Spanish-Portuguese Arthurianism. Giving itself out for the first part of a Grail-trilogy, it is not actually followed by the other parts, but ends in a colophon. It is considerably shorter than the third part of the trilogy, which frequently boasts its equal divisions. Though the name of Juan Bivas has been found by K. Pietsch embedded in the text, the translation or transcription that the schoolmaster Sánchez "caused to be done" in 1313 contrasts with that which Bivas dedicated to a king, presumably Sancho IV. about 1291. It is probable that we have here the Portuguese rendering of the first part of Bivas' *Demanda del Sancto Grial*, but full certainty in this matter must await a satisfactory description of the manuscript.[1]

The history of the Holy Grail was assuredly found complete in Castilian and Portuguese literature. It is cited in the *Cronica General de* 1404 under the title *Estoria del Sancto Grayal et de rrey Artur*,[2] and the three parts of the *Demanda del Sancto Grial*, bound up in two volumes in white leather covers, stood in the library of Queen Isabel the Catholic.[3] The first branch has, however, become severed from the others, with the exception of a summary treatment of the introductory chapters by a manuscript

[1] See Appendix.

[2] Fol. 25r. On fol. 26: "Como Inglaterra fue conuertida dos vezes a la fe: la vna por Josephas, fijo de Joseph de Varametia e la otra por sant Agostin." This mingles the *Estoire del Saint Graal* and the *Historia Regum Britonum*.

[3] Clemencín, in *Memorias de la Real Academia de Historia*, vi., cites: "142. Otro libro de pliego entero de mano escripto en romance, que se dice Merlin, con coberturas de papel de cuero blancas, e habla de Josepe de Arimathia. 143. Otro libro de pliego entero de mano en romance, que es la tercera parte de la demanda del santo Grial, las cobiertas de cuero blanco."

of Leonese provenience. This is a scrap-book, bearing the title of *Leyes de Palencia* and the signature 2–G–5 of the Palace Library at Madrid, and was completed in 1469 or 1470 by Pedro Ortiz, clerk (of Palencia?).[1] Its miscellaneous contents include a *Libro de Josep Abarimatia*, a *Libro de Merlin*, and a *Tratado de Lanzarote*. The last is too brief to be of much service as a classifier, but corresponds, so far as it goes, to the Castilian-Portuguese *Demanda del Sancto Grial* in the sections dealing with the commencement of the *Mort d'Arthur*. The middle section corresponds accurately with the Castilian *Baladro del Sabio Merlin*, and is of sufficient fulness to be compared textually with the first twenty-six chapters of the Pseudo-Robert de Boron. It follows that the *Libro de Josep Abarimatia* may be assumed in all confidence to be the survivor of the manuscripts which originally formed the first part of the Boron-trilogy in Spain. The 8th chapter (how Vespasian put Caiaphas into a ship) is caught up by the 227th of the Castilian *Demanda*. Under fifty-five headings the fragment sets out from the imprisonment of St. Joseph, the expedition of Vespasian, and the destruction of Jerusalem. Joseph of Arimathia

[1] Title, *Leyes de Palencia*. *Ad init.*, "E este libro se acabo Año domini MCCCCLXIX p. ortis clericus"; *Ad fin.*, "Escriptus fuyt año domini MCCCCLXX petrus ortis"; Contents: Fols. 1–44, "flor sanctorum (libro de fueros)"; 44–213, "vida de Barlan e de iosafa"; 213–238, "libro de la vida de los santos padres"; 238–251, "libro de fray juã de rocaçisa"; 251–282, "libro de josep abarimatia"; 282v–296, "libro de Merlin"; 296–298, "tratado de los articulos de fe de los christianos"; 298v–302v, "tratado de lançarote." *Cf.* O. Klob, *op. cit.*; K. Pietsch, *Concerning MS. 2–G–5 of the Palace Library of Madrid*, in *Modern Philology*, xi. pp. 1–18; *id. On the Language of the Spanish Grail Fragments*, in *Modern Philology*, xiii. pp. 369–378 and 625–646; *id.*, *The Madrid Manuscript of the Spanish Grail Fragments*, in *Modern Philology*, xviii. pp. 147–156, 591–596; and *Spanish Grail Fragments*, i. (Chicago, 1924); H. O. Sommer, in *Romania*, xxxvi. pp. 393–394.

and Vespasian leave Jerusalem together in the 12th chapter, and in the 16th the saint reaches Sarras. Armed with the miraculous powers of his sacred charge, he enters Evalach's council-chamber and preaches the Gospel and the mysteries of our Faith. Christ Himself fills chapters 38–48, as He consecrates Josaphas and explains the doctrine of the Eucharist. The 49th chapter begins the conversion of Evalach, and the remainder (many of which are unsupported rubrics) bring the fragment to an end in the thanksgivings of that monarch after his victory over Tolomer.

IX

THE ARTHURIAN NOVELS IN CASTILE AND PORTUGAL: THE "HOLY GRAIL"; "MERLIN," "QUEST"[1]

THE story of the Holy Grail survives in a vast and disorderly romance, which we may entitle (after Nicolás Antonio) the *Merlin y Demanda del Santo Grial*, or, for short, *Merlin y Demanda*, its component

[1] MANUSCRIPTS: *Cronica de* 1404, fols. 25–6; *Historia dos cavalleiros da Mesa Redonda e da Demanda do Santo Graal*, Vienna, Palace Library, MS. No. 2594; *La estoria de Merlin*, Madrid, Palace Library, MS. 2–G–5, fols. 282v–296 ("Aqui comieça la estoria de merlin y cuyo fijo fue, e del rrey artus y de como gano la grand bretaña que se dize ĩglaterra"); *Tratado de lançarote*, Madrid, Palace Library, MS. 2–G–5, fols. 298v–302v.

EARLY EDITIONS: *El Baladro del Sabio Merlin con sus profecias*, Burgos, Juan de Burgos, 1498; *Merlin y Demanda del Sancto Grial*, Seville, 1500 (cited by Moratín, Diosdado, N. Antonio; not now available); *La Demanda del Sancto Grial con los maravillosos fechos de Lanzarote del Lago y de Galaz su hijo*, Toledo, Juan de Villaquiran, 1515 (*Demanda* survives); Seville, 1535 (*Baladro* and *Demanda* survive).

REPRINTS: R. Menéndez Pidal, *La Crónica General de* 1404, in *Revista de Archivos*, 1903; K. von Reinhardstoettner, *Historia dos cavalleiros da Mesa Redonda e da Demanda do Santo Graal*, Berlin, 1877, 1 Band (Vienna MS., fols. 1–70); O. Klob, *Dois episodios da Demanda do Santo Graal*, in *Revista Lusitana*, vi. (Vienna MS., fols. 183v–185v and 192v–195r; the whole MS. has been transcribed by Wechssler and by Klob, but not published); O. Klob, in *Zeitschrift für rom. Phil.*, xvi. pp. 192–205 (extracts from 2–G–5); K. Pietsch, *Concerning MS.* 2–G–5 *of the Palace Library at Madrid*, in *Modern Philology*, xi. pp. 1–18, and *Spanish Grail Fragments*, i. (Chicago, 1924); G. Paris et J. Ulrich, *Merlin, Roman en Prose du xiiie siècle* (Paris), i. pp. lxxxi–xci (*Baladro*, 1498, prefaces, contents, conclusion); Bonilla, *Libros de Caballerías* (Madrid, 1907), i. pp. 1–338 (*Baladro* and *Demanda*, Seville, 1535). *Cf.* also *Del Santo Greal, Comedia*, seventeenth century, cited in Paz y Melia, *Cat. de los MSS. de la Bibl. Nac.—I. Teatro*, No. 3040, and La Barrera.

CRITICISM: G. Paris, O. Klob, K. von Reinhardstoettner, *opp. cit.*; K. Pietsch, *opp. cit.*, and *On the Language of the Spanish Grail Fragments*, in *Modern Philology*, xiii. pp. 369–378 and 625–646; E. Wechssler,

sections being the *Baladro del Sabio Merlin con sus profecias* and the *Demanda del Santo Grial.*[1] Originally translated as a trilogy (*Joseph*, *Merlin*, *Demanda*) under the title of *Historia de la Demanda del Santo Grial*, the first book is now but a fragment, and the latest edition allows of but two parts. The remainder correspond in style, development, and other characteristic marks of authorship, but are not logically complete in themselves nor consistent with each

Ueber die verschiedenen Redaktionen des Robert de Boron zugeschriebenen Graal-Lancelot-Zyklus, Halle-a-S., 1895; Brugger in *Zeitschrift für franz. Spr. und Litt.*, xxiv. *ff.*; H. O. Sommer, *The Quest of the Holy Grail*, in *Romania*, xxxvi. pp. 369–402 and 543–590; *id.*, *Die Abenteuer Gawains, Ywains und le Morholts*, in *Beihefte zur Zeitschrift für rom. Phil.*, xlvii., 1913; *cf.* also A. Pauphilet, *La Queste du Saint Graal du MS. Bibl. Nat. fonds fr.* 343, in *Romania*, xxxvi.; F. Lot, *Études sur le Lancelot en Prose* (Paris, 1918), p. 384; J. D. Bruce, *The Development of the Mort Arthur Theme in Mediæval Romance*, in *Romanic Review*, iv. (1913), pp. 401 – 471; *id.*, *The Evolution of Arthurian Romance*, 2 vols. (Göttingen and Baltimore, 1923); and Miss L. A. Paton, *Notes on Manuscripts of the Prophécies de Merlin*, in *Publications of the Mod. Lang. Assoc. of America*, xxviii. (1913), pp. 121–139.

[1] Internally, there are notes of a different division of books in the Boron-trilogy, but these indications are anterior to the Spanish stage of their history. For the Spanish or Portuguese mind, the trilogy was composed of Joseph, Merlin and Quest, probably without restriction as to correspondence in length. Combining the indications of the *Cron. de* 1404, and the Vienna MS., we get the fullest title for the group: *Historia de los caballeros de la Mesa Redonda y de Rey Artus y de la Demanda del Santo Grial*. This was abbreviated as *La Demanda* (less often *La Estoria*) *del Santo Grial* (or *Grayal*, whence *Grial* and *Graal*). The *primera parte* was *El Libro de Joseph Abarimatia*. The *segunda parte* varied. The fullest title is that of 2–G–5: *La estoria de Merlin y cuyo fijo fue e de rrey Artus*, etc. So in the *Tristan* we read: *Coronica del Rey Artur*. But it was generally named from its conclusion, which is extracted from the *Conte del Brait* ("este libro ha nonbre el BALADRO"). So *Valadro de Merlim* (*Cron. de* 1404); *Baladro del Sabio Merlin con sus profecias* (1498); or even *Profecias de Merlin* (? *cf. Profacies de Merli en frances*, Martin I.'s library). *Cf.* further *El Libro de Merlin* (Benavente, *c.* 1444), *Merlim* (D. Duarte's collection, *c.* 1437). The *tercera parte* was *La Demanda del Sancto Grial*, amplified: *con los maravillosos fechos de Lanzarote del Lago y de Galaz su hijo*. Villaquiran's edition ends: "Aqui se acabe el segundo y postrero libro," etc.; the edition of 1535 more explicitly: "Aqui se acabe el primero y segundo libro," etc. But there is no internal consistency in these late editions. *Bal.*, cap. 218, refers to cap. 297 as *El Segundo Libro del Sancto Grial*; and *Dem.*, cap. 355, refers to *las primeras* (plural); *cf.* cap. 423.

other. They imply the existence and currency of the romances[1] of Lancelot and Tristan, to which they make frequent reference, and they presume the reader's knowledge of the older and more spiritual Grail-story of Walter Map. There is, in fact, almost nothing with which the author seems to be less concerned than with the High History itself in any of its parts, and this neglect has been still further extended by the Castilian redactor. The so-called Robert de Boron is wholly insensible to the logic and meaning of the legend, and repeatedly turns away from it in order to lose himself in a catalogue of fantastic happenings and insensate battles. Belonging to the same category of romances as the Huth-*Merlin*, Malory's first four books, and certain manuscripts of the Bibliothèque Nationale,[2] the Castilian-Portuguese *Merlin y Demanda* is a pastiche of heterogeneous

[1] "La gran historia que llaman de Tristan" (*Dem.* c. 2, *cf.* 22; *Bal.* 332). "Lanzarote, que es ramo de la historia del sancto Grial, que anda por su parte" (*Bal.* 301), and "La grande historia que dize de los hechos de Lançarote, e de su nascencia, e de los nueuos linajes de nacion, assi como lo deuisa la alta historia del santo Grial" (*Bal.* 298, *cf.* 144; *Dem.* 40, 62, 323). The phrase "segun adelante oyredes," or an equivalent, is used of Tristan (*Bal.* 332) and Lancelot (*Bal.* 144); and of Galahad's birth and all Lancelot's history we are supposed cognisant (*cf. Dem.* 40). Map's *Quest* is termed "el otro libro" or *El Libro de Galaz* (*Dem.* 226: "lo auemos escrito en el libro de Galaz," 229, 241, 249, 358). A *Livro de Galaz* (language not specified) stood in the library of King Duarte of Portugal. *El libro del Baladro* (*Bal.* 338, *Dem.* 358 thrice, 373, 423, 424 twice, 426) refers always to the *Conte del Brait* of Hélye, an extensive romance covering (it would seem) the adventures of Bandemagus, Entombment, etc., of Merlin, Quest, and Death of Arthur. This title (taken from *Bal.* 338) came to be later applied to the *Historia de Merlin*. The *Cuento del Bastardo* (*Dem.* 36) is cited for "La Cote Male Taile" and "Guinglain." There was also *El Libro de las Aventuras*, an imaginary work (*Bal.* 240, *Dem.* 344), and *La gran historia de Llain* or *Clain* (*Dem.* 294). For events of *Joseph Abarimatia*, cf. *Bal.* 25–6, *Dem.* 49, 368. For the mutual relations of the *Baladro* and *Demanda*, cf. *Bal.* 72, 87; *Dem.* 181 *ff.*, 221, 277–279. Charlemagne's conquest of Britain is supposed in *Dem.* 287, 288, 316. All references here and later are to the chapters of Bonilla's edition (*Libros de Caballerias*, i.).

[2] Bibl. Nat., Paris, f. fr., Nos. 112, 340, 343.

parts, pseudonymously ascribed to Robert de Boron, which contain the following details: I. The story of Merlin and the Elevation of Arthur; II. The Prophecies of Merlin; III. The *Suite du Merlin*, an involved romance of diverse adventures, and especially of Balin and the Dolorous Stroke; IV. The *Conte du Brait*, extracted from Hélye de Boron; V. The Boron-*Quest*, a scatter-brained narrative which adds to the true *Grail* the knight-errantries of Galahad, passages in detraction of Gawain, and copious extracts from *Tristan* and *Palomedes*; VI. The *Mort d'Artus*, ending with the death of King Mark.

I. The *Livre de Merlin* narrates the diabolical begetting of that prophet, how he visited Vortigern and prophesied his destruction, how he assisted King Pendragon, how he triumphed over a malicious baron who tried to convict him of false prophecy, how he helped Uther, and how he presided over the birth and education of King Arthur. Finally, it tells how he devised the test which led to the coronation and universal acceptance of that monarch. II. During the whole of this section Merlin contributes liberally his predictions of events in Arthurian time; but after the insidious stratagems of the baron, he resolved to speak no more prophecies which could be known before the event. The prophecies in his new and obscure style are omitted from the Huth-*Merlin*, and also from the Spanish *Baladro*, except (says the latter) a little of what he said to Uther.[1] III. Then follows

[1] Huth-*Merlin*, i. pp. 85–6: "Ensi fu commenciés uns livre que on apelle par nom le livre des prophecies Merlin, de chou que il dist des rois d'Engleterre et de toutes les autres choses dont il parla puis." *Baladro*, cap. 75: "mas en este libro no dize sino lo que dixo claramente, sino vn poco que dixo a Uter." This section presumably gave the name to Martin I.'s *Profacies de Merli en frances*, which otherwise appears to have resembled the Pseudo-Robert de Boron.

the *Suite du Merlin*, an enormous jumble of adventures. Arthur begets Mordred by Helaine; and is declared son of Uther Pendragon. The Blatant Beast is seen; and the entry of *le chevalier nafré* leads Giflet and Arthur into sundry battles, until the latter acquires from the Lady of the Lake his invincible Excalibur. The king's attempt to murder all Mordred's contemporaries is frustrated by the providence of God, and Mordred is reared by the father of Sagramor. We are then mainly concerned with Balin le Savage, who is singularly unlucky in his attempts to convey his *protégées* on their quests, who captures King Rience and aids in the rout of Nero and Loth (the killing of the latter by Pellinor leads Gawain to swear revenge, and his oath is bloodily maintained in the sequel); he bears two swords, stands powerless to prevent a damsel's sacrifice of a dish of her blood in a vain attempt to do what Percival's sister alone could achieve, slays Garlan [1] at Pellehan's court, and wounds the latter with the Holy Lance,—and this is the Dolorous Stroke which leads to the wasting of the lands, and the commencement of the Adventurous Times. As for Balin, he dies by the hand of his brother Balan, whom he slays; and Merlin enchants the island of their tragedy and the sword of its execution. Arthur obtains Queen Guenevere, and institutes the Round Table with 148 knights. Gawain, Tor and Pellinor engage in a triple adventure. Merlin travels with Niviene, and by her is entombed in the Cave of the Lovers. Arthur fights and defeats Five Kings. He is in graver peril from Sir Accolon of Gaul. Another triple adventure (of Morholt, Gawain and

[1] Momentarily confused with Gawain in *Baladro,* cap. 268.

Ywain or Uwain) is commenced from the moment when the two latter found twelve damsels deriding Le Morholt's shield; and some other episodes (such as the murders of Pellinor, Lamorant and Agloval by Gawain) are required in order to complete the catalogue of things assumed by the *Quest*. IV. After the battle of the Five Kings, Tor was preferred to Bandemagus, and the latter left Camalot in a fit of temper. His adventures are omitted by Malory and the Huth-*Merlin*, in the latter of which the reader is referred to the *Conte del Brait*.[1] Bandemagus, in fact, set out from Camalot, and soon fell—I know not how—into the prison of Urien's father. Being liberated by a damsel, he fled, lost her to Le Morholt, who hated all damsels because his father had been killed on escort duty, and who specialised on collecting them in Irish castles as slaves; Bandemagus recovered her, somewhat unfairly, proceeded to Merlin's tomb, and heard the prophet's terrible cry. He returned to Morholt, dismissed the damsel, and travelled to court. V. The *Demanda* is chiefly distinguished from the Vulgate *Quest* by its weakened sense of the mystical, and its reinforcement of extraneous and extravagant matter. Without any previous notice of Galahad or his father, the former reaches Camalot and fills his Seat Perilous. All the knights swear to the Quest, Gawain leading. Galahad and Melian, his squire, find

[1] Huth-*Merlin*, ii. pp. 172–3: "A tant se met Baudemagus a la voie entre lui et son escuiier. Mais de chose ne d'aventure qui li avenist en toute la voie ne parole mes livres, car mes sires Helyes mes compains a empris sa matiere . . . car mes sires Helyes en a commenchies l'ystoire a translater, et si di ge malement l'ystoire, mais la branke, car chou est droitement une des brankes del graal, sans quoi on ne porroit pas bien entendre la moiiene partie de mon livre ne la tierche partie."

sundry adventures. Gawain murders Ywain, Patrides, Sagramor, Erec and Bandemagus; and in the assembly of the first year his name is mentioned to his shame. Previously thereto the dispute of Bors and Leonel occurs. In the second year of the Quest Tristan was wounded and lay in an abbey; and Galahad visited Corbenic, where he paid little attention to its mysteries, but chastised the impertinent Eleazer. He made some cures, and came on Caiaphas and Solomon's Vessel. Mark captured Joyous Guard in Tristan's absence, seized Iseut, and sorely pressed King Arthur, who was relieved by a combination of Galahad, Palomades and Arthur the Less. After this defeat, Mark made a wicked attempt to poison the sainted Galahad; the modesty of the latter became the mockery of Gawain and his brothers, till they were overwhelmed in personal combat and later had to be released by their butt from the Castillo Follon. Some 350 damsels were released on this occasion, which was fittingly commemorated in a statue raised by Charlemagne to Galahad. After informing Tristan of Mark's outrages, Galahad righted the wrongs of a disinherited widow, and knighted Samaliel son of Frollo, who proved to be worthy. Lancelot obtained a partial and temporary view of the Grail, and Hector and Gawain were repulsed. Palomades the Pagan defeated or matched Gareth, Gawain and Lancelot, but under Galahad's strokes he turned Christian, and so ended his quest of the Blatant Beast. Galahad, Bors and Percival came again to Corbenic, where they found nine other knights; the first-named saw the Grail and cured the Maimed King; the trio remained in the castle when the others departed, Palomades perishing shortly after. The Questers were educated in the puzzles of the Blatant Beast, the Healing Fountain and the Lady of the Chapel; and when Galahad and Percival in Solomon's Vessel departed for Sarras, Bors returned to Camalot. VI. The story then plunges without preamble into an abbreviated *Mort d'Artus*, which follows in its general lines the Vulgate *Lancelot.* After Arthur's death, those of Guenevere, Lancelot and King Mark follow in rapid and dolorous succession.

This combination of the *Merlin*, *Conte del Brait*, and *Livre des Prophecies* is nowhere extant, nor ever existed with all the details just given; for what we have set down is an inclusive scheme for the related romances. It is, however, most nearly realised in the Spanish and Portuguese Grail-fragments. The three parts of the Boron-trilogy occur together only in the manuscript 2–G–5 in the Royal Library at Madrid; but they are fragmentary, and of little service in reconstituting the archetype for Spain. Two parts, the *Baladro* and the *Demanda*, are still extant, proceeding from a Sevillan edition of the year 1535, under the title, *La Demanda del Sancto Grial con los maravillosos hechos de Lanzarote del Lago y de Galaz su hijo*; and the British Museum contains a copy in which the *Baladro* of 1535 has been bound up with a *Demanda*, the surviving moiety of a *Merlin y Demanda*, printed by Juan de Villaquiran at Toledo in 1515. Though the correspondence of the Sevillan and Toledan editions amounts almost to identity, it is probable that they are both reprints of the same *Merlin y Demanda del Sancto Grial* (Seville, 1500) seen by N. Antonio, Moratín and others. The *Baladro del Sabio Merlin con sus profecias* was issued separately at Burgos by Juan de Burgos in 1498; and the manuscript No. 2594 of the Palace Library at Vienna, containing *A Historia dos Cavalleiros da Mesa Redonda e da Demanda do Santo Graal*, has been reproduced in part by Reinhardstoettner and Klob, and has been collated by H. O. Sommer. The *Baladro del Sabio Merlin*, or *Segunda Parte de la Demanda del Santo Grial*, contains: I. The *Merlin*, II. The *Profecias*, III. The *Suite du Merlin*, IV. *Conte del Brait* (extracts); the *Demanda*, or *Tercera Parte*, embraces: V. The Boron-*Quest*, and VI. his *Mort d'Artus*.

By comparing the contents of the editions of 1498 and 1535, we may determine the fifteenth-century form of the *Baladro del Sabio Merlin*; but the evidence of the Portuguese *Cancioneiros* indicates a French source that differs from this consensus of the *Baladros* by the addition of certain elements, and we may reasonably suppose that this was also the form of the first translator's manuscript, when he laid down his pen. His work would also show more agreement with its congeners north of the Pyrenees, in proportion as they each approached nearer to their original source, and he would especially stand closer than the texts now stand to Malory and the Huth-*Merlin*. In an admirably abbreviated form Malory gives all the adventures of Boron's narrative up to the conclusion of Gawain, Ywain and Le Morholt's adventure; but he omits all that precedes Uther's intrigue with Igerne, nor does he give the Prophecies or the *Conte del Brait*. He adds to the narrative an account of Arthur's war with Eleven Kings, drawn out of a Vulgate *Merlin*. The Huth-*Merlin* contains the *Merlin* and *Suite du Merlin*, but no Prophecies or *Conte del Brait* or Vulgate incidents; it extends to the commencement of the triple adventure of Gawain, Ywain and Le Morholt, as far as the episode of the damsels who dance in scorn of the shield, and at that point breaks off to follow the Grail. The triple adventure itself has to be supplied from the manuscript 112 of the Bibliothèque Nationale. Compared with these compeers, the distinguishing mark of the Spanish romances is that they include some of the Prophecies and an extract from the *Conte del Brait*: the French compiler of their original has, in fact, verified the allusions of the Pseudo-Boron. The Prophecies fall most naturally after cap. 75 of the *Baladro* where preparation is made for their reception,[1] but they appear to have been attracted into Merlin's conversation with Vortigern in cap. 52; with the *Conte del Brait* the narrative is concluded.

The *Cronica de* 1404, which briefly alludes to the reigns of Vortigern, Pendragon, Uther and Arthur (capp. 52–180 of the *Baladro*), confirms the existence of the Peninsular romance as far back as 1390, the year in which the chronicler collected his materials in Castile. The description of the Blatant Beast (cap. 145) is confirmed by Fernand' Esquio's poem in the *Cancioneiro da Vaticana*, which humorously plays on the attention to colour of the description given in

[1] In the Italian life of Merlin (Venice, 1480) and a manuscript at Parma, certain prophecies occur at this point. It was here, too, in all probability that Maistre Anthoine was found, though later transferred to the purely Spanish appendix of prophecies. *Cf.* Miss. L. A. Paton, in *Publ. Mod. Lang. Assoc. of America*, xxviii. p. 216. An edition of the *Prophécies de Merlin* by Miss Paton is now in the press.

the romance.[1] The notice of Le Morholt's death (cap. 245) is, as we have seen, the subject of an allusion by the translator of *Tristan de Leonis* (cap. 70); and the oft-quoted poem of Estevam da Guarda in the *Cancioneiro da Vaticana* (No. 930) is a secure notice not only of the entombment of Merlin as related by Robert de Boron, but also of Hélye's *Brait*, one of the distinguishing marks of the Peninsular versions (cap. 338).[2] These references confirm the existing text so far as it goes, and retract it to the early fourteenth, or even late thirteenth, century; but the second *lai de Bretanha*,[3] confirming the text

[1] *Canc. Vat.*, 1140:

"Disse un infante ante sa companha
Que me daria besta na fronteira;
E non sera ja murzela, nen veira,
Nen branca, nen vermelha, nen castanha,
Pois amarela nen parda non for,
A pran, sera a besta ladrador,
Que lh'adurran do reino de Bretanha."

Cf. Baladro, cap. 145: "vna bestia . . . la mas dessemejada que nunca vio . . . blanco como nieue . . . negras como carbon . . . estraña de fuera y de dentro . . . en el reyno de Londres." The name *Bestia ladrador* does not occur in *Tristan*.

[2] *Canc. Vat.*, No. 930:

"Com'avẽo a Merlin de morrer
Por seu gran saber que el foi mostrar
A tal molher que o soub'enganar,
Per essa guisa se foi cofonder
Martin Vaasquez—per quanto lh'eu oí—
Que o ten mort'ũa molher assi
A quen mostrou, por seu mal, seu saber.

Sei que lh'e muito grave de tẽer—
Por aquelo que lh'el foi a mostrar,
Con que sabe que o pod'ençerrar
En tal logar u conven d'atender
A tal morte de qual morreu Merlin,
U dara vozes, fazendo sa fin;
Ca non pod'el tal mort'estraer."

Cf. Canc. Baena, No. 331, and Fernández de Oviedo, "Quinquagenas," in *Canc. Baena*, ed. Pidal, Ochoa and Gayangos, p. 681, n. 200.

[3] *Canc. Col. Branc.*, No. 2:

[Rubric] "Esta cantiga fezeron quatro donzelas a Marot d'Irlanda en tempo de Rei Artur, porque Marot filhava toda-las donzelas que

with its rubric, demonstrates at the same time the imperfect conservation of the final episodes.

If we take up the hint of the Pseudo-Boron, and combine the *Merlin* with the *Brait*, the concluding adventures should make the following scheme: 1. Entombment of Merlin; 2. the Five Kings, 3. Adventures of Bandemagus and Morholt; 4. Bandemagus and Merlin—the *brait*; 5. Accolon; 6. Morholt and the damsels; 7. Gawain, Ywain and Morholt's triple adventure; 8. other episodes. But it was the idiosyncrasy of the Boron-trilogy that it insisted on

achava en guarda dos cavaleiros, se as podia conquerer d'eles. E enviava-as pera Irlanda pera seeren sempre en servidon da terra. E esto fazia el porque fora morto seu padre por razon de ũa donzela que levava en guarda." [Colocci, from an old rubric] "Esta cantiga é a primeira que foi feita e fezeron-na quatro donzelas en el tempo del Rei Artur a Maraot d'Irlanda por la . . . tornada em lenguagem palavra por palavra e diz assi. . . .

'O Marot haja mal grado . . .'" etc.

Cf. Baladro, cap. 255: "e Morloc embiaualas todas a Irlanda, e fazialas todas meter en vn castillo donde no podian salir despues; y esto hazia el por su padre e por dos sus hermanos, que eran buenos caualleros, que fueran muertos en vn torneo por juyzio de dueñas e donzellas que dieron en el reyno de Londres."

Bibl. Nat., f. fr., MS. 112: "Apres heure de tierce leur auint quilz vindrent deles .j. bois et trouuerent damoiselles qui karoloient entour .j. arbre, et pourient bien estre iusqua .xij. Et deuant elles auoit .ij. cheualiers tous armes sur .ij. grans cheuaulx. Et estoient amduy si apreste quil ny failloit fors du poindre. Et a cel arbre (entour) cui les damoyselles karoloient auoit .i. escu pendu tout blanc sans autre enseigne nulle. Et ainsi comme chascune damoiselle passoit par deuant lescu, elle crachoit dessus et disoit: 'Dieux donit honte a cellui qui te souloit porter, car il nous a mainte honte pourchassee.' Et lors recommencoit sa chanson et respondoit auec les autres. Gauuain vient pres des damoyselles et escoute ce quelles dient. Et quant il la bien entendu, il demande a son cousin: 'Entendes vous ceste chanson?' 'Oil bien,' fait il, 'elles dient que mal gre en ait le Mor(h)olt.'" (Sommer, in *Beihefte zur Zeitschrift für rom. Phil.*, xlvii. pp. 3–4; *cf.* Huth-*Merlin*, ii. pp. 232 *ff.*, and Malory, iv. chs. xvi. *ff.*) While there is hardly room to dispute the origin of the *cantiga* and its two rubrics, the latter are probably a somewhat faulty report of the episode; "iiij donzelas" for "xij damoyselles"; Marot, Maraot (also adopted by *Amadis*) for Morloc (Morlot, Morolt, Morholt); death of Morholt's father reported with a difference, which could, however, be added as an emendation to the *Baladro*, referring the tourney to his brothers.

the equality of its divisions; so that changes made in any part had to be balanced by symmetrical changes elsewhere. The end of the *Merlin*, being a string of disconnected episodes, offered itself to the knife, and it seems to have been pruned by each transcriber. Malory reports 1, 2, 5, 6, 7, with a passing allusion to 3 and 4. Nowhere is 8 preserved. The Huth-*Merlin* has 1, 2, 5, 6, and refers its readers to Hélye for 3 and 4; it then hastens into the *Grail*, leaving the triple adventurers with their hands in their pockets. The *Baladro* of 1535 has 1, 3, 4, and Bandemagus returns from Merlin to Camalot; the *Baladro* of 1498 has 1, 2, 3, 4, and Bandemagus returns to Morholt before going on to court, so that Morholt is left standing in the field; moreover, both *Baladros* agree to put 3 (Bandemagus' adventures) into the middle of the compilation, but in the edition of 1498 his departure for these adventures occurs at the end of the book. The Portuguese lyric

O Marot haja mal grado

is assuredly taken from 6 (Morholt's shield and the damsels), to which Colocci's rubric refers. The first rubric is taken from 3 (Bandemagus and Morholt), which must have stood within a reasonable distance of 6; that is to say, it can hardly have been displaced by half a volume as in the extant texts, nor is it likely that 5 (Accolon) intervened to break the sequence of Bandemagus and Morholt's affairs in 3, 4, 6. Further, in the *Baladro* of 1498 Le Morholt is obviously ready to undertake the adventure of the shield and damsels. There is no evidence that 7 (the triple adventure) or 8 (undiscovered adventures presumed by the *Quest*) formed part of the Peninsular text: 7, 8 and 5 (Accolon) had probably been pared away to compensate for the increased bulk of this book that arose out of the adoption of 3 and 4 from the *Conte del Brait*, and some prophecies. We conclude that the French original of the Castilian-Portuguese story consisted of: I. *L'Estoire de Merlin*; II. *Prophecies*; III. *Suite du Merlin*, as far as 1, the Entombment of Merlin, and 2, the Five Kings; IV. Extracts from the *Conte del Brait*, namely 3, Bandemagus' adventures, and 4, Bandemagus and Merlin, followed by 6, Morholt and the damsels, from the *Suite du Merlin*.

We now compare the three texts of the *Baladro del Sabio Merlin* or *Estoria de Merlin y de rrey Artur*.

The manuscript 2–G–5[1] contains: I. *Merlin*, a somewhat abbreviated transcript of the first twenty-six chapters, concerning the wizard's birth, his mother's peril, and his conversation with Blaise. A string of headings cover Merlin's intercourse with Vortigern (capp. 27–54), and there is no allusion to his prophecies. From the *Suite du Merlin* (III.) this manuscript alludes under a string of headings to the meeting of King Arthur and the Blatant Beast and that of Arthur and Merlin, that is, the matter of chapters 144–150 of the *Baladro*. Where it is possible to compare the phrases of this abstract with the language of the editions, it has the advantage of a more archaic style; but it is much contracted and shows many omissions. Its dialect, a Castilian infected with Leonese, is of considerable interest, as giving

[1] 2–G–5 has been compared with the *Baladro* of 1535 by O. Klob, in *Zeitschrift für rom. Phil.*, xxvi., and by K. Pietsch, in *Modern Philology*, xi. pp. 1–18. See also Pietsch, *Spanish Grail Fragments*.

a hint of the commerce of these Arthurian stories with the old dialects of the Peninsula, while these had some autonomy. On the other hand, 2–G–5 is of little weight as evidence of the form and construction of the novel.

The *Baladro* of 1498, extant in a unique example in the library of the Marquis of Pidal, is as yet known to us only through the extracts forwarded by Menéndez y Pelayo to G. Paris, and published by the latter in his edition of the *Merlin* of Pseudo-Boron. They include two prefaces which are not to be found in other editions, a table of contents, and a portion of the last chapter; and it is in this last only that we can make a textual comparison of the issues of 1498 and of 1535. The earlier edition shows some superior readings and a greater measure of stylistic correction, so that its language approximates to that of *Don Tristan de Leonis*. Both romances were issued by the same printer, Juan de Burgos, the *Tristan* in 1501 at Valladolid, and the *Baladro* in 1498 at Burgos; and to his improving or destructive pen we must be indebted for their similarity of style. The contents of the *Baladro* of 1498 are distributed among 40 chapters and 105 folios; the edition of 1535 consists of 341 chapters and 97 folios: their matter, therefore, must have been almost the same, but with a slight advantage in favour of the earlier text. The forty chapters of Juan de Burgos' text consist of thirty-eight numbered headings, and two—between 9 and 10, and between 37 and 38—that have not been numbered, and which we may conveniently term 9A and 37A; the rubrics are most frequent in the earlier pages of the novel, but later become more widely spaced and correspond indifferently to the probable contents of the chapters. It is not safe, therefore, to presume the absence of any of the episodes which are to be found in the edition of 1535; and we should probably look to the 28th and 29th chapters, although their rubrics refer only to Bandemagus and Le Morholt, for the later adventures of Balin le Savage,—the slaughter of Garlan, the Dolorous Stroke, the death and burial of the brothers. The two editions exhibit in common three characteristics which probably do not ascend to the Peninsular archetype. The obscure prophecies of Merlin,[1] which should have been placed in King Pendragon's reign and delivered to Uther (cap. 75), have been attracted to the interview between Merlin and Vortigern, where they interrupt the sense. As both the manuscript 2–G–5 and the *Cronica de* 1404 are too brief to inform us of the state of their text of these prophecies, we are perhaps arbitrary in supposing that a correct order was ever known south of the Pyrenees. The blunder is, however, entirely characteristic of the Arthurian traditions of Spain and Portugal; and it is accompanied by two others of Peninsular origin. They agree to transfer Bandemagus' adventures from their connection with the visit to Merlin to a place which bisects those of Balin and Balan;[2] but in so doing they are neither consistent with each other nor with themselves. The Dolorous Stroke (cap. 283) begins the Adventurous Times, but some of its first adventures are achieved by Bandemagus more than thirty chapters previously

[1] 9A. Cap. (s. num.): "Como Merlin dixo al rey Berenguer ciertas profecias." *Cf.* ed. 1535, cap. 52.

[2] *Baladro*, 1498, capp. 28 and 29; 1535, capp. 241–61.

(cap. 250).[1] The redactor of 1535 does not know how or when Bandemagus left court, nor how or why he came into the prison of Urien's father: according to Juan de Burgos, however, Bandemagus left Camalot in the chapter we have numbered 37A, and his adventures occur in those numbered 28 and 29.[2] This enumeration[3] may explain the error. The adventures of Bandemagus followed the defeat of the Five Kings in a sequence of chapters, numbered in the Roman style, xxxvii., xxxviii., xxxix., and xl.; but the two internal figures were corrupted to xxviii., xxix., and transferred to the middle of the romance, cancelling the rubrics of xxviii. and xxix. which referred to Balin and the Dolorous Stroke; xl. would then be re-numbered xxxviii. The same result, however, might possibly result from some similar error of foliation, and in the absence of a satisfactory account of the *Baladro* of 1498 it may not be wise to pin our faith to any one explanation. It is, however, undoubtedly a mechanical error that has arisen within the Spanish period of the romance, for the two texts show slightly different readings.

[1] *Bal.* 1535, cap. 283: "Agora comiençan las auenturas del reyno auenturado." Cap. 250: "y este Bandemagus fue de los primeros que las auenturas e marauillas del reyno de Londres comenςaron."

[2] *Bal.* 1498, cap. s. num. (37A): "como Baudemagus salio de la corte del rey Arthur muy despechado por que no le habian fecho caballero de la Taba redonda, e al rey e a los otros grandes les peso."

[3] The numbers are given in the Roman style:

Cap. xxxvii.: "como el rey Artur fizo batalla con los cinco reyes."

Cap. s. num.: "como Baudemagus salio," etc.

Cap. xxviii.: "como Baudemagus se combatio con su primo Anchises."

Cap. xxix.: "como Morlot llevo de las tiendas una donzella."

Cap. xxxviii.: "como Baudemagus tomo a Morlot de Irlanda una donzella."

Cap. xxvii. contains the visit of Ebron's wife to King Arthur and the knighthood of Brehus *sans pitié* (ed. 1535, capp. 238–40). As this incident is not found in Malory or the Huth-*Merlin*, it also, perhaps, should be referred to the *Conte del Brait*.

That of 1498 opens its chapter 38 with the words: "Despues que Baudemagus tomo su donzella que no respondio a Morlot ninguna cosa de lo que le decia . . ."; it then proceeds to the meeting of Bandemagus and Merlin. But in terms of the edition of 1535, this involves the juxtaposition of chapters 261 and 333. The third common feature of the *Baladros* is that they have cut short the romance with the conclusion of the *Conte del Brait.* According to the edition of 1498, Bandemagus returns to his damsel, who has been much terrified by Merlin's cry, conducts her to Le Morholt, dismisses her, and returns to King Arthur's court, leaving Le Morholt still in the field: according to that of 1535, Bandemagus returns to his damsel, whom he finds dead of fright;[1] there is, therefore, no need to revisit Le Morholt, and he makes his way straight to the capital. The principal difference in content between the two romances is that the earlier still preserves the episode of King Arthur's war with the Five Kings (cap. 37), which has been omitted in the later issue in order to bring Bandemagus' visit to Merlin (capp. 333–340) into immediate contact with Merlin's entombment (cap. 332). Accidental differences are the superiority of the style of Juan de Burgos' work, and the circumstance that this edition possesses two prologues and an epilogue which are wanting to the other. Conversely, the Spanish prophecies of Merlin are peculiar to the Sevillan copy.[2]

[1] "muerta . . . por miedo de los baladros." A metaphor taken literally.

[2] Both *Baladros* contain 1, 3, 4; both omit 5, 6, 7, 8, and misplace 3. The ed. of 1498 has 2 and a hint of 6, lost to the ed. of 1535. The ed. of 1535 has lost all 2 and the first half of 3.

Thus the comparison of the two Castilian versions of the *Baladro del Sabio Merlin* indicates a point of contact between their textual traditions within the Peninsular period of the romance. When collated with French and Portuguese parallel passages or novels, this earlier Castilian story shows traces of two kinds of peculiarities: there have been certain deliberate alterations, and especially abbreviations; and there have been mechanical errors of ignorance. The evidence of the *lai de Bretanha* is to be valued not as necessarily indicating the language and circumstances of the first translation, but as giving a report of a text earlier than that of the consensus of the extant *Baladros*; for if, as we have contended, the translation of the *matière de Bretagne* was accomplished while the two countries still enjoyed an unbroken unity of culture, then it is equally reasonable that divergences of tradition should be referred to the time of that unit's scission. The same interest and importance attaches to the *Historia dos Cavalleiros da Mesa Redonda e da Demanda do Santo Graal.* That fifteenth-century manuscript is neither the original translation nor an accurate copy; but it still preserves the original form and expression, where the Castilian work has been severely re-edited. The separation from the Castilian works occurred most probably in the first half of the fourteenth century; since which date, the Castilian *Demanda*, like the Castilian *Baladro*, has been exposed to intentional and mechanical change.

The Portuguese *Demanda do Santo Graal* has preserved, without essential modifications, the combination of the *Quest* and *Mort d'Artur* which had been imagined by the self-styled Boron.[1] Assuming, and largely incorporating, that history which was attached to the Prose-*Lancelot*, the compiler worked in hints from the Prose-*Tristan*, *Palomède*, and *Méraugis de Portlesguez*. He had little sense of the meaning of his original, but sometimes invented episodes in explanation of what he could not fathom. Nobody cares for the Holy Vessel; nobody has any purpose save cuffs and blows. Galahad is as absurdly pugilistic as any other knight. As the fabricator could presume on the acquaintance of his readers with *Lancelot du Lac* and the *Queste del Saint Graal*, he could sever the logical connection of the two works, introducing his chief actors unannounced, contradicting himself, leaving unfinished his own hints, directing continually his readers' attention to external literature, but always with the impudent insinuation of his own authorship or that of his fellow-conspirators, Hélye de Boron and Luce de Gast. None the less, the congruity of the two parts of the trilogy is assured by their citations of Robert de Boron and of the *Conte del Brait*, by their hostility to Gawain, by their agreement with the *Tristan*, *Palomède* and *Méraugis*, by the prominence allotted to these heroes and to Bandemagus, and by the infallible evidence of their dissipated style and rambling construction. Such points of contact are greater than marks of internal contradiction, because (as A. Pauphilet has well said) it is of the very nature of the Boron-*Quest* that it should not be invariably constituted.

Such is the Boron-*Quest*, and such the Portuguese

[1] See A. Pauphilet's excellent critique in *Romania*, xxxvi. pp. 591–609.

Demanda. The scribe has no liberty in face of his text. A few folios have, however, dropped out: a passage on the death of Erec (Spanish, capp. 165–8), another on Galahad's storm of the Castillo Follon (capp. 285–8), and the episode of the Disinherited Widow (capp. 292–6) are wanting. Pursued into yet minor particulars, the Portuguese writer displays some uncertainty as to whether his original should be a Latin work or a French, demonstrating that it was probably neither; he fails to name himself or his language, has a precarious grip on proper names, commits extraordinary "howlers," and seems unable to check his work by other Arthurian originals: in all which respects the Castilian texts, despite the stringent editing from which they have suffered, show a healthier scribal tradition.[1]

The surviving editions of the Castilian romance, 1515 and 1535, present a united front in the matter of the *Queste del Saint Graal.* Their most conspicuous feature is the accidental loss of some fifty folios relating to Bors, Percival and Bandemagus;[2] and this, together with many other excisions and losses,

[1] *Cf.* H. O. Sommer, in *Romania,* xxxvi.: p. 548, Ptg. "destoria, aquella domaa, ante a jnsoa grande," for Sp. "descocia, en aquella demanda, ante la joyosa guarda"; Ptg. "gram batalha," Sp. "gran bretaña"; p. 549, "the corruption of proper names is in S., and more especially in P., developed to an incredible degree" (*e.g.* Ptg. "Gadram" Sp. "Tristan"!); p. 561 (cap. 184), Ptg. "mais nom vos direi como, ca o nom achei em frances nem Boirom diz que en mais achou na grande storia do latim de quanto eu vos conto," Sp. "ca ya deuisado lo ha en el cuento como murieron & los otros falle en françes & no lo escreui en castellano. Mas habla la gran hystoria de Llayn de quanto yo cuento"; pp. 555–7 (cap. 52), Ptg. "madar, filho sofria," Sp. "mudar, philosophia"; Ptg. "nem eu direy mais, . . ." Sp. "ni yo Joannes Biuas no vos dire ende mas de lo que vos el dize: ca so frayle & no quiero mentir"; Ptg. "de frances em latim," Sp. "en françes."

[2] After cap. 126, corresponding to fols. 51–103 of the Portuguese text. The error may have been confirmed by the similarity of GALUAN&gARiETe (cap. 126) to GALUAN&EREC (127).

has reduced the romance to no more than two-thirds of its original extension.[1] Gestures of impatience are not infrequent: the reviser puts a limit on "significances" and unnecessary anagnorises, and he is unwilling to repeat what has been said in other parts of the trilogy. He economises space on specifically Grail episodes, not because of a practical temper which sees no interest in such mysteries, but because he found in them duplicates of the Map-*Quest*, which he declares himself to have already transcribed. Its influence begins in the middle of his romance (cap. 226), and by reference to it he is enabled to elide passages concerning the ship of Solomon, Caiaphas, and the navigation of Lancelot. Map's history is termed by him *El Libro de Galaz*, and the Boron version is *La verdadera hystoria del Sancto Grial*; but in chapter 358 Boron's work is the *Libro de Galaz*. For at that moment the redactor was preparing to mystify his readers. The twelve knights assembled at Corbenic should have (and in the Portuguese version do) achieved the Quest, cured the Maimed King, and departed, leaving the three heroes to conclude the work. But the Castilian reviser wrenched off this conclusion, merely naming the company; in chapters 359–72 he continued to follow the Pseudo-Boron for the adventures of Palomades

[1] The omissions are: cap. 31, 3 paragraphs; 49, 5 paragraphs referring to the *Joseph*; 52, 3 paragraphs of "senificanças"; 126, 52 folios; 141, 1 paragraph; 194, 6 folios; 201, 22 lines; 225, 23 lines; 226, 3 folios concerning Solomon's ship; 229, 8 folios, Caiaphas; 241, 3 folios; 291, 2 folios, Lancelot and Galahad's navigation; 358, 3 folios, Corbenic; 373 *ff.*, Boron's conclusion, 6 folios. In capp. 226, 229, 241, 291, 358, the omission is justified by a reference to the *Libro de Galaz* (226: "lo auemos escrito en el libro de Galaz"), which is in the first four instances the Map-*Quest*, and in the fifth, in order to mystify the reader, the Boron-*Quest*.

and the exposition of the marvels, and at the end of 372 led them once more out of Corbenic. After three years' wandering without cause or record, and despite a phrase which limits the whole book to a year and a half, he brings the questers back to Corbenic to conclude their adventure (373–90) in the manner approved by Master Walter Map, whom he names.[1] This conclusion is more happy than the book, but the Spanish version has heightened the stupidity of Galahad by making him stumble on his goal not twice, but thrice. The style is disorderly and incoherent; the rubrics are frequently wrong;[2] and the reader will note that the *Baladro* opened with the 540th year of our era, while (as time rolled back!) the *Demanda* commenced in the 454th.[3]

The *Mort d'Artur* of the Pseudo-Boron occupies chapters 391–455 of the Spanish *Demandas* and folios 187–99 of the Portuguese text, without divergences of note. In 2–G–5 the opening incidents are quoted in a passage that extends from the conspiracy of Agravain and his brothers to the rejection of Lancelot's terms of peace (capp. 391–417); but the greater part is mere summary, space being allowed only to the revelation of the queen's adultery and the message of reconciliation, and a lesser liberty being allowed to the ambuscade, Lancelot's flight, and the fight at the place of execution. Yet these chapters have the peculiarity of being accessible in four texts, three dialects, and two centuries, and they help to

[1] Cap. 385: "segun lo dize maestre Gualter."

[2] For instance, that of cap. 58 refers to capp. 292 *ff*.

[3] *Baladro*, cap. 26: "a quinientos e quarenta años despues de la pasion de Jesuchristo." *Demanda*, cap. 6: "a .ccccl.iiij años complidos de la muerte de Jesu-Christo."

document what we have already noticed in the *Tristan*, the constant process of modernisation which affected the Spanish romances of Britain in their history of two and a half centuries.[1] The narrative is an abbreviation of the Vulgate story as attached to *Lancelot du Lac*, but it ends with King Mark's treacherous invasion of Logres, and his ignominious death.

Having examined the available texts of the trilogy in Spain and Portugal, we must endeavour to ascertain their genealogy, authorship and date,—hazardous operations of which the prize is mere probability. The original translation (O), corresponding precisely with its French model, must have contained the *Joseph* (α), *Merlin*, etc. (β) and *Quest* (ϵ) of Boron, together with the *Conte del Brait* (γ) of his companion in arms and the *Prophecies* to Uther (δ). There is no evidence of a Vulgate or Map *Joseph* (η) nor *Merlin* (θ), but a corresponding *Quest* (ζ) is partially reproduced by the reviser of the Spanish *Demanda*. The conformity of the editions of 1515 and 1535 probably ascended to the now inaccessible *Merlin y Demanda del Sancto Grial* of 1500 ($\beta\gamma\delta\epsilon\zeta$), which had lost the first part of the trilogy, the Five Kings, the episode of Morholt's shield, and the Boron termination of the Holy Grail, but possessed the Spanish prophecies of Merlin and the Map visit to Corbenic. The *Baladro del Sabio Merlin con sus profecias* (1498) is, of course,

[1] *Cf.* K. Pietsch, in *Modern Philology*, xi. p. 4, who cites: ed. 1515, "asonada, ledo, honrro, afijado, feziste, fecho, vos"; ed. 1535, "juntada, alegre, honro, ahijado, heziste, hecho, os." He also notes their concurrence in misprints. *Cf.* also O. Klob, in *Zeitschrift für rom. Phil.*, xxvi. pp. 200–1; MS. 2–G–5 (1469–70): "y si el al diz que esta guerra començo por la muerte de sus sobrinos. . . ." Ptg. *Demanda* (fifteenth century): "E se diz que começou esta guerra por morte de seus sobrinhos. . . ." Sp. *Demanda* (1535): "Y si os dixere que esta guerra començo por la muerte de sus sobrinos. . . ."

not available for comparison with the third branch; the sole indication of the Spanish prophecies is in the title, which may be taken as referring to those which Merlin spoke to Uther; but it possesses a fuller conclusion than its peers. The *Merlin y Demanda*, 1500, and the *Baladro del Sabio Merlin*, 1498, jointly indicate a yet earlier work (Z), bipartite or tripartite, which exhibited their common peculiarities (α?βγδεζ?). But this hypothetical Z cannot have been the Castilian original, to which its transpositions are manifestly posterior; we, therefore, posit an earlier Y. The manuscript 2–G–5 is of an ambiguous position. Its readings are too scanty to be quoted in evidence, and they touch on none of the characteristic marks of the other extant texts; and it could derive equally well from either the Castilian or the Portuguese tradition, and equally from Y or Z: so that when we attribute it to the former and, on the doubtful support of its silence as to the prophecies, assign it to Y, our action is to some extent arbitrary. It is practically certain, however, that Y was not destitute of a *Joseph Abarimatia* (αβγδεζ?). A similar conciseness in the *Cronica de* 1404 prevents our classifying the text which that author handled in 1390. The Portuguese *Demanda* (ε), of the fifteenth century, presumes the existence of a corresponding *Romanço do Brado*, which is hinted at in Nos. 1140 and 930 of the *Cancioneiro da Vatiçana* and No. 2 of the *Colocci-Brancutti*. The *Liuro de Josep Abaramatia* preserves Boron's first branch (α). The *Josep*, *Brado* and *Demanda* combined point to a romance of all three parts (X) and of a tradition more ancient than Z or even, perhaps, Y (αβγδ?ε). Finally, as it is certain that the novels of both languages ascend to a single translation, we place another unknown (O) at the head of the table, which will assume the following form:

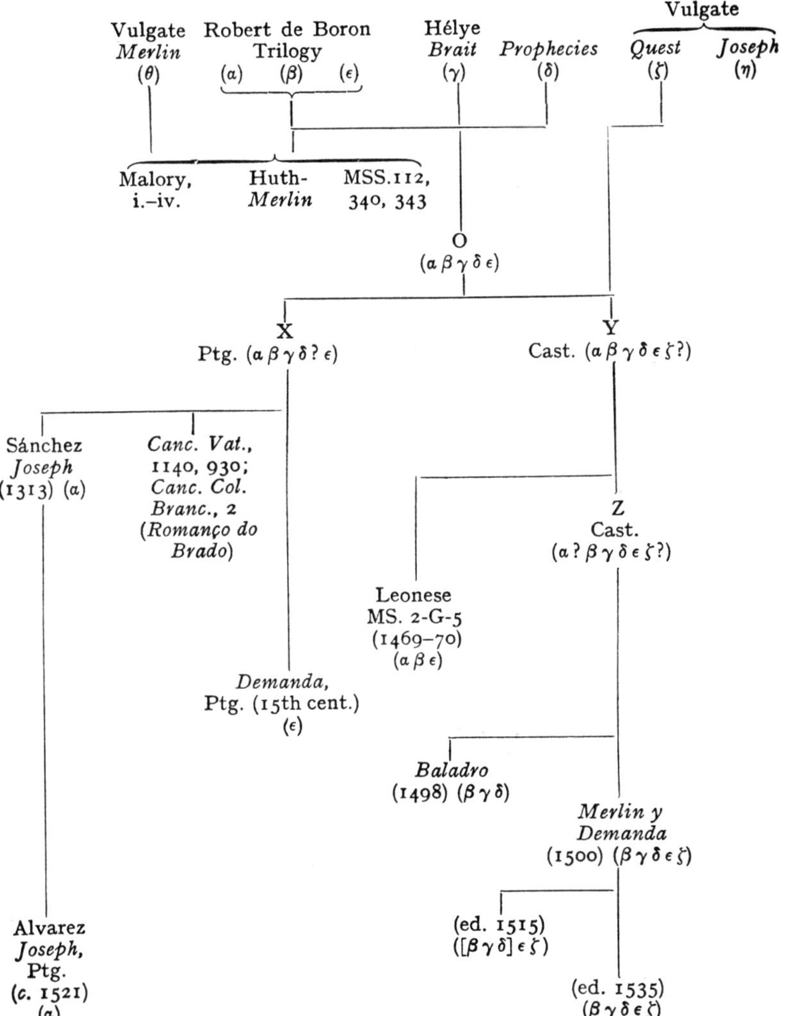

To have assumed four unknowns (OXYZ) may seem to be an embarrassment of the pedigree with uncertainties, but they must be taken as but typical of numerous redactions suffered by our manuscripts and not as an exhaustive statement. After the introduction of the art of printing into Spain, and in the face of Amadis and his children, the decaying *Merlin y Demanda* achieved four editions in forty years; but in the period of its efflorescence, the fourteenth century, when every copy was in some detail a modification of the original, and every scribe a compiler, the issues must have been more frequent and the process of change more rapid. We have, in fact, only the relics of a considerable literature of the same thing, an unknown number of versions in both Peninsular speeches deriving ultimately from O. In what language or dialect was O written? By whom? At what time?

On the first two points the Castilian *Demandas* are explicit: they were written in Castilian by Fray Juan Bivas.[1] We might, of course, have considered Bivas the author of the redactions Y or Z, had the Portuguese version known by whom it was translated or from what foreign language; but in the former respect it is simply anonymous, and in the latter it vacillates towards the opinion that Boron wrote Latin.[2] When we recall to mind the better scribal

[1] *Demanda*, cap. 52: "ni yo Joannes Biuas, no vos dire ende mas de lo que vos el dize, ca so frayle e no quiero mentir." The name is now confirmed by Prof. Pietsch's discovery of "Joam Biuas" in the text of the *Josep*.

[2] Contrast: cap. 35, Sp., "mas porque la ystoria deuisa en frances," Ptg., "mas porque a estoria nom nomeou"—an error; cap. 52, Sp., "mas esto no lo oso tresladar ruberte de brunco en françes," Ptg., "mas esto nom ousou Madar [*sic*] ruberte de borem de françes em latim . . . nem eu nom direy mais segundo meu poder"; cap. 194, Sp., "los

tradition of the Castilian text, despite drastic revision; when we consider that the power to contaminate implies a freer access to Arthurian texts, we shall probably concede to Bivas' claim intrinsic verisimilitude as well as textual authority.

Against the name of Bivas, nothing being known, nothing can be objected. Against his language Professor Pietsch has addressed two philological articles,[1] the first of which established the dialect of manuscript 2–G–5 as Leonese or infected with Leonese, and the second discusses the "presence of certain Portuguese words and particularities of Portuguese syntax" in this and the Spanish *Demandas*. The former is based on morphology; the latter is supported by a vocabulary of some thirty-six words or particles, of which fourteen occur in the *Demanda*. Not all of these are equally conclusive; and if we are as indifferently posted in the mediæval vocabularies as with the modern,—and surely for that period we possess no word-list that compares even with the insufficient *Diccionario* of the actual speech,—then we must deduct some credit from the remaining instances

otros falle en françes & no lo escreui en castellano. Mas habla la gran hystoria de Llayn de quanto yo cuento," Ptg., "Mais nom vos direi como, ca o nom achei em frances nem Boirom diz que en mais achou na grande storia do latin de quanto eu vos conto"—the Ptg. is quite wrong; the Sp. is correct if emended "los otros *no* falle . . ."

[1] K. Pietsch, *On the Language of the Spanish Grail Fragments*, in *Romance Philology*, xiii. pp. 369–78 and 625–46. Prof. Pietsch now holds that they are written in a mixed language, basically Castilian, but tinged with Leonese and Galician elements, and he champions the theory of Castilian priority. See Appendix. The above criticisms, therefore, have no strict reference to his views, but they may well stand in opposition to views that others have based on his linguistic data. It also seems that Pietsch has himself suffered some modification of opinion in the three decades of his study of this manuscript. His programme in 1911 was certainly to deduce a Portuguese conclusion from relics of Portuguese words and syntax—"*por el hilo se sacará el ovillo.*"

offered in support of the theory; and, after all, it is the whimsical condition of our studies that the worst old authority is better than the best modern inference. In face of the assertions of the text, and of what we have already observed as to the respective traditions of Castile and Portugal, we require a broader basis for any theory which attempts the paradox of deducing the existing Castilian from the non-existent Portuguese; the position of 2–G–5 is not itself sufficiently determined owing to want of material on which to found a judgment; and if we go so far as to modify Bivas' "castellano" in favour of any other dialect, we should certainly hesitate to place it west of Leon.

As the date of the translation does not appear to be indicated or implied in the text of the *Merlin y Demanda*, we are compelled to interrogate the accidents which accompany it. Such sources of instruction are obviously not of the most trustworthy, for we may be misled by forgeries or interpolations; but they are, after all, customary. In dealing with a modern translation, it is usually from the prefaces alone that we can deduce the date and authorship of the version and the progress of its editions; nor is it always easy, as may be seen from certain recent reprints, to inform oneself on such details when a publisher has chosen to cover his tracks. The mediæval translator, on the other hand, was less accountable for his fidelity to his original, and seldom failed to leave indications of his identity and circumstances in the text, but these marks have tended to disappear from the romances with which we are concerned; and in the reproduction of the work he was totally without protection against the private interests of book pirates.[1] But these reservations notwithstanding, merely to deny the utility of the accidental matter in the translation of the trilogy would not be an intelligent position, and it is incumbent on us to give a fair hearing to whatever witness may remain to us in the prefaces, epilogue, and prophecies attached to the various editions.[2]

The *Profecias de Merlin*, attached to the *Baladro* of 1535, give the later history of the work, and we must recapitulate what has already been said concerning them. They are written in a difficult or confused style, which it is frequently impossible to construe; they are not chronologically arranged; they are profuse of dates, which, however, partly from the corruptibility of Roman numerals, and partly from conversion from the Julian to the Christian era, are wholly unreliable; they have been tampered with on various occasions, and it is possible that their earliest matter may be found mingled with their latest. But we can venture on a few generalisations. The latest allusions cover the whole of the fifteenth century, and reach as late as 1488; they predict the reunion of Christendom, the ruin of Africa, the empire of Spain,

[1] In the case in point, the translator of the trilogy has seen fit to suppress Boron's name in a number of instances, and one Portuguese translator has suppressed that of Bivas.

[2] K. Pietsch, in *Modern Philology*, xi. p. 15, n. 2: "It is true that the redactor of B (*Merlin*, i. p. lxxxviii) says, concerning his work: 'yo no de mio este libro copile, mas transferile de una lengua en otra.' (Similarly in 'Prologo,' p. lxxxiii.) But it will be sufficient to quote Gayangos, *Libros de Caballerias*, xlvi.: '(es) sabida la invariable costumbre de los escritores de este género de libros, quienes, sin excepción alguna que sepamos, pretendieron siempre haber hallado sus originales en lengua caldea, griega, húngara e inglesa' (add: arábiga—*Leopolemo* i, *Don Quixote*)." But it is seldom sufficient to quote Gayangos, least of all out of his context. The *Tirant lo Blanch* may be no translation; but such the Arthurian novels undoubtedly are, and it is wholly capricious to discard any source of instruction with regard to that work.

and such other matters as Gutierre Diez de Games has taught us to expect.[1] In references to the later fourteenth century we seem to discern the bitterness of contemporaries in the mention of D. Pedro el Cruel,[2] and contemporary knowledge in that of Enrique III;[3] the latter is destined to mend the ruins made by the former,[4] and the two passages might be written by some "prophet" who, like Ayala, carried the rancour of the civil war into the reigns of the Trastamaras. These passages, and those of the fifteenth century, use a menagerie of lions (crowned, young, fierce, etc.), wolves, ounces, horses, cubs and asses, which derive from the obscure prophecies of Merlin to Uther in the *Livre des Prophecies Merlin*; and this menagerie is first let loose on the struggles of Alfonso XI.'s minority, when the fiction of Maestre Antonio's visit to Merlin covers and authorises a series of utterances which extend from his accession to his victory at Río Salado (1312–40). Maestre Antonio has also some things to say concerning Don Rodrigo, Pelayo, Alfonsos I. and III., and other kings; but these paragraphs are superficial and his real knowledge of events is put forth only on the reign of the eleventh Alfonso. In cap. 341, which may be the earliest of his utterances, he names the Leona de Molina (Queen María) and the date 1350: a figure which, though

[1] For instance, p. 161 (ed. Bonilla): ". . . y esto sojuzgara todas las tierras de Africa vn reino en la ysla. Y en este tiempo descendera el Imperio en el reyno de España . . . e la su morada sera en la tierra santa de Jerusalem . . . y en aquel tienpo sera la yglesia de Sant Pedro mas honrada. . . ."

[2] P. 158: "asno de maldad, conplido de toda crueldad."

[3] P. 159: "vn pollino leon se leuantara en este tienpo, perezoso, adormido, e con grandes llagas."

[4] P. 159: "los quales el asno de gran maldad e lleno de toda roña, con su solo bramido vuo sacado e descortezado."

cited as a Christian year (which is absurd), may be read as a Julian date, *i.e.* A.D. 1312, and it is possible that some of the other gibberish of the chapter may be read as an allusion to the obliteration of the Templars in that year.[1] However this may be, Maestre Antonio's interest in Alfonso XI.'s reign and his zoological style are confirmed, as we have seen, by Rodrigo Yáñez, who wrote about 1344, and speaks in a past tense. While it is not possible to bring forward proof of their coherence with the *Baladro* at so early a date, we have no reason to doubt that they always formed one corpus; for their authority depended intimately on that of the *Livre des Prophecies Merlin*, partially incorporated with the *Baladro*, and we have seen that, at a date not much posterior to Yáñez, Villasandino's copy probably contained the *Baladro*, *Profecias* and *Demanda* in immediate contact.

In both matter and style these prophecies of Maestre Antonio stand in marked contrast to those which Merlin delivered one day in the palace of King Arthur,[2] and some of which were revealed by a friar of Molina to D. Manuel at Seville. In these the style is open and clear, somewhat moral and supercilious, antidynastic; the matter concerns Alfonso X., Sancho IV. and Fernando IV. Its intelligibility exposed it to the ravages of the emendator, and some partisan of the Trastamaras is certainly to be held responsible for the mention of the deposition of Pedro (1369).

[1] Cap. 341: "Desde diez y nueue fasta en veynte vno e tres dias del mas del millar e los trezientos cinquenta años de mas de la era de Jesu Christo, en estos tiempos, en los canpos de Italia, en la cabaña de Romulo el pastor, sera tornado el leon muy cruel, e no se fartara, e rompera las greyes de sus ouejas por quatro partes, . . ." The Christian era was not formally adopted in Castile until the Cortes of Segovia of September, 1383 (*Cron. de D. Juan I.*, año 1383, capp. v.–vi.).

[2] Pp. 155–7: "Estando Merlin vn dia en el palacio del rey Artur."

A date, 1467, has crept into the text; but dates are precarious. It is more serious that these prophecies have incorporated two famous anecdotes, which can hardly be contemporary with their subjects. The amusing story of how Alfonso the Wise declared that, had he stood by God at the Creation, he would have corrected His mistakes, is cited by Byron and generally attributed to Pedro IV. of Aragon (1337–57) or to his colleague in the chronicle, Descoll; but the witticism is too good not to be anonymous. The *Cronica de D. Fernando IV.*, the *Livro das Linhagens*, and this section of the Spanish prophecies contain the anecdote of Fernando's summons before the Judgment Seat within thirty days of a judicial murder; and though obviously copied from a similar tale concerning Philippe le Bel, its Castilian application need not have been much later than Fernando IV.'s death. There are thus reasons for doubting these prophecies of Merlin in London; but have they no basis of fact? They have felt the influence of the Trastamaras, but they are not a perfect piece of propaganda for the new dynasty, which had no real quarrel with the three kings here mentioned. On the other hand, they do represent, with sufficient accuracy, the anti-dynastic policies of D. Manuel, here cited, and D. Juan Manuel, which might serve as a precedent for subsequent rebels. D. Manuel was in Seville about 1283, when the intrigues around Sancho's rebellion against his father were thickest; and his policy was to befriend both in expectation of the ruin of both,[1] and the same covert or open hostility to the dynasty was continued

[1] *Cron de D. Alfonso X.*, p. 65: "commo quier que dijeron que les placia, non era ansi, antes les pesaba, que rrescelaban de la avenencia que serie contra ellos."

by his famous son, D. Juan Manuel, into the succeeding reigns. Even the mention of Molina has some intrinsic probability, seeing that its seizure by Sancho in his wife's name was the storm-centre of a number of intrigues. In short, these prophecies seem to be capable of construing into a pamphlet on behalf of D. Juan Manuel in the contests over the regency of Queen María de Molina, but whether it be conceded or not that they have a core of contemporary fact, the activities of Maestre Antonio are enough to carry us to the early years of Alfonso XI. The composition of the work took place, therefore, in the reign of one of his predecessors, Alfonso X., Sancho IV., or Fernando IV.

It is from the Prologues and the Epilogue of the *Baladro* of 1498 that we must hope to identify this monarch. Juan de Burgos lies heavy on them all. He has some feeling for style; his language is, so far as we can judge, purposeful, and he can pervert a rambling text into a workmanlike prose.[1] He was accustomed to misapply his industry in attempts to provide works with prologues, or to give uniformity to those he found; and by so doing, has undoubtedly obliterated some valuable indications with regard to the *Tristan* as well as this text. His first prologue he lifted bodily out of the manuscript of *Tristan* which he published in 1501 (cap. 28). This related the

[1] Thus he turns an endless sentence into a compliment to his reader; *Baladro*, 1535, cap. 338: "E por esto llaman este libro en romance: El Baladro de Merlin, que sera de grado oydo de todos caualleros e honbres buenos que del oyeron fablar, ca los buenos caualleros *de aquel tiempo* nunca fazian villania ni la dirian si lo entendiessen," etc. But ed. 1498, cap. 38: "Por esto lo llaman el Baladro de Merlin en romance, el qual sera de grado oydo de muchas gentes, en especial de aquellos caballeros que nunca fizieron villania, sino proezas e grandes bondades de caballeria, e cosas extrañas que fizieron los caballeros de la Tabla Redonda."

wars of Evalach and Meridiantes down to the conversion of the former and his imprisonment; but instead of proceeding to the birth of Palomades, whose paganism was attributed to this persecution, the redactor introduced a "maestresala que havia nombre Jaquemin," whose business it was to write the second Prologue. The Epilogue "imposes silence on the pen" (as does that of *Tristan*) and refers absurdly to the king's "purpose *or imprisonment*"; and it is doubtful whether we can salvage from the Epilogue more than the reference to "royal majesty" and the statement that the whole is a translation.[1] The second Prologue is manifestly the source of the first. In it a subject addresses a king, dedicating to him a book; there is no mention of prison, but he speaks feelingly of the horrors of a war raging in the territory of his patron. The account of the war contains the *locus* concerning the mother who devours her children, and the enemy, who should have been Meridiantes, is inconsequently styled the Duke of Berri. But Berri was not a dukedom before 1360, and neither the first nor the second duke[2] had, or could have had, any such devastating importance for Castile; on the other hand, a kingdom of Berri had flourished in Arthurian times as the relentless enemy of the House of Ban and of all true chivalry, and the name might be used to cover some historical figure. Juan de Burgos has been busy with this Preface too, but the inconsistencies he has left show that it cannot be wholly his work. It belongs to the translator, who addresses a king who has suffered severely at

[1] "a vuestra real majestad suplico lo mande corregir e emendar que yo no de mio este libre copile, mas transferile de una lengua en otra." The Epilogue of *Tristan* leaves the work of emendation to its readers.

[2] Jean (1360–1416); Charles (1447–72).

the hands of a prominent adversary, and who could be congratulated on his success and courage.[1] Of the three monarchs to whom the *Profecias* direct us, the one to whom these few indications point is Sancho IV. (1284–96), whose capture of the rebel Infante D. Juan and simultaneous peace with France, Aragon, Portugal and Granada (1290–1) brought the nation through one of the most severe crises of her history, and whose ferocious courage was recognised in his sobriquet of *el Bravo.*

To the reign and patronage of Sancho IV., and to a date about 1291, we would assign the translation of the trilogy into Castilian by Fray Juan Bivas. To D. Juan Manuel, perhaps, to some retainer of Alfonso XI. or Maestre Antonio himself, to a contemporary of Ayala, and to later writers from the reign of Juan II. to that of Carlos Quinto, we attribute redactions of the *Profecias*, and so of the whole work. Two books of this trilogy, and probably all three, were turned from Bivas' version into Portuguese during the fourteenth century, and both of these survive in a relatively primitive form; but on the numerous and drastic Castilian revisions, it is clear from the indifference of the *Profecias* that the Portuguese texts exerted no influence.

[1] "E como deseoso me hallase de la tal disposicion, vino a mi memoria, entre otros libros que pasado he, un libro del sabio Merlin [only?], e paresciome que para exercicio de vuestra majestad seria bien transferirle en otra lengua que le he leydo, para que entenderse pueda, como quiera que vuestra excelencia tenga e aya visto famosa libreria de muchos e diversos libros asi catholicos como del militar officio . . . entre otros muchos infortunios, que vuestra excelencia pasado ha, uno que poco tiempo ha que padecistes con los del duque de Berri, que vistes a vuestros subditos sufrir infinitas miserias en tanto grado que no dubdavamos de comer diez mil desventuras. . . . E mi opinion es que no ha sido en estos tiempos rey ni principe ni señor que con tanto animo oviese sofrido los infortunios nombrados."

X

MINOR GRAIL HEROES: GAWAIN, PERCIVAL. THE "FAULA" OF G. TORROELLA

SPAIN and Portugal were in this manner acquainted with Galahad's achievement of the Holy Grail as it was related by Robert de Boron, and a considerable knowledge of Walter Map's alternative version; they also knew, to some extent, the other Grail heroes, Gawain and Percival. In the Prose-*Lancelot* Gawain has the misfortune to blunder into the Adventurous Palace, and his discomfiture, which the author of the *Demanda* supposes us to know,[1] is the result of his irreverence. When the Holy Vessel is borne into the banqueting hall by a maiden, her beauty alone attracts his eyes, so that he neither bows the knee nor prays; as he lies in his presumption on the Adventurous Bed, a mysterious lance stabs him; his rest is perturbed by voices, thunders, the combat of a lion and serpents, the lamentations of women, and a desperate personal struggle against an armed stranger. To the eyes of the hero, now lying bleeding and

[1] *Demanda*, cap. 323: "como Galuan e Gariete se fueron al palacio auenturoso. . . . Dixo Galuan: '¡Ay Señor Dios! si vos plugiere, dexadme entrar en el palacio auenturoso, e salir dende con mayor honra que *otra vez* sali.'" The extract from *Lanzarote de Lago* (Bibl. Nac., Madrid, MS. 9611, fols. 281–5) has been printed in the appendix to Bonilla, *Leyendas de Wagner* (Madrid, 1913), pp. 94–109. For Gawain as Grail hero see *Encyclopædia Britannica*, s.v. GRAIL. The Spanish account is the same as that in P. Paris, *Romans de la Table Ronde, Lancelot*, laisse cxxviii., or Sommer, *Vulgate Version of the Arthurian Romances*, iv. pp. 345–9.

gasping, the mysterious procession appears and passes; Gawain's wounds are healed, but he cannot see his antagonist. An angry multitude seizes him, binds him to a cart and drives him from the town in insult; and a hermit diagnoses his failure and predicts the death of King Arthur.

Perhaps the best evidence of the circulation of Percival's *Quest* in Portugal and Spain during the fourteenth and fifteenth centuries must still be drawn from the popularity of his name in baptismal registers; in respect of other information, we have none that refers unmistakably to a manuscript of that date. The Portuguese *Demanda*, it is true, in a place corresponding to the lacuna of the Castilian texts, cites an *Estoria de Parcival*, but the allusion implies nothing for the Peninsular literatures. There was a *Historia de Perceval de Gaula, caballero de la Tabla Rotonda, el cual acabo la demanda y aventuras del santo Grial* published in the year 1526 at Seville by Cromberger or at Salamanca by Varela;[1] and this text, though no longer available, may have presented to the Spanish readers the substance of *Perceval le Gallois*. Yet it is through the name of Percival that Spain comes — passively it is true—into touch with one of the highest creations of the Middle Ages, the great allegory of Wolfram von Eschenbach. The identification of his imaginary Grail kingdom with parts of Spain, though supported by the stage directions of Wagner and repeated in our own century by M. Barrès, is more indebted to German Romantic prejudice than to an accurate appreciation of the text. Monserrat or

[1] Bonilla, *op. cit.*, p. 48; *Tristan* (1501), Intro. *Cf. Grundriss der rom. Phil.*, II. ii. p. 214, n. 4.

Monsagro, which have been put forward as the originals of Munsalvæsche, depend on an etymology *Mons Salvationis* which is hardly tenable; and a similar scruple forbids linking Salvatierra and Terre de Salvæsche.[1] Zazamanc and Azagouc are to be sought for in Africa, and so can hardly be identified with Salamanca and Zaragoza,[2] but with the Garamantes and Azachæi of Solinus. But the "starken Berbester" of *Titurel* 42 is a recollection of the famous siege and sack of this fortress by Guillaume de Montreuil in 1064, and Rotrou de la Perche's brilliant capture of Tudela in Navarre (Tuteleunz) in 1114 would preserve that name in a French memory. The same campaign might suggest that "stolze künec von Arragûn" (67. 14) who beat down Uther Pendragon at the tournament of Kanvoleis. Pontevedra (Vedrun) was one of the ports at which neighbours of the English Channel were accustomed to disembark for the shrine of St. James at Compostela; it would be a familiar name also to Crusaders from the same regions, who were regularly wont to disembark at one or other of the Galician ports on their way to Palestine,—of such were the 14,000 English, Normans and Flemings who had opportunity to praise Portuguese gallantry at the siege of Lisbon in 1147.[3] Nor could Toledo (Dôlet) be forgotten, seeing that its capture was effected in 1085 by the help of an unusual concourse of French Crusaders, some of whom settled down to

[1] Bonilla, *Leyendas de Wagner*, has an ingenious theory in support of a castle of Monsagro, near Oviedo, where certain Grail-like relics from Toledo were conserved.

[2] Milá y Fontanals, *De los Trobadores en España* (*Obras*, ii. p. 51 n.), Barcelona, 1889. *Cf.* Bonilla, *op. cit.*, pp. 40 *ff.* For Wolfram's *Parzival* I have used chiefly E. Martin's edition (Halle-a-S., 1903), and Miss Weston's translation.

[3] *Parz.*, 66. 28: "si wellnt durch schilde stechen."

fiefs and others to benefices in Spain. In Toledo men found master-armourers,[1] and Jewish or Moorish interpreters, who might tell the stranger of the splendours of Az-Zahra[2] in its days of glory, of the seething commercial activity of Seville,[3] and of the Commander of the Faithful (*mahmumelîn*, Sp. *miramamolín*) who ruled in Morocco. During the twelfth century Toledo was frequented by many clerics from the north, who translated into Latin the books of Al-Kindî and Ibn-Thâbit,[4] studied astronomy,[5] and nigromancy,[6] and exported their labours to France, Britain and Germany. It is in this spirit and tradition that "Kyôt der meister" declares that he found the first hint of the Holy Grail in a cosmological work by one of Solomon's descendants (presumably Ibn-Thâbit, in whose pedigree the son of Bathsheba figured); and he names his authority Flegetânîs (*Felek thânî*, *Sphæra altera*).[7] He pursued his researches among Latin books, reading the chronicles of England, France and Ireland; but he ran down his reference at length in Anjou. The writer's knowledge of Spain is not intimate, but it is unified. He has the standing

[1] 261. 2–4:

"sîn schilt was ze Dôlet
in Kailetes lande
geworht dem wîgande
rant und buckel heten kraft."

[2] 736. 16: Assigarzîonte, capital of the Arab count Gabarîns. Elsewhere Azzaria, Assigarzîunde.

[3] Sibilje Wolfram reckons a seaport, and with some reason.

[4] 643. 17: "Kancor unt Thêbit."

[5] 782; the seven planets are named by their Arabic names.

[6] 453. 15–18:

"der karakter â b c
muoser hân gelernet ê,
ân den list von nigrômanzî."

Chaucer's "clerk of Orliens" used "Tables Toletanes." D. Juan Manuel's sorcerer is "don Yllán, el gran maestro que moraba en Toledo."

[7] See *Parzival*, 452–5, with E. Martin's notes and introduction.

of a Norman or Northern Frenchman, who fought by land in the Spanish Crusades, travelled by sea to Galicia, or occupied a Spanish benefice with a view to advancing his studies; and though Guyot de Provins is hardly likely, on the evidence, to have seen Spain in these capacities, he had learned so to see it through the eyes of his acquaintances. From his evident attachment to the interest and policies of the House of Anjou, he may have obtained his few notes of the politics of Spain. Kailet von Hoskurast and Gahmuret the Angevin are friends just as Henry Plantagenet and Alfonso VIII. after the marriage of Leonor of Aquitaine (1170); and some obscurer allusion, perhaps Henry's good offices in the marriage of Mathilda of Portugal to Philip of Flanders (1184), seems to underlie the love of Kailet and Alyzen. Kiot von Katelangen is a considerable personality in the romance, and covers possible allusions to Raymund Berenguer IV. and the monk-king Ramiro of Aragon. These Peninsular princes are but units of the vast dynastic complex which centred in Henry II. and Queen Eleanor of Aquitaine and Provence.

The story of the Holy Grail had no posterity in Castile or Portugal; but in Catalonia it was found in one other form, and with a native hero. Guillem de Torroella[1] was, as the reader will recall, the principal figure of his *Faula*, where he chased a parrot, and was inadvertently carried eastward by a whale to many hundreds of miles from Majorca; landing on an island at darkness, he saw a fair meadow at dawn, and proceeded to a splendid palace, where Arthur is

[1] Professor E. G. Gardner will, I understand, treat more fully of this Sicilian tradition in his *Arthurian Legend in Italian Literature*.

tended by Morgane la Fée; two queens, Love and Valour, attended at the king's sick-bed; Arthur asked the poet's name and was duly informed; to the Catalan's question as to how Arthur lived it was answered that he lived by the annual visit of the Holy Grail; and at length Torroella was dismissed with a message for mankind. In its simplest form this tale referred to the immortality of the stricken king in Avalon, where Morgane waited on him.[1] Geoffrey of Monmouth's *Vita Merlini* already identified Avalon with the Fortunate Islands;[2] and other legends assigned to Arthur and his barons a number of hills for their other-world residence—the Eildons, Arthur's Seat, Cadair Arthur. Nor was the hero quite unapproachable, seeing that the foresters of Britain and Brittany were wont to hear the sound of a hunt at midday or under a full moon, and to speak to the knights of his court. Passing with the Normans from England to Sicily, this narrative coalesced with some debased form of the Classical myth of Vulcan's forge, and it adapted itself to the scenery of the island—the town of Catana, the volcano of Etna, its barren slopes, and the rich meadows whence Proserpine was plucked by gloomy Dis. According to Gervase of Tilbury,[3] a groom of the

[1] Gervase of Tilbury, *Otia Imperialia*, II. xvii.: "Alteraque pugna revocata, Arcturus vulneratur, omnibus hostibus ab ipso peremptis. Unde secundum vulgarem Brittonum traditionem in insulam Davalim ipsum dicunt translatum, ut vulnera quotannis recrudescentia subinterpolata sanatione curarentur a Morganda fatata: quem fabulose Brittones post data tempora credunt rediturum in regnum." *Cf.* Rhys, *The Arthurian Legend* (Oxford, 1890), pp. 334 *ff.*, and Wolfram von Eschenbach, *Parzival*, ed. E. Martin (Halle-a-S., 1903), ii. pp. lxiii–lxx, or E. Martin, *Zur Gralsage* (Strassburg, 1880), pp. 32 *ff.*

[2] "Insula Pomorum quæ Fortunata vocatur,
Ex re nomen habet, quia per se singula profert," etc.

[3] *Otia Imperialia*, II. cap. xii.: "Hunc autem montem vulgares Mongibel appellant. In hujus deserto narrant indigenæ Arturum

Bishop of Catana was popularly supposed to have seen the king. While he was grooming a horse near Etna or Mongibello, the latter suddenly galloped away; the ostler followed along the shadier parts of the mountain side, until he came to a fair field full of all delights, where there was a palace. In the palace Arthur lay in a royal bed, his wounds ever fresh. The king inquired his name and business; satisfied with the serving-man's replies, he dismissed him with the horse and gifts for the bishop. The tale presents the essentials of Torroella's poem, but a few further details may be noted in the eighth riddle of the *Wartburgkrieg*, which gives the opening scene of the legend of Lohengrin.[1] The notice of St. Brandan assures us that we are in the Fortunate Isles; the hill and Arthur are likewise mentioned. But Arthur is openly identified with the Maimed or Fisher King of

magnum nostris temporibus apparuisse. Cum enim uno aliquo die custos palefredi episcopi Catanensis commissum sibi equum depulveraret, subito impetu lasciviæ pinguedinis equus exsiliens ac in propriam se recipiens libertatem, fugit. Ab insequente ministro per montis ardua præcipitiaque quæsitus nec inventus, timore pedissequo succrescente circa montis opaca perquiritur. Quid plura? Arctissima semita sed plana est inventa; puer in spatiosissimam planitiem jucundam omnibusque deliciis plenam venit ibique in palatio miro opere constructo Arturum in strato regii apparatus recubantem. Cumque ab advena et peregrino causam sui adventus percontaretur, agnita causa itineris, statim palefridum episcopi facit adduci, ipsumque præsuli reddendum, ministro commendat, adjiciens, se illic antiquitus in bello cum Mordredo nepote suo et Childerico duce Saxonum pridem commisso, vulneribus quotannis recrudescentibus, saucium diu mansisse, quinimo, ut ab indigenis accepi, xenia sua ad antistitem illum destinavit, quæ a multis visa et a pluribus fabulosa novitate admirata fuerunt. Sed et in silvis Britanniæ majoris aut minoris consimilia contigisse referuntur, narrantibus nemorum custodibus, quos *forestarios*, quasi indaginum ac vivariorum ferinorum aut regiorum nemorum, vulgus nominat, se alternis diebus circa horam meridianam et in primo noctium conticinio sub plenilunio luna lucente sæpissime videre militum copiam venantium et canum et cornuum strepitum, qui sciscitantibus, se de societate et familia Arturi esse, affirmant."

[1] K. Simrock, *Der Wartburgkrieg* (Stuttgart and Augsburg, 1858), Nos. 82–7.

the Grail stories; the land is waste; and it is as Lord of the Grail Castle that he sends forth Lohengrin to defend Elsa of Brabant. Consequently, when the question is asked, "How does the king live?"[1] the answer, though withheld, cannot be other than that he lives by the Grail. Two queens wait upon him, Felicia and Juno,[2] who are evidently the figures of an allegory; and an hundred knights, named by St. Brandan[3] but not by the poet, dwell in the Grailberg with the king.

The tale came into Sicily with the Normans. When the Normans were succeeded by the Hohenstaufens, it travelled into Germany and begot, probably, the similar legend of Barbarossa's stay in the Kyffhäuser, as immortalised by Rückert. Torroella's original appears to have contained the features which characterise both the versions which we have adduced, and differs from the primitive story of Gervase by the addition of an allegory in the thin style of the *Roman de la Rose*. This may be his own addition; in which case we might suppose that the myth came to Catalonia through the Aragonese conquest of Sicily in the later years of the thirteenth century. If, as is very likely, he depended on some French predecessor, it was set in indirect motion towards him by the Angevin domination.

[1] No. 83: "Die vrâgt ich wie der küninc lebe."

[2] No. 83:

> "Feliciâ, Sibillen kint,
> und Jûnô, die mit Artûs in dem berge sint."

[3] No. 84:

> "der schreip mit sîner hant vil gar die spæhe
> wie Artûs in dem berge lebe und sîne helde mære,
> der si mir hundert hât genant,
> die er mit im vuorte von Britanien lant."

The romance of the *Chevalier au Cygne* is linked in the Spanish tradition as in the French with the ancestry of Godfrey de Bouillon, not with Lohengrin (*Grand Conquista de Ultramar*, lib. i. capp. 47–135).

XI

THE ARTHURIAN NOVELS IN CASTILE AND PORTUGAL: "LANCELOT"[1]

THE poets of the *Cancionero de Baena* frequently bracket Lancelot, Tristan and Amadis as types of

[1] MANUSCRIPTS: D. Pedro de Barcellos, *Nobiliario*, titulo ii., Torre do Tombo, Lisbon, 16th century; *Cronica General de* 1404, Vindel MS., Portuguese and Castilian, fifteenth century; *Lanzarote de Lago*, Bibl. Nac., Madrid, No. 9611 = Aa 103, paper, sixteenth century, 355 fols., 1 col., 315 × 215 mm. (fol. 1r: "Aqui comiença el libro segundo de Don lançarote de lago"; fol. 277r: "Aqui se acaba el segundo libro de Lançarote"; fol. 355v: "Aqui se acaua el segundo y tercero libro de don lancarote de lago y a se de comenzar el libro de don tristan y acabose en miercoles veinte y quatro dias del octubre año del nasçimiento de nuestro saluador Jhuxpo de mill e quatroçientos y catorze años. finis."); *Historia de Leonel, Galvan y Lanceloto*, en portugués. MS. en pergamino; no tiene principio (Caj. L., núm. 3, Library of the Conde-Duque de San Lúcar in the Convento del Ángel, Seville; cited by Gallardo, *Ensayo*, iv. col. 1506).

EARLY EDITIONS: *El libro de Galaz*, fragment, in *Demanda del Sancto Grial*, capp. 373–90; *Lanzarote*, en castellano, 1528 (?) (Clemencín, *Don Quijote*, iii. p. 457, notas); *Artus*, 1501 (?).

REPRINTS: *Portugalliæ Monumenta Historica,—Scriptores*, i., ed. Herculano, Lisbon, 1860 (*Nobiliario*); R. Menéndez Pidal, *La Crónica General de* 1404, in *Revista de Archivos*, 1903; Bonilla, *Leyendas de Wagner*, Appendix (1, fols. 119r–121v: Lancelot at the tomb of King Galahad; 2, fols. 261r–266v: Gawain and the Broken Sword; 3, fols. 281r–285v: Gawain at Corbenic;—from MS. 9611); O. Klob, in *Zeitschrift für rom. Phil.*, xxvi. (fol. 105r: Lancelot at Gorre; fol. 310v: Lancelot and Pelles' daughter). Fols. 352–5 are reprinted in *Revista de Filología Española*, xi. (1924). A collation with the Vulgate has been promised by Bonilla, and an edition by E. de Laiglesia.

CRITICISM: Varnhagen, *Cancioneirinho de trovas antigas*; H. O. Sommer, in *Romania*, xxxvi.; O. Klob, in *Zeitschrift für rom. Phil.*, xxvi. p. 191. I also use my own summary of the MS. 9611, and transcript of fols. 871–911; which has recently been described by P. Bohigas Balaguer, *El Lanzarote español del manuscrito* 9611 *de la Biblioteca Nacional*, in *Revista de Filología Española*, xi. (1924), pp. 282–97. *Cf.* also Menéndez y Pelayo, *Antología*, xii. pp. 473–6; E. de Laiglesia, *Tres hijuelos habia el rey*, in *Revista Crítica Hispano-Americana*, iii. pp. 3–56; and my *Adventure of the "Cerf au Pied Blanc,"* in *Modern Language Review*, xviii. (1923) pp. 436–48, and works there cited.

perfect knighthood and love; Lancelot, as duplicated in Galahad, and Tristan are leading figures of the *Demanda del Sancto Grial*; Merlin's name and fortunes are the result of the *Baladro del Sabio Merlin*. The four novels of chivalry to which the poets of the court of D. Juan II. give prominence—namely, *Tristan de Leonis*, *Merlin y Demanda*, *Lanzarote de Lago*, and probably *Amadis de Gaula*, its derivative—were likewise known to their Galician predecessors of the fourteenth century. Of *Tristan de Leonis* much has survived; of the *Merlin y Demanda* we may even speak with confidence; of the *Amadis de Gaula* we possess the whole content, though its history be dark; but of *Lanzarote de Lago* no more than fragments have been left over, and these have not been offered to the modern world of scholarship. Its incidents are for the most part little distinguishable; its hero is ubiquitous: so that the allusions, being generally limited to the name of the hero and heroine, entirely fail to document its path through the centuries. It is first cited as a book in the *Rimado de Palacio* of the chancellor López de Ayala, who regretted a youth misspent among frivolous readings and proved fictions such as *Amadis* and *Lanzarote*.[1] Copies of the romance were found in the libraries of Carlos III. of Navarre (1387 – 1425),[2] Queen Isabel,[3] and the Conde-Duque de San Lúcar;[4] and

[1] *Rimado de Palacio*, copla 162:
"Libros de devaneos e mentiras probadas,
Amadis, Lanzarote . . ."

[2] "Un romans de Lancelot. Item un Romanz Pampeluno vieio de Lanzelot et de Bors su compaynero."

[3] No. 144: "Otro libro de pliego entero de mano en papel de romance, que es la historia de Lanzarote, con unas coberturas de cuero blanco."

[4] Gallardo, *Ensayo de una Biblioteca Española*, iv. col. 1506.

they would seem to have been written in Navarrese, Castilian and Portuguese respectively, while there is, perhaps, still some hope of the recovery of the last-named from the library of the Convento del Ángel, at Seville. Among printed books the *Artus* (1501)[1] and the *Lanzarote* (1528)[2] are hardly more than rumours. Thus we are reduced for our direct knowledge of the Castilian or Portuguese romance to a single fragmentary example, the manuscript *Lanzarote de Lago* which is possessed by the National Library at Madrid. To it we may add certain isolated citations of episodes concerning this hero. None of the passages, which we shall allege, contradict the data of the manuscript, and may be held to complete its information; but we must acknowledge with regret that the union of each separate branch with the main stem involves a separate hypothesis. The sum of the existing manuscript and the fragments from other sources forms the image of a large cyclic romance, sufficient to bear the weight of Lancelot's reputation and of the direct imitation of his qualities by *Amadis de Gaula*;[3] but the sceptic is at liberty to deny either the necessity of this cyclic romance, or the adhesion thereto of any particular detail. To the latter nothing

[1] *Grundriss der rom. Phil.*, II. ii. p. 214, n. 4.

[2] "Imprimióse después la versión castellana y hubo un ejemplar en la biblioteca que formó en el Nuevo Bastán el siglo pasado el Conde de Saceda: de allí ha desaparecido, y no tengo noticia de donde existe ningún otro ejemplar."—*Don Quijote* (1833, ed. Clemencín), iii. p. 457.

[3] Miss G. S. Williams' opinion (*The Amadis Question*, in *Revue Hispanique*, xxi. p. 146) is that the author of the Peninsular novel drew directly on French sources. It is doubtful whether the Spanish are well enough known to justify their exclusion, and, in regard to *Tristan de Leonis*, the thesis has been contested (Bonilla, *Tristan de Leonis* (1501), 1912, Introduction). But the success of the imitation certainly depended on that of its model, and the *Amadis* is especially indebted to the *Lanzarote*.

very satisfactory can be answered; to the former objection our experience of the *Tristan* and the *Merlin y Demanda* replies that the texts are curiously, though not absolutely, conformable with each other, and would tend to discourage multiplying the models of any romance.

The surviving *Lanzarote de Lago*,[1] a manuscript executed with some haste by four hands during the sixteenth century, professes to be a transcript of the second and third books taken from an original that was completed on Wednesday, 24th October, 1414; and as the day coincides with the date, the claim is to be allowed. The narrative of the second book opened immediately after the great assembly of the Roche aux Saisnes; Gallehault obtained permission to depart with Lancelot for his own kingdom of Sorelois. Shortly after, Queen Guenevere is brought into peril of her life by the plot of Bertolais and the False Guenevere; which adventure being concluded by the strength and loyalty of Lancelot, he next conquered the outrageous Carados. When Meleagance had secured possession of the Queen, Lancelot rescued her and, at length, slew that knight; and during this period suffered the disgrace of being conveyed in a cart (*La Charette*). The ἀρίστεια of Bors occupy a few chapters, leading up to the birth of Helain le Blanc, the future Emperor of Constantinople; and after Lancelot has freed Meleagance's sister from deadly peril, and has visited Gallehault's tomb, the remainder of the book is possessed by Sagramor and Mathamas, Dodinel, Gawain and Hector. The conclusion is given

[1] The manuscript extends from iv. p. 87–v. p. 315 or 316 of P. Paris, *Romans de la Table Ronde*, or iii. p. 429–v. p. 193 of Sommer's *Vulgate*.

abruptly by the disgrace of the last couple in a churchyard, and the whole book covers the distance between vol. iii. p. 429 and vol. iv. p. 341 of H. O. Sommer's *Vulgate Version of the Arthurian Romances*. The third book, which is much more brief, carries the narrative on to vol. v. p. 193. Gawain visits Corbenic, and is ejected without honour. Hector and Ywain occupy a couple of folios; then Lancelot is poisoned, and cured by a damsel who swears to be ever a virgin for his love, he aids an old damsel against Duke Calles, is enchanted by Morgane la Fée, escapes, and takes part in the tourney of La Harpe. Visiting Corbenic, he becomes unwittingly the father of Galahad; and when he has left the castle, he meets Hector's mother, enters the Foreste Perdue, wins a magic chessboard, is imprisoned, and avenges a murdered dame on a caitiff cavalier. His extraordinary prowess at the tourney of Camalot leads to his identification, and he recapitulates his adventures, to which Gawain, Bors and Garieth add their own. After this incident the Vulgate Romances relate that Lancelot sallied forth in quest of Hector and Leonel, who were still roaming the earth in search of him; but the Spanish novel avers that a damsel came to the hero from Sir Tristan, that he resolved to quest for the Cornish knight, that he passed over an iron bridge, rested on Merlin's bed, entered into a ship with twelve damsels, and so set out to sea. The compiler then announces a *Libro de Tristan*, which, by Malory's chronology, might begin mid-way in the second book, or at the commencement of the third, of that romance.[1] In either case, this work cannot be

[1] Fol. 352v: "como la donzella vino a la corte del Rey Artur por

identified with the extant *Tristan de Leonis*, which lacks these incidents, and conducts the warrior in a single volume from the cradle to the grave.

When collated with the *Vulgate Version of the Arthurian Romances*, this *Lanzarote de Lago* proves to be almost featureless. It is shorter throughout, probably because some passages have been abbreviated by the Spanish authors or their models,[1] and certainly because of the omission of entire *laisses*. Among the latter, the adventures of Gawain at the Pont Perdu[2] are absent from most manuscripts of the romance; a long sequence concerning Gawain and his brothers[3] has fallen out through accident or design; as also a fruitless visit by Bors to Corbenic.[4] The concluding half of the third book of *Lancelot du Lac* has been omitted,[5] and preparation made for the insertion of part of a Prose-*Tristan*. Some folios are blank,[6] and the additions[7]—if there be any—are of no consequence. The names of lesser characters are not always easy of recognition, nor consistently transcribed; and in the narrative concerning the two Gueneveres the Spanish

mandado de don tristan." 353v: "de como don lançarote dixo que queria yr en busca de don tristan." 354r: "como don lançarote paso la puente de fierro." 354v: "como don lançarote fue a la mar y fallo vn barco con doze donzellas y entro en el mar." 355v: "aqui se acaua el segundo y tercero libro de don lançarote de lago y a se de comenzar el libro de don tristan . . ."

[1] Thus fols. 318v–322v are made to cover Sommer's *Vulgate*, v. pp. 124–38.

[2] *Vulg.*, iv. pp. 182–96. Sp. fol. 125v.

[3] *Vulg.*, iv. p. 358–v. p. 67. Sp. fol. 288v.

[4] *Vulg.*, v. pp. 138–47. Sp. fol. 322v.

[5] *Vulg.*, v. pp. 193–409, which take the story to the opening of the *Quest*. Sp. fol. 352v.

[6] Fols. 9v–10r, 21v–22r, 35r and v, 48r and v, 277v. There are no fols. 278–9, and 142 is repeated thrice.

[7] Fol. 24r: "como galeote enbiara el amo de lançarote e de la rreyna." Fol. 142 ter: "El mayordomo llego ende e dixo a lançarote. . . ." Fol. 351: Bors and Garieth are added to Gawain. *Cf. Vulg.*, iv. pp. 26 and 212, and v. p. 192.

romance shows the transposition of some elements.[1] A closer examination of the details of the text might establish other points of divergence. In expression the Spanish romance is naïve and unadorned; and whatever literary merits it may possess—nor are they inconsiderable, especially in the more active passages—presumably belong to its original, for the translator seems to have but a feeble control on orthography, punctuation or phrase.

The Spanish translators of the *matière de Bretagne* were probably very much at the mercy of their originals. In the versions of Arabic works which were made by the Toledan School, a rendering was rough-hewn by some Jewish or Mozarab interpreter and it was polished into a translation by some competent latinist; in drawing upon classical and other sources for the *Cronica General* or other historical and legal works, we have evidence of the existence of a *borrador*, or rough copy, as well as the revised editions approved by the royal editors: but the translators from contemporary languages of Europe would show, then as now, more initial accuracy and less final perfection. There was then no literary criticism, and the scale of value was one of imputed doctrinal utility; and low in the scale, or beneath its reckoning, were works whose end was pleasure. They pleased; they were not esteemed. So the first Arthurian renderings were the children of chance, naïve, paratactic, garrulous, verbatim, unrevised. Successive editors or scribes

[1] Fol. 15 (Bertolais plot) should follow 33v (*Vulg.*, iv. p. 45). 34r and v (Gallehault's intention of kidnapping Guenevere) is postponed from 16v (*Vulg.*, iv. pp. 17–18). 23r and v (Prophecy of Galahad, *Vulg.*, iv. p. 26) is taken after the matter of *Vulg.*, iv. pp. 30–31. 38v–39r (Arthur's complaisance with the False Guenevere, *Vulg.*, iv. p. 50) are taken after *Vulg.*, iv. pp. 51–2.

continued to modernise them with a coat of the vocabulary of the day, though it is threadbare in places. More rarely would they fall into the hands of a renovator like Juan de Burgos, who is perspicuous and purposeful when he is interested, and even eloquent when aroused; and none of them had the good fortune of *Amadis de Gaula*, which chanced on a transcriber who presented it anew in a manner of speech that became a model and an inspiration to succeeding ages. Yet Montalvo's *Amadis* is but the end of a process which begins approximately in the *Merlin y Demanda's* languid and literal incoherence; nor is the *Lanzarote de Lago* greatly altered, save in vocabulary, from its first verbatim nakedness.

The manuscript 9611 of the National Library at Madrid is a fragment, the transcript of another fragment. He who wrote the colophon dated 24th October, 1414, mentions the second and third books as his task; but we must reasonably suppose that the first translator presented to his patron or readers a complete work, and possibly a complete cycle. What were the constituent parts of this work? We cannot give an infallible answer; but we can collect the scattered members of Lancelot stories, and order them according to the schedule of the Vulgate *Lancelot*; and we may then, according to our individual estimates of probability, associate some or all of them into a complete romance of *Lanzarote de Lago*. It is, at all events, a circumstance worth noting, that none of them (unless in the case of one ballad which has not yet been properly explained) involve any contradiction with the manuscript, nor lead to any result which is intrinsically improbable in one and the same romance.

I. *Lestoire del Saint Graal.* The introduction to either Map or Boron's cycle of Grail stories is the same *Estoire del Saint Graal* which is found in the *Liuro de Josep Abaramatia*, made to the order of Juan Sánchez in 1313. An altogether orthodox first part of the Holy Grail, the *Joseph* comes to a close in a colophon which seems to cut it off from all succeeding romances; and its citation of Juan Bivas, the translator of Boron, excludes it from the cycle of *Lanzarote de Lago.* There is thus no evidence of this branch in connection with the Peninsular *Lanzarote.*

II. *Lestoire de Merlin.* In Malory's compilation, which is often suggestive to one studying the Spanish romances, the orthodox *Merlin* was almost entirely elided against the *Merlin* of the Pseudo-Boron; in Spain and Portugal it is not to be traced. The *Artus* (of 1501), of which a mere rumour remains, might have been *Le livre d'Artus.*

III. *Le livre de Lancelot del Lac, partie I.* It is to be presumed that this work existed earlier than 1414. It would have extended up to the assembly at the Roche aux Saisnes, and in this respect it would be similar to the French manuscript, No. 485 of the National Library at Madrid.

IV and V. *Le livre de Lancelot del Lac, parties II. et III.* These are partially conserved in the two extant books of *Lanzarote de Lago.* The close of the second part has been moved forward. It should be found in the lacuna after folio 288, and its anticipation at folio 277 seems to have the intention of concealing the changes made in the third book. To the second book we ought, perhaps, to attach the ballad:

Nunca fuera caballero de damas tan bien servido
como fuera Lanzarote cuando de Bretaña vino
(*Primavera*, No. 148);

which Cervantes delighted to quote. It states that Lancelot, coming from Britain (or Brittany) was well received; that Guenevere complained of an outrageous gallant; that Lancelot cut off the insolent's head under a green pine, and returned to the embraces of his lady. It has been suggested that this episode is written in general imitation of the hero's exploits, and that it more especially represents the impertinences of Meleagance and his death at Lancelot's hand; while the duenna Quintañona who strains the wine is a popular version of the Lady Mallehault (Sp. Malagud). But if the ballad be a free adaptation of Arthurian situations, its composition differs strangely from the method employed by both the other ballads of this cycle, and by the majority of ballads of any Spanish cycle: for the custom was to work from a text, often in prose, to conserve phrases and situations, and to employ the lesser liberties of contamination and contraction. Shorn of its augments, which have grown on the primitive form by a logical series of popular suggestions, the ballad of Tristan and Iseut consists, as we have noted, of a fair representation of three chapters of the romance, reduced into a half-dozen lines and eked out with hemistichs from the ballad-monger's stock-in-trade, and the same is true of the ballad of the white-hoofed stag. Even the five *lais de Bretanha* and their rubrics, though the latter are not exact in every particular, bear upon specific episodes. The solution of the difficulty may lie, as in the Tristan instance, in the discovery of variant readings which would lead to an intelligible text; but its requirements, as it stands, are best met not by any incident in the history of Sir Lancelot, but in the life of Tristan. When the latter was residing at Joyous Guard with Queen Iseut, a Scottish knight named Dagarius had the impertinence to make love to the Queen; but Tristan, when apprised of the matter, cut off his head, and returned to the castle. The incident was much discussed at court on the day of Pentecost.[1]

The third book is now a mere torso. Halved by the loss of the final *laisses*, it is again reduced by a third through the loss of several episodes at the commencement, and one in the course, of the narrative; but there are indications of a longer form. If Gutierre Diez de Games had the authority of a Spanish *Lanzarote de Lago* for his mention of Arthur's battle with Frolle—and he expected to be understood—his copy must have been more complete than that which now survives; but the matter is doubtful.[2] Shortly after the return

[1] The former explanation is that of Menéndez y Pelayo, *Antologia*, xii. p. 476. The episode of Dagarius (Löseth, para. 349) is cited in *Demanda*, cap. xi.: "La otra silla fue de vn cauallero d'Escocia que auia nonbre Danarin, que matara Tristan en aquella demanda ante la Joyosa Guarda, porque aquel Danarin demandara su amor a la reyna Iseo," and the reference is given to *La Gran Hystoria de Tristan*. Of Tristan's stay at Joyous Guard Malory says (X. cap. lii.): "And wit ye well that castle was garnished and furnished for a king and a queen royal there to have sojourned. And Lancelot charged all his people to honour them and love them as they would do himself." Brangain is a better Quintañona than Lady Mallehault. She even served wine: "Tristan . . . fizo aparejar a Brangel pan e vino e ceuada" (*Tristan de Leonis*, cap. 59).

[2] *El Vitorial*, Bibl. Nac., Madrid, MS. 17648=Gay. 209, fol. 92v: "avnque otras guerras ovo ante quando el rrey Artur mato a Frole rrey de Françia, que tenia el rreyno por los emperadores de Rroma." *Cf. Vulg.*, v. p. 373.

from the French war,[1] Lancelot was tricked into a visit to Helaine in the very apartment of the Queen. Unable to bear Guenevere's contempt, he lost his reason; but after long wanderings, he was brought to the castle of Corbenic and cured by the visit of the Holy Vessel. He felt no confidence of the Queen's mercy, and so consented to go with Helaine to live in the Isle de Joie, where he set up his shield on a tree, ornamented with the figure of a knight imploring the mercy of a lady; but Helaine was happy and her damosels danced round the shield, singing that Sir Lancelot was the best knight in the world.[2] The *Chevalier Mesfait* defended his shield and island against not less than two thousand knights before he was reconciled to the court by the good offices of Hector and Percival. This incident, which is also the last immediately before the feast of Pentecost, is the subject of the fifth *lai de Bretanha*—a dance of damsels in praise of a hero, as the second had been danced and sung in scorn of a monster.

[1] *Vulg.*, v. pp. 379–403.

[2] *Cancioneiro Colocci-Brancutti*, No. 5: "Este laix fezeron donzelas a don Ançaroth quando estava na Insoa da Lidiça quando a rainha Genevra o achou con a filha de rei Peles e lhi defendeo que non paresçesse ant'ela."

(Colocci notes): "Don Tristan per Genevra."

The refrain is:

"Ca este escudo e do melhor
omen que fez Nostro Senhor."

Cf. Vulg., v. p. 403: "Et dirent que voirement estoit il li mieldres cheualiers del monde. Ensi demoura lancelot en lille de ioie. . . . Ni ia si grant yuer ne feist que elles ne venissent chascun iour caroler au pin entour lescu qui y pendoit. Par coi cil del pais lapelerent lille de ioie."

Castilian and Portuguese readers must have been familiar with this madness of Lancelot, if they were to comprehend the more deliberate fooling of Beltenebros in Peña Pobre (*Amadis de Gaula*, ii. cap. 8). From Beltenebros, in comic but just descent, we come to the antics of the Knight of the Sorrowful Countenance in the Sierra Morena (*Don Quixote*, i. chap. 25, etc.).

VI. A *Libro de Don Tristan* was inserted, on the faith of our manuscript, in the middle of the third book of *Lanzarote de Lago*. We have no means of determining its contents, but into it we would naturally gather such fragments of that hero's adventures as are not to be explained by *Don Tristan de Leonis*. We are hardly entitled to argue into it the references which the *Demanda del Sancto Grial* and *Baladro* make to *La gran Hystoria de Tristan*; but as the book opens late in Arthurian time, a few months before the Holy Grail begins, we could hope to find in it the Dagarius episode which was contemporary with the festival of Pentecost; the battle with Helys II. (the first *lai de Bretanha*) and the third lyric of the *Cancioneiro Colocci-Brancutti*, which happen in the first year of the Quest; and the song sung in Brehus' house (No. 4), after Mark had carried off Iseut from Joyous Guard early in the second year.

VII. *La Queste del Saint Graal.* The reviser of the Castilian version claims to have translated, or at all events transcribed, Map's *Quest* in a work entitled *El libro de Galaz.*[1] In support of his assertion, he displays his knowledge of the alternative account of the second year's adventures, and adds to these proofs a considerable extract from its conclusion. By referring to the *Libro de Galaz* he can avoid specifically Grail incidents, and economise his interest for chivalrous exploits. It is clear that the redactor of the *Demanda* trusted to his readers' familiarity with the Map-*Quest*, which is nowhere so well supported by a cycle of Sir Lancelot.

[1] *Demanda*, capp. 226 ("lo auemos escrito en el libro de Galaz"), 229, 241, 291 (358). Capp. 373–90 follow Map (385: Maestre Gualter). The Portuguese MS. does not share this peculiarity.

VIII. *Le Cerf au Pied Blanc.*[1] After the achievement of the Grail, and before the tragedy of King Arthur, a breathing space is found into which disconnected adventures may be inserted. There Malory relates the pathetic story of the Lady of Astolat, and the Dutch *Roman van Lancelot*[2] recounts the hero's adventure with a white-hoofed stag. The Dutch poet tells how a damosel came to court to complain of the injuries wrought by such a stag, guarded by seven lions, upon the territories of a queen, and she promised that lady's hand to her deliverer. Keu boasted his merits and was guided by a lap-dog to a water; but he was afraid to follow the creature across. Lancelot took up the task as soon as he heard of it,—for he had but recently arrived—slew the lions and the stag, cut off its hoof, and sank down overcome by exhaustion and fatigue. A craven knight, who was then passing, snatched from him the hoof, and by that token claimed the lady and her kingdom. But Gawain became suspicious of the absence of Lancelot, discovered and cared for him, and exposed in single combat the fraud. It is then in Lancelot's power to obtain the queen and the realm, but he prefers to impose on her a perpetual virginity. The conclusion is clumsy and ungracious, and is borrowed from the instance of the damsel who vowed perpetual virginity for love of Lancelot,[3] and its awkwardness is a sufficient proof that the tale cannot end in a satisfactory manner unless by a marriage and a reign.

[1] *Cf. The Adventure of the "Cerf au Pied Blanc,"* in *Modern Language Review*, xviii., 1923, pp. 436–48, where the documentation is given in full. A different view is expressed by E. de Laiglesia, *Tres hijuelos habia el rey*, in *Revista Critica Hispano-Americana*, iii. pp. 3–56.
[2] *Roman van Lancelot*, ed. Jonckbloet, ii. pp. 151–7.
[3] *Lanzarote de Lago*, fol. 296v; *Vulg.*, v. p. 83.

The Dutch poem is of the thirteenth century: an earlier version of the fable is found in the *Lai de Tyolet.*[1] In that poem the unhappy lady is a princess, not a queen; but her marriage with Tyolet and their joint reign are the immediate consequence of the adventure. Tyolet, like Lancelot, is not long come to court; but for the better reason, that he is a novel knight begotten *ad hoc ipsum.* The princess makes her appeal in person, and so promises her own hand. Other details—the lap-dog, the boastful Lodoer, the false pretendant, and Gawain—are the same as in the Dutch. But *Tyolet* has an introduction which tells of his woodland upbringing and skill in woodcraft. His special qualification is a manner of whistling that brings his quarry to him, so that he is astonished when one stag neglects his lure, escapes across a water, and is metamorphosed into an armed knight. In the conversation that follows Tyolet displays the same naïveté as Percival, and the knight-beast advises him to seek knighthood at King Arthur's court. The Arthurian details, and the comparative irrelevance of this introduction, are signs that the *Lai de Tyolet* is already not an unsophisticated romance. There remain hints, however, that the stag with the white hoof who dwells by the ford of the Perilous Water and the stag-knight who is found there are not different persons but the same thing; so that the two parts of the tale can be pressed into a simpler form of which the moral is initiation. For, a hero can do many things through his own natural powers, but he cannot do all. He is initiated. He succeeds and receives his reward.

[1] *Romania,* viii. pp. 40–50; *Histoire Littéraire de la France,* xxx. pp. 113–18.

The identity of the stags is the first assumption of the Spanish ballad of

Tres hijuelos habia el rey   tres hijuelos, que no mas;

the rest is debatable. According to the narrative, some lady complains of the stag and offers her hand in exchange for its hoof; Lancelot accepts the mission but not the offer. He sets out with some hounds (*sabuesos*, plural); he finds a hermit who describes the stag, and (for the first time!) its attendant lions, who are seven, as well as a whelped lioness, and the good man exclaims against the malevolence of her who had sent him on such an errand. A concluding couplet is easily recognisable as the work of the Spanish poet:

¡ Ay dueña de Quintañones   de mal fuego seas ardida
que tanto buen caballero   por ti ha perdido la vida!

The dueña de Quintañones comes from the neighbouring ballad where she represents either the Lady Mallehault or Brangain, and her interference here, offering her hand to Guenevere's lover, makes nonsense of the situation; while the sentiment merely underlines the last words of the hermit. Now, why does Lancelot meet a hermit and ask him for directions? Clearly because at this point he must be beside the ford of the Perilous Water: the *brachet* of *Tyolet* and the Dutch *hondekin* swam right across the water, because they had a magic sense of hostility to the stag which made them independent of scent; but Lancelot's leash of hunting-dogs is at fault. Who is the lady? We know from *Tyolet* and the *Roman van Lancelot* that the fable requires a marriage and a reign, or the possibility of these things; she must, therefore, be either a princess royal or a queen. On the whole, seeing that she appears in person and offers her own hand, we set her down as the princess, daughter of *the* king of the story, who may be already dead, or dies with convenient alacrity.

We may now brave the greater perils of the opening quatrain. This informs us that *the* king had three sons and no more; that he cursed them in his wrath; and that the sons turned respectively into a stag, a dog and a Moor. But this is very elliptical, and casts only darkness on the rest of the poem. The verses intend to tell us the relation of the princess and the stag; but they completely fail to do so. We are here given, however, that the stag is *a* son of *the* king; we have inferred that the lady is *the* daughter of *the* king; they are brother and sister. But if full brother and full sister, then the sister has no right against her brothers, as she simply passes from the *patria potestas* into the *fraterna potestas*: she is the heiress (or the story has no ending), and they must be her brothers by the bar sinister. This situation is an entirely probable one, not within the distant conventions of folk-lore whether Celtic or other, but in the everyday experience of the Middle Ages. It is a simple case of inheritance. Three illegitimates attempt to exclude the princess royal from her heritage; their father curses them, probably from his death-bed, where curses are notoriously effective; but though now metamorphosed from men into beasts, they continue their hostility, and the eldest, the stag, wastes her lands and compels her to seek knightly aid. As for the dog (*can*) and the Moor (*moro*), they have little objective existence and no influence on the story; their value is that of a compound epithet (*perro moro*, *chien de païen*, heathen dog) which puts the stag—a noble beast—into the wrong.

Sr. de Laiglesia has advanced, however, another theory, which is based not only on the three narratives already cited, but also uses episodes from *Tristan*, *Morien*, *Perceval*, *Parzival*, *Mule sanz frainz*, and *Le Chevalier au Cygne*. For him the problem is to disenchant the stag. This is done by the third brother, the Moor, guided by the second, the dog, and summoned by the messenger damsel, whom he duly marries. The Moor, he thinks, was Morien, because in the *Roman van Lancelot*, though at the distance of many thousand lines from this episode, Morien is said to be black like any Moor.[1] So we cancel Lancelot from the story on the authority of the Dutch novel, when the Dutch novel adjudicates the adventure to him! The net, cast so widely, seems to bring in more fish than we want. We are to understand the disenchantment of the stag, when the three principal authorities, who are also the only relevant ones, demand his death. If the dog, or second brother, is the *brachet* or *hondekin* that guides the quester, how does he become a whole leash of hounds in the course of one ballad? And who is this messenger damsel, who so far forgets her anonymity as to offer to marry a hero, and who stirs up a man to revenge his own wrongs? And to what kingdom does the quester succeed, when he has disenchanted two brothers who can rely on primogeniture? But the

[1] Citing from vol. i.:

> "Die Moriaen was geheten . . .
> . . . Was enen moer gelijc,
> Ende alse sward alse een raven."

gravest criticism of Sr. de Laiglesia's theory is that its method is too free for application to the ballads. There is no question of reconstructing a folk-tale, for which the most distant and least proved analogies may be sufficient evidence, but of determining an episode contained in a Prose-*Lancelot* of the thirteenth century in France and the fourteenth in Spain, which is itself unknown, but can be inferred from two parallel and earlier verse forms, and one later ballad based textually upon it. The *romance* is constructed on the same lines as other Spanish ballads, by cutting prose into tirades of assonanced verses, by compression, contamination, ballad formulas, explanatory phrases and conclusions.

The *Tres hijuelos* is found extant in twenty-seven lines of sixteen syllables each, arranged in three tirades, and four logical divisions. We have: (1) the introduction, in the assonance á; (2) the scene at court, assonanced a—o; (3) Lancelot and the hermit, in i—a; and (4) the moral, in the same assonance. But the famous grammarian, Antonio de Nebrija,[1] gives a variant of Lancelot's conversation with the hermit in the assonance a—a; so that we ought probably to add yet another scene, viz., (1) introduction, á; (2) court scene, a—o; (3) Lancelot sets out, i—a; (4) Lancelot and the hermit, a—a; and (5) the poet's moral. The rapid changes of assonance, as well as the unintelligibility of the actual form, are clear proof that the ballad is a reduced form of an earlier ballad,[2] now lost, which was presumably intelligible in all its parts; the

[1] Nebrija, *Grammatica*, II. capp. vi. and viii.

[2] The earlier form must have referred "que no mas" to the princess, presumably by means of the clauses (which were not in contact with

primitive ballad, like *Ferido esta don Tristan*, would be a rapid summary of several chapters of prose. The variations of assonance have indicated four possible rubrics.

IX. *La Mort de Roy Artus*. In the *Merlin y Demanda* Spain and Portugal had a satisfactory account of the deaths of Arthur, Guenevere, Lancelot, and King Mark; but there was also another history. This, taken from the *Suite du Lancelot*, that is to say, a manuscript similar to the original of Malory's twenty-first book, touched on the death of Gawain, the interview of Arthur and Mordred, the fatal misunderstanding caused by the appearance of a snake in their conference, the battle, and Arthur's removal to Avalon. A summary was made of this book in Castilian, and it has been handed down to us independently by the second titulus of D. Pedro's *Nobiliario* (*c.* 1325), and by the author of the *Cronica General de* 1404. Was there ever a translation at full length, prepared, perchance, for the *Grande et General Estoria*?

We may sum up our authorities for *La Gran Historia de Lanzarote de Lago*:

1. *Primer libro de Lanzarote de Lago.*
   Lost. Extended to the Roche aux Saisnes.
2. *Segundo libro de Lanzarote de Lago.*
   Bibl. Nac., Madrid, MS. No. 9611, fols. 1–277.

each other): "Tres hijuelos habia el rey . . . *y una fija* que no mas." The second hemistich would then recall, as it ought, *Tyolet*, lines 340–2:

> "Fille de roi et de roine
> Et de Logres est roi mon pére;
> N'ont plus enfanz li ne ma mére."

There is no point in emphasising the trinity of the brothers; had they been thirty, the tale would have proceeded the same.

For the influence of this ballad on others, *cf.* Laiglesia, *op. cit.*, and add Braga, *Romanceiro Geral*, i. (1906), pp. 345–8.

Ballad: "Nunca fuera caballero" (?). *Primavera*, 148.

3*a*. *Tercer libro de Lanzarote de Lago, primera partida.*
Bibl. Nac., Madrid, MS. No. 9611, fols. 280–355.

4. *Libro de don Tristan.*
Dagarius episode? *Canc. Col.-Branc.*, Nos. 1, 3, 4?

3*b*. *Tercer libro de Lanzarote de Lago, segunda partida.*
Frole? *Canc. Col.-Branc.*, No. 5.

5. *Libro de Galaz.*
Cf. Demanda, capp. 226, 229, 241, 291, 358, 373–91.

6. *El Ciervo del Pie Blanco.*
Ballad: "Tres hijuelos habia el rey." *Primavera*, 147.

7. *Muerte de rey Artur.*
Nobiliario, tit. ii. *Cronica de* 1404, fol. 25v.

In fixing the date of the translation, the different sections of the cycle determine different terminals. On the 24th October, 1414, the history of Sir Lancelot was already a fragment consisting of the second and half the third books, with or without a book concerning Tristan: its original must be carried back into the fourteenth century, where it meets with the period vaguely fixed by Ayala's allusion in the *Rimado de Palacio*. The ballad of *Tres hijuelos* in its present state is certified by Antonio de Nebrija in 1492 to be "old"; on a conservative estimate we refer the present state of this ballad to the early fifteenth century. But in the present form it is no longer intelligible, but implies a longer development, which, if we allow time for decay, must surely attain to the later fourteenth century; and the earlier ballad is carved from a prose text of, at latest, the middle of that century. If the

Muerte de rey Artur be part of the original translation, its mention by D. Pedro de Barcellos points to the first quarter of the fourteenth century, or the last years of the thirteenth; the *Lanzarote de Lago* must have preceded the *Amadis de Gaula*, which is mentioned in 1345–50, and was composed, we believe, between 1304 and 1312; and the fifth *lai de Bretanha* is evidence in the same direction. The name of D. Pedro de Barcellos connects the *Lanzarote de Lago* with the courtly and literary systems of Alfonso X. and Sancho IV., from whom he derived much of his material.

The *Demanda del Santo Grial* makes claims to have been composed by the same writer as the *Gran Historia de Lanzarote*;[1] but the agreement of the Castilian and Portuguese texts throws back the impertinence to the Pseudo-Boron. On the other hand, the *Lanzarote de Lago*, like the *Tristan de Leonis*, has been equipped with an allusion to the *Baladro del Sabio Merlin*, for the translator refers the Dolorous Stroke to the Knight of the Two Swords.[2] This not

[1] *Bal.*, cap. 144: "como dira despues encima de la gran historia de Lançarote de Lago"; cap. 332: "como adelante oyredes." *Dem.*, cap. 40: "llego la donzella alegre, ella que os dixe que mostrara Erec e firiera a Lançarote con el freno"; Ptg., "Aqui uos, vem a donzella laida, que uos dise, que doestara Erec e que firiera lançarot com o freo." The latter is an allusion to the Vulgate *Tristan.*

[2] *Lanzarote de Lago*, fol. 301v: "por el qual cuidaba ser tornada la tierra en su estado bien como de primero que por el doloroso golpe que el cauallero de las dos espadas fizo fue tornada en pobreza y en lloro ansi como la gran historia del santo greal lo deuisa" (*i.e.*, *Baladro*, cap. 283: "Como el cauallero de las dos espadas firio al rey Pelean con la lança vengadora." This is not the *Gran Historia* but the *Verdadera Historia del Santo Grial*). The "cauallero que traia dos espadas" (fol. 262r, *Vulg.*, iv. p. 324) was another than Balin le Savage, who died at the beginning of the Adventurous Times. Contrast with the reading of the Spanish MS., *Vulg.*, v. p. 110: "dont tous li pais deuoit reuenir en sa premiere biaute qui par le dolerous cop de lespee auoit este desertes & escillies. Si comme li contes a deuise apertement en lystoire del saint Graal" (the reference is to *Vulg.*, i. p. 290).

only is in direct contradiction to the Vulgate story, but it partially negatives a passage in the second book of *Lanzarote de Lago* in which a different Knight of Two Swords is introduced; and for these reasons the error should be kept within the Peninsula. We have also seen that the redactor of the *Demanda* claims to have written the ordinary Lancelot story of the Holy Grail in the *Libro de Galaz*, and that he offers substantial proof of his assertion; but he unfortunately forgot to state whether by "*auemos escripto*" he meant "we have translated" or "we have transcribed"; nor is there any means of determining when the revision of the Castilian *Demanda* took place. But we can say, with some confidence, that the translation of *Lanzarote de Lago* occurred at about the same time, and under similar influences, as that of the *Merlin y Demanda* and *Tristan*. There is not much risk in assigning the date *circa* 1300, with some fifteen years for a margin of error.

XII

SECONDARY ARTHURIAN AND OTHER ROMANCES IN CASTILE AND PORTUGAL: "AMADIS"

SAGRAMOR'S name can be found in any of the chief Arthurian cycles, but it is in the *Lanzarote de Lago* that he develops characteristics which make him one of the most interesting of the younger personages. As such he was revived by the *Memorial da Segunda Tavola Redonda*, or, according to Barbosa Machado's reading of the sub-title, the *Triunfos de Sagramor em que se tratão os feitos dos cavalleiros da Segunda Tavola Redonda* (Coimbra (1554?), 1567 and 1867), by Jorge Ferreira de Vasconcellos.[1] Beginning with King Arthur, his departure, and the prosperous reign of Sagramor, it is chiefly occupied by the Knight of the Crystal Arms, amid a whirl of mortal combats with knights, centaurs, giants and dragons. It ends in a description of the tournament of Xabregas (5th August, 1552), at which the ill-fated Prince João, who died in 1554, was the principal figure. The novel is a curiosity in literature, and gives the last date of the life of Arthurian fictions in the Peninsula.

The Provençal *Istoria de Jaufre* circulated, as we have seen, in Catalonia from the date of its inception; but for Castile it does not appear to be attested at any time during the mediæval period. The *Cronica de*

[1] A. F. G. Bell, *Portuguese Literature* (Oxford, 1922), pp. 168–9.

los muy notables caualleros Tablante de Ricamonte, y de Jofre hijo del conde Donason (Salamanca, 1513) was the only Arthurian or semi-Arthurian romance with which Cervantes was acquainted.[1] Its action passed between Camalot and Richmond, and concerns the liberation of Don Millan from the power of Tablante by the young Jofre. The first few lines rehearse a number of the most prominent Arthurian names, and cite the *Baladro del Sabio Merlin* and the *Demanda del Sancto Grial.*

Some novels, which are not Arthurian, profess to be based on the chronicles of England, and they helped to spread absurd conceptions of our nature and history among Spaniards of the Middle Ages or early Renascence. Of such was the *Historia de los nobles caualleros Olīueros de Castilla y Artus Dalgarbe* (Burgos, 1499),[2] which furnished a prologue to the *Tristan de Leonis.* It is the old story of *Amis et Amiloun* translated from a prose romance of the fifteenth century, and it reappears in Lope de Vega's dylogy *Don Juan de Castro.* The *Espantosa y terrible vida de Roberto el diablo* (Burgos, 1509)[3] is perhaps the best Sunday-school story ever written; the badness and goodness of *Robert the Devil* are of a naïveté and whole-heartedness that exceeds the power of Mark Twain's *Good and Bad Little Boys*, and it has the advantage of being related in cold seriousness. The

[1] *Don Quixote*, i. chap. 16. The *Tablante* is reprinted from the edition of 1564 by Bonilla, *Libros de Caballerías*, i. pp. 459–99 (Estella, Adrian de Anvers).

[2] Facsimile by A. M. Huntington, New York, 1902; ed. Bonilla, *Libros de Caballerías*, ii. pp. 446–523 (Burgos, 1499).

[3] Bonilla, *op. cit.*, ii. pp. 405–21 (Barcelona, A. Lacaballeria, 1683). It was translated into Portuguese by Jeronimo Moreyra de Carvalho as late as 1733 (*Historia do grande Roberto, duque de Normandia e emperador de Roma*, Lisbon, 1733).

Chronica del Rey don Guillermo (Toledo, 1526) and the *Estoria del rey Guillermo de Inglaterra* (fifteenth century) are translations of different stages in a French *rifacimento* of St. Eustace's legend,[1] which had already been followed in the first part of *El Cauallero Cifar*. They give a strange, devout and patient complexion to our Conqueror.

The Carolingian legends circulated in a number of popular chap-books of the sixteenth century both in Castile and in Portugal. But prosifications of the *chanson de geste* entitled *Mainete y Galiana* are to be found as early as the *Primera Cronica General* and the *Gran Conquista de Ultramar*. The latter also includes in its capacious body the legend of his mother Berthe aux grands pieds; and his wife Sebile is the heroine of the fifteenth-century *Noble cuento del Emperador Carles Maynes de Rroma e de la buena Emperatriz Sevilla*.[2] The romance of *Flores y Blancaflor*, attached to the grandparents of Charlemagne, was familiar to the readers of the Archpriest of Hita, to whom *Tristan* was a comparative novelty, and it was popular among the poets of the *Cancionero de Baena*. These *trobadores* also knew and admired the *Historia de Enrrique fi de Oliva*,[3] a version of *Doon de la Roche*. The legend of the *Chevalier au Cygne* is given in the *Gran Conquista de Ultramar*; and it is possible to cite a number of other French tales—*Clamades y Clarimonda*, *Partinuples*, *Pierres de Provenza y la linda Magalona*, *Ottas de Roma* (*Florence*

[1] Both published by H. Knust, *Dos obras didácticas y dos leyendas sacadas de MSS. de la Biblioteca del Escorial*, *Madrid*, 1878 (Soc. de Bibliófilos Españoles).

[2] Bonilla, *op. cit.*, i. pp. 503-33.

[3] *Don Quixote*, i. chap. 16: "and that other book which recounts the deeds of count Tomillas."

de Rome), *Melosina*, *Paris y Viana*,—in which the chivalresque interest is subordinated to the fantastic or sentimental order. As prose, the *matière de France* lacked unity of matter or intention. The novels are decentralised, and so fail to be significant in proportion to their bulk for literature and society; but the numerous fine ballads of the Carolingian series, torn from forgotten epics, were and are a perpetual support for Carolingian themes. In a more ephemeral manner the epics of Italy begot Spanish and Portuguese imitations in the later sixteenth century, when the rage for prose chivalry was almost glutted; and they brought with their Carolingian subjects a style of treatment that was Arthurian.

In sharp distinction from the *matière de France*, and weak in ballads because they were never epical, the British fictions were strong and persistent in prose; their chief product being the romance of *Amadis de Gaula*.[1] Three books of this heavy tome are devoted to the triumphs of Amadis over the obscure circumstances of his birth, over personal enemies, enchanters, hosts embattled, the suspicions of his lady and the envy of his king, until at last he is in possession of his Oriana, having snatched her from a hated marriage; during all this time his right arm is never withstood, his faith dims but once, and—in contrast to the French champions—his moral character is of a middle-class respectability. The fourth book, fabricated from elements of the other three, reconciles Amadis to his father-in-law and hallows and regularises his possession of Oriana. In its general plan the

[1] Gayangos, *Libros de Caballerias* (*Bibl. de Aut. Esp.*, No. 40); G. S. Williams, "The Amadis Question," in *Revue Hispanique*, xxi.

novel follows that of the *Lancelot* through imprisonments, enchantments, temptations, and lover's lunacy; the hero marks his career by a succession of sobriquets that resemble those of King Ban's son (el Doncel del Mar, Beltenebros, etc.), but the earliest of them, Amadis Sin-Tiempo, is suggested by the play on Tristan-Tantris. There is no Holy Grail and no theory of adulterous love, apart from a convention that heroes must be so born as to be ignorant of their parentage; but the chivalrous manners and gallantry are Arthurian, and there is the same preference for decoration over reality, for sentiment over genuine emotion. The setting and scenery is Arthurian; the time bisects the interval between the *Estoire del Saint Graal* and the *Livre de Merlin*; the names of persons and places derive by suffixes from well-known models. Don Galaor, the fancy-free, is Gawain; Merlin passes from the supernaturally beneficent into the supernaturally bad as Arcalaus el encantador, and Morgane la Fée aids virtue under the name and style of Urganda la Desconocida. The first sentence is suggested by the *Destruction de Jerusalem*; and the first chapter announces a "cruel custom" borrowed from the *Merlin*. The imitations are too continual and the relations between whole groups of incidents too constant to admit of any doubt as to their model having been the romances in complete form as we have them, whether found in some such compilation as that of Rustician de Pisa, or separately: though the author is no mere journeyman, but is an artist who has his own design. It is not certain whether he drew on French originals or on the Castilian-Portuguese translations, seeing that the latter are too fragmentary to put the matter to the proof; but the author's touch, unlike that of *Cifar*, is so secure, his course so even, his contact with the reader's mind so steady and intimate, as to imply for himself a long familiarity with his sources and for his public an awakened and established taste.

It is from the edition of *Amadis de Gaula*[1] in four books, made by Garci-Ordóñez de Montalvo about the year 1492, and issued in 1508 or earlier, that all the succeeding novels of Renascence chivalry in Spain and Portugal descend, including those also which pretend, like *Palmeirim da Inglaterra*, to be based on the authentic chronicles of England. But the manuscript editions of the great romance embraced only three books, which were presumably the same as those now so numbered, and they are mentioned to Pero López de Ayala by Pero Ferrús before the year 1379;[2] Ayala himself had read the *Amadis* at the same time as *Lanzarote*, and in Castrogeriz' translation of the *De Regimine Principum*, which we have already mentioned in another connection, *Amadis*, *Tristan* and *Cifar* are named together as extant about 1345–50. By the year 1372 his fame had transcended the

[1] For the *Amadis*, the reader will consult Miss Williams' article, and Dr. H. Thomas' admirable *Spanish and Portuguese Romances of Chivalry*, 1920.

[2] *Cancionero de Baena*, No. 305:

"Amadis el muy fermoso,
Las lluvias e las ventyscas
Nunca las fallo aryscas
Por leal ser e famoso:
Sus proesas fallaredes
En tres libros e dyredes
Que le de Dios santo poso."

Cf. Nos. 38, 72 (Macandon, *Amadis*, ii. cap. 14), 188, 226, 249, 301, 572; *Revue Hisp.*, xv. p. 815; *Canc. del Palacio*, p. 70 (Insola del Ploro, *Amadis*, II. cap. i); Ayala, *Rim. de Palacio*, copla 162; Rubió y Lluch, *Docs. per l'hist. de la cultura*, ii. p. 327, n. 1.

frontiers of Castile and reached the court of Barcelona; and the allusions to the novel refer not only to the hero and heroine, but also to the sexagenarian knight Macandon, and to the adventures of the Insola Firme under the older name which that passage borrowed from the Spanish *Tristan*—Insola del Ploro. We are assured, therefore, of a three-volume *Amadis de Gaula* of approximately the same contents as the actual first three volumes, written in Castilian and read by Castilians in the first half of the fourteenth century.

The plot of the romance advances with the confidence of an established and understood convention, and it shows none of the vacillations of original Arthurian compositions; but in the fortieth chapter of the first book we catch a momentary, but precious, glimpse of the labour of composition. At that point of the tale the Amazon Briolanja falls dangerously in love with Amadis de Gaula, as so many women had done with Lancelot; but it is as essential to the character of the Spanish as of the French knight that he reject her advances. Amadis rejects Briolanja. But the Infante D. Affonso of Portugal commanded that the matter should be differently expressed, and in so doing (says a voice which can hardly be other than that of the author) he pleased himself but spoiled the tale.[1] The hero's character now suffered from a fatal contradiction, and it was inevitable that attempts should be made to rectify the Prince's blunder. In a new paragraph some redactor proposed to save Amadis' reputation for constancy by immuring

[1] *Amadis*, i. cap. 40: "En esto hizo lo que su merced fue, mas no aquello que en efecto de sus amores se escribia."

him in a tower where Briolanja besieged him with her passion, until Oriana, in sheer pity for his sufferings and emaciation, authorised him to satisfy the Amazon's demand. And again, Montalvo (who reveals himself by appealing to the authority of the fourth book, his creation) declares that Briolanja herself relented and only detained the hero until the arrival of Don Galaor, who readily consented to espouse so charming a maiden! We have thus four stages of the episode, along with a comment on the second by him who wrote the first. The Infante D. Affonso of Portugal has been explained to be the son of King Diniz who reigned as Affonso IV. from 1325 to 1357; but we are inclined to think that Snra. de Vasconcellos is right in identifying him with the D. Affonso de Portugal, brother of King Diniz, who lived from 1263 or 1265 to 1312, and who was a Castilian subject for the last eight or nine years of his life. He was the brother-in-law of D. Juan Manuel, and the affairs of his house seem to have interested the Astorgan translator of *Josep Abaramatia* (1313).

In proposing to identify the Infante D. Affonso with the brother-in-law of D. Juan Manuel, Snra. de Vasconcellos' hope and effect was to put new life into the theory of the Portuguese authorship of this novel; for there is a theory of Portuguese priority with regard to the *Amadis de Gaula*, which embraces, exceeds, and is the motive cause for, the claim to priority in the *matière de Bretagne*. Portuguese authors, of whom the earliest wrote about a century later than the allusions of Castrogeriz and Ayala, persistently throw up Lobeiras of differing Christian name to serve as the originators of this novel. The least substantial of these is Pedro de Lobeira of Evora, who is said to have translated the work out of the French about 1449; the authority is the seventeenth-century antiquarian Jorge Cardoso.[1] Gomes Eannes de Azurara,[2] writing about the year 1450, assigns the novel to Vasco de Lobeira, who was knighted on the field of Aljubarrota, 1385, and died in the year 1403. He is supposed to have written the work during the reign of Fernando the Handsome (1367–83). If Vasco de Lobeira received his honour at anything like the normal age, he would not be born at the time when Ayala and Castrogeriz read the book; if we are to identify his fortunes, as some suggest, with those of the sexagenarian Macandon, he would still be in his teens when the romance was well known in Castile, and the revision by either Infante Affonso must have preceded his birth. If this Vasco's name is to be retained in connection with the *Amadis de Gaula*, it cannot be as author, but Azurara's authority might be held sufficient to name him as the writer, *i.e.* translator, of the Portuguese version. No such version exists; two copies have been mentioned, the one by a sixteenth-century prevaricator, and it was destroyed by an earthquake, while a revolution has obliterated another that lay unnoticed until 1683. But it would be dangerous as well as superfluous to deny a Portuguese *Amadis de Gaula*, nor need we exclude the possibility of its translation during the reign of Fernando by Vasco de Lobeira.

The Lobeiras were, however, a hardy race, and of them Dr. Braga has discovered a whole genealogy, all

[1] J. Cardoso, *Agiologia Lusitana*, i. p. 401.

[2] Gomes Eannes de Azurara, *Chronica do Conde D. Pedro de Menezes*, i. cap. 63; *cf.* Fernam Lopes, *Chronica del Rei D. João I.*, ii. cap. 39.

detailed off to various duties in the creation or transmission of the romance, but whom there is no compelling reason to discuss here. Much more important is the *trovador* João Pires de Lobeira of Galicia, the natural son of Pero Soares de Alvim and the vassal of the afore-mentioned D. Affonso. His life is known between the years 1258 and 1285 from a scanty documentation, and among other contributions to the Portuguese song-books he was responsible for an air

Leonoreta fin roseta,

which is repeated and adapted in *Amadis*, ii. cap. 11. Leonoreta, we there learn, was the little sister of Oriana; she demanded a love-song from Amadis, and he gave her this lyric, with a conclusion which referred his expressions of passion from her to another object. The passage may well have been an interpolation into the original text, designed to cover the introduction of Lobeira's lyric; for Leonoreta has otherwise no importance whatever for the romance neither before nor after this incident. The lyric, on the other hand, bears no rubric; in this respect it differs from the five *lais de Bretanha* which are certainly extracted from chivalrous novels. João de Lobeira *may* have been the author of both lyric and romance, and he *may* have quoted the lyric from the romance or fashioned the romance to suit the lyric; or the Infante D. Affonso of Portugal *may* have interfered in Book II. in favour of his protégé's poem, as he had done in the first book to further his own ideas of propriety; or the passage concerning Leonoreta *may* have been inserted in any of the many redactions which were required to keep the novel alive until Montalvo's day. Snra. de Vasconcellos[1] is of the opinion that the lyric is taken from the romance, that the romance was in existence in the thirteenth century and was composed in Portuguese, and that the removal of D. Affonso to Castile in 1304 provided an opportunity through D. Juan Manuel for a Castilian translation which could be seen by Castrogeriz and Ayala. But these are hypotheses in tiers! It is not certain that Lobeira was author of both the lyric and the romance. Were that granted, it would still be doubtful which was written first. It is not certain whether D. Affonso's marriage brought the novel of *Amadis* into Castile, or brought that prince into contact with *Amadis*. It is not certain that the first draft must have been Portuguese even if the writer were a *trovador* of the *Cancioneiros*; Alfonso X. was a Galician in his poetry, but a Castilian in his prose. Snra. de Vasconcellos' researches have brought together the names of D. Affonso and João de Lobeira, and the citations of the Leonoreta lyric and of *Amadis*, i. cap. 40, and ii. cap. 11; they also point to the importance of D. Affonso's marriage and change of nationality in 1304; these are all facts of importance in the determination of the circumstances under which the romance was composed, but we lack guidance as to the manner in which they ought to be interpreted.

For our part, seeing that it is desirable to express some view, the fact which dominates the situation

[1] C. M. de Vasconcellos, *Lais de Bretanha*, and *Grundriss der rom. Phil.*, II. ii. p. 216 *ff.*: "Die früheste verlorene Redaktion aber gehört noch dem 13 Jh. an, ist, aller wahrscheinlichkeit nach, das Werk eines portugiesischen Troubadours, und ursprünglich in portugiesischen Sprache geschrieben."

is the assured existence of the book in Castile from the first half of the fourteenth century; its presence in Portugal has never been more than an inference. Bearing this circumstance in mind, we find it too much of a paradox to expatriate the work from Castilian literature. As the *Amadis* is based on the Arthurian translations, it must have followed the more significant cycles, which were rendered into the Peninsular vernaculars, as we have seen, mainly during the reign of Sancho IV. of Castile and under the inspiration of the Alfonsine literary movement. To assign this romance to the thirteenth century seems, therefore, considerably to antedate its composition. It would be better to connect it with the later phase of the same Alfonsine movement which is typified in D. Juan Manuel; and the intervention of D. Affonso of Portugal, his brother-in-law, does us the service of placing the composition between the years of his residence in Castile, viz. 1304–12. João Pires de Lobeira wrote the lyric. It was adapted, perhaps through his patron's influence, to furnish an episode in the novel; but if Lobeira effected this interpolation, or if he wrote the romance, it is in a high degree improbable that for this purpose he employed the Portuguese language. On the other hand, João Pires de Lobeira's is the only name which any evidence, valid or invalid, connects with this authorship.

XIII

THE INFLUENCE OF CHIVALROUS LITERATURE IN THE SPANISH PENINSULA DURING THE MIDDLE AGES

Amadis and the novels of the *matière de Bretagne* form a corpus of chivalrous doctrine and example, intimately dovetailed, united in purpose, invention, expression and effect, equally popular and efficient in the Spain and Portugal of the fourteenth and fifteenth centuries, and equally prompt in their appeal to the new public of the printing press. It is there that they separate. In their joint history as manuscripts the original Arthurian novels enjoyed the greater repute, viz., *Tristan de Leonis*, *Merlin y Demanda*, and *Lanzarote de Lago*. At that period they were the possessions of the upper ranks of society, who are always in some degree cosmopolites and who might feel pleasure in the consciousness of a foreign derivation; but Gutenberg's discovery brought literature to the middle classes, and the national appeal of the native romance, strongly reinforced by Montalvo's new prose, drew that novel ahead of its compeers. They are not the begetters of Spanish chivalry save through their creation of *Amadis de Gaula*; not the parents, they are the grandsires of *Don Quixote*. Chivalry is a doctrine of heroism and of society conventionalised in love. As sources for heroism the characters of this group were classed with the Carolingian paladins of the ballads, and with the *matière de Rome la grant* as represented by the *Libro de Alejandro* and the *Cronica Troyana*; wherever chivalry is love, their effects and manner were similar to those of *Flores y Blancaflor*, *Paris y Viana*, and other sentimental productions. Akin both to heroism and sentiment, the Amadis-Arthurian group is the nucleus of mediæval fiction in Spain and Portugal, the best and weightiest exemplar of the prose whose purpose is pleasure, the corrector and educator of the chroniclers and moralists of the time, the needed antithesis to the picaresque and practical temper of the Castilian mind. The manners of the Burgalese epics no longer expressed the facts of social life, nor was their simple directness any more the characteristic mould of thought; they gave place to the refining influence of chivalry and to the nimbleness of Arthurian prose.

This prose, as we have seen, first spoke to readers in the centre and west of the Peninsula through the *Historia Regum Britonum* of Geoffrey of Monmouth, which appeared at the court of Alfonso VIII. or Enrique I., having been introduced, in all probability, in the trousseau of Leonor of Aquitaine (1170). French romances and poems may have accompanied her, but they left no traces on a literature still too rudimentary to record their impression; Queen Leonor lived too soon to read the late and developed originals of the extant translations. These were gathered together in the court of Alfonso the Wise, either by his own initiative or on that of his literary colleagues and executors; and we have seen reason to believe that the *Livre monseigneur Edouart* or original of

Don Tristan de Leonis was in his hands by the year 1260. We are not informed as to whether the wise king attempted the translation of any part of Arthurian romance, though his was the energy which diffused them among his kinsfolk in either nation; it is possible that his superior culture felt little need for versions of that which he might as conveniently read in the original, nor could he easily find time in his life for the addition of French translations to his heavy labours in the classical tongues of three religions, Latin, Hebrew and Arabic, nor for novels in addition to his contributions to historical, legal, theological, social and physical science. In the *Gran Conquista de Ultramar*, however, he planned a work in which history verges on fiction; and when continued by Sancho IV., it included some Carolingian summaries, an Arthurian reference, and the complete novel of *Le Chevalier au Cygne*. To Sancho IV., as we believe, the *Baladro del Sabio Merlin* and its other two parts were dedicated by Fray Juan Bivas about the year 1291; and we have likewise noticed that the novels of *Tristan* and *Lanzarote*, which have no intrinsic connection with the Pseudo-Boron, are equipped with allusions to his cycle in Spain. It is possible that either or both of these books may have preceded the translation of the *Baladro*, and that the references which they give ought to be connected with its French original; and it is highly probable that the three books of *Lanzarote de Lago* led on to an orthodox Map-*Quest* entitled *El libro de Galaz*, to a *Mort d'Artus* similar to that of Malory, and were accompanied by a *Libro de Tristan* now lost. Boron's trilogy was also longer than it now is, as it possessed some concluding incidents of the *Baladro* and all the *Josep Abarimatia*. The other *Livro de Josep Abaramatia*, executed by or for Juan Sánchez (de Velasco?) of Astorga in the year 1313, seems to belong to a second epoch of Castilian-Portuguese Arthurianism. At about the same time the faction of D. Juan Manuel and the prophet of Alfonso XI., Maestre Antonio, appear to have influenced the *Profecias de Merlin*, and his kinsman tampered with the first draft of *Amadis de Gaula*. At the same time, or a few years earlier, *El Cavallero Cifar* (*c.* 1305) seems to show knowledge of the lays of *Lanval* and *Graelent*.

The romance of *Amadis de Gaula* implies the existence, in one or other of the vernaculars of the centre and west, of the main cycles of Arthurian chivalry, and the process of their translation was probably complete before the entry of the fourteenth century. The poets of the *Cancioneiros* had access at that time to a *Libro de Tristan*, a *Lanzarote de Lago*, and the *Baladro del Sabio Merlin*; the *lais de Bretanha* may have been designed to occupy blank spaces in the prose texts;[1] and the use of British allusions, which was at first a badge of Provençalism among the *trovadores*, descended to become familiar to the humblest retainers of the court of King Diniz. The absence of any guidance over the Leonoreta poem prevents our determining the relationship of the *Cancioneiros* to *Amadis de Gaula*, which is not men-

[1] In translating Geoffrey for the *Grand et General Estoria*, Alfonso X. left a blank space for "los viessos de latin" of Diana's oracle to Brutus, intending to fill them later, but he gave a prose paraphrase. Translation from prose and from poetry was not necessarily one operation. Is it possible that the Arthurian translators wished to render the lyrics of their texts into the *lyric dialect*?

tioned in Portuguese literature until the *Cronica de D. Pedro de Menezes* (*c.* 1450) and the pedants of "O cuidar e sospirar" in the *Cancioneiro de Rezende*; but it circulated actively in Castile from the middle of the fourteenth century. The *Nobiliario* advances our knowledge of the *matière de Bretagne* in Portugal and indicates its path of entry: while, on the other side of the border, the *Profecias de Merlin* continued to receive additions, and the *differentia* of the surviving texts were caused by the ignorance, negligence or caprice of the scribes or by the decay of their copies.

Having commenced with the monarch, pervaded the court, and reached the nobility in the course of the fourteenth century, the Breton fictions had descended by the early fifteenth to the squirearchy and to the fringe of the manuscript-reading public. In the two hundred years of their progress we can name royal readers like Pedro IV., Juan I. and Martin I. of Aragon, João I. and Duarte of Portugal, Alfonso XI., Juan II. and Isabel of Castile; we note the greater nobles, Ramón Perellós, Pero López de Ayala, Nun' Alvares Pereira, Benavente, Santillana and Pérez de Guzmán, the lord of Batres. There are chroniclers like Lopes and Azurara, Muntaner, Rodrigo Yáñez, and Diez de Games; court poets such as Pero Ferrús, Villasandino, Baena, Diego Martínez, Nicolás de Valencia, and forerunners of the Italian movement in Spanish thought—Miçer Francisco Imperial and Ruy Paes de Ribera. The manuscripts are copied in Spain, Portugal and Catalonia—*Lansalot* in 1380, *Lanzarote de Lago* in 1414, the *Tristan* fragments of the Madrid National Library and the Vatican, the Vienna *Demanda*, the fragmentary Grail-trilogy by Pedro

Ortiz (1469–70). Still more significant than these is the attempt to carry some knowledge of this literature by means of ballads to the unlettered masses, seeing that a process so uncongenial to the temper of courtly conventions could only arise out of a compelling enthusiasm, and we have a strange reading of Lancelot's futile chivalry, a deeply pathetic version of the tragedy of the Cornish lovers, and a racy and wholly Spanish *tercera* in the duenna Quintañona.

During the latter half of the fifteenth century it is possible that, as Baist has argued,[1] the interest in chivalresque fiction was nearing a point of exhaustion; and that other writers as well as the Catalan Martorell might have felt an inclination to look for some more adequate, if less ideal, interpretation of society. But the introduction of the art of printing, which converted into readers those who had been hearers only, permitted a new and wider appeal; and the marvellous history of national unification, foreign conquest and trans-oceanic discovery stirred and engendered a new belief in the strange, the ideal, the adventurous and the improbable. The romances of *Tristan* and the *Merlin y Demanda* gained half a century of life, and the *Josep Abaramatia* and *Lanzarote de Lago* were, at all events, copied and read; the *Amadis* was reborn like the phœnix, and became the most striking literary event of the century. It was the father of an innumerable progeny; but even the way-weary and shattered remnants of Arthurianism had still strength to produce *Tristan el Joven* (1534) and *Os Triunfos de Sagramor* (1567). King Arthur's court, however, was

[1] Baist, in *Grundriss der rom. Phil.*, II. ii. p. 441: "In der zweiten Hälfte des 15 Jhs. muss die Schätzung der *Amadis* etwas nachgelassen haben."

foreign and over-populated with famous names, and his legend was closed by the annihilation of all that he had defended. But the *Amadis de Gaula* left in the tail of each part the romantically-begotten hero of succeeding volumes: his enormous family buried not only our Legend but himself; and the youth of Cervantes witnessed their decline and fall. After 1588 novels of chivalry are intermittent; by 1600 they are *in articulo mortis*; and 1605 wrote their epitaph.

A *floruit* of two and a half centuries during the formative period of the national mind should discourage the objections that Arthurian chivalry was unpopular[1] or late and uncongenial in Castile,[2] or that the *matière de Bretagne* was but a bibliographical curiosity which can safely be omitted from the history of its literature.[3] To compare, as does Durán, the numerous Carolingian ballads with the solitary three of the Breton tradition, and to deduce from that a measure of degrees of popularity, is to introduce the fallacy of setting one type of expression in judgment on another; and the same ratiocination would demonstrate the "unpopularity" of Chaucer on the evidence of Percy's *Reliques*. The Carolingian matter was epical and favoured epic moulds, but the Arthurian was romantic, demanding a deliberate

[1] So Durán, *Romancero General*, note on Nos. 351–3: "Para prueba de lo poco que encarnó en España ese espíritu caballeresco feudal de las fábulas bretonas, basta observar que de ellas sólo se tomaron los tres romances de esta sección."

[2] Milá, *De la poesía heroico-popular* (*Obras*, vii.), pp. 380–1; the same view underlies Menéndez Pelayo's discussion of them.

[3] Fitzmaurice-Kelly, *Historia de la literature española* (Madrid, 1921–2), p. 121. *Cf.* his *Spanish Literature* (Oxford, 1922), where they are omitted; and Mérimée, *Précis de l'histoire de la littérature espagnole*, where they have one footnote. But Prof. Kelly's observations in *Encyclopædia Britannica*, xxv. p. 580, apart from the Portuguese heresy, hardly differ from our own.

and decorative treatment. The reproach of lateness and uncongeniality to Castile is a more subtle attack, especially as it is usually accompanied by contrary assertions with regard to Portugal. Foreign they indisputably are, and they represent modes of thought which conflict with the sincere practicality of the *cantares de gesta* and even, as may be conceded, with the principle of realism that supports and informs the most successful and characteristic productions of the Castilian genius, in arts or politics or literature. But neither is Castile the whole of Spain, nor is the human mind incapable of contraries, nor is all that may be foreign distasteful. The Breton fictions which penetrated society from the court down hardly infringed on the province of the decadent tirades and ballads of the streets and squares, whither the old Castilian forms were tending even in the thirteenth century; nor did they conflict with, but rather complemented and corrected, the view of the world to which the Spanish mind seems always most prone to recur. The *matière de Bretagne* was not uncongenial to the circles it affected, and no type of literature can effect more. In like manner it was not late, any more in Castile than in Portugal and Galicia. Late, of course, it may be, if we compare it with the land of its origin, or even with similar translations in England, Holland, Germany or Italy, but only in the same measure as the Hispanic literatures themselves are late; for both in Spain and Portugal they are found as early as the emergence of a prose competent for their presentment and of a public with leisure for their enjoyment. The narrative metres of the thirteenth century, whether those of the *mester de clerecía* or the *mester de juglaría*, were no fit vehicles for these polished fictions, which were compelled to await the rise of the Toledan prose of Alfonso X. Nor did any class of Spanish society enjoy leisure and means to cultivate the graces of life, until the great victories of Fernando III. ended the continual peril from the Moor. But this very king, great in war, was the first to turn the advantages of his conquests into the victories of peace; he schemed an awakening of the national mind which his son carried forward and his grandsons and great-grandsons completed in all the Spains. When the wealth and culture of Cordoba, Seville and Cadiz had poured into the hands of the great nobles of the Reconquest, and when the cessation of yearly battling had given to them an unwonted superfluity of time and desires, then it was necessary to learn the art to live with elegance; and as the human species never makes what it may borrow, the Spanish nations turned inevitably and with eagerness towards the *courtoisie* of the wealthiest and most polished society within their ken. Wealth and leisure were diffused more generally as the Iberian civilisation broadened through the centuries, and the code and practice of courtesy permeated all ranks.

But the most unfortunate result of prejudging thus the history of Arthurian romances in Castile has been the discouragement of their study precisely in the region where their material remains are most considerable. In Portugal and Catalonia they have been read, in recent years, with enthusiasm and industry; facts are tracked with assiduity and interpreted, according to the nature of the critic, into proportionate or magnified conclusions; they are considered and cherished as valued portions of the early experience of the nation. But the Castilian, who is led to expect no national advantage from his studies, seems to pursue them with indifference and to be content with hearsay. The *a priori* doctrine of the lateness and uncongeniality of the Castilian novels is bolstered up by an equally *a priori* theory of the priority of other nations; indifferent to the evidence of his eyes, he does not boggle at the paradoxical notion of attributing a literature now mainly Castilian to an origin wholly Portuguese. The question has been fogged by the elementary fallacy of imposing the yellow and green of a modern political map on the literature of an earlier age. Spain and Portugal are not terms for ever fixed, but each is the result of the confluence of many separate streams. In the epoch of the Arthurian translations the dialects were still alive, and could still be applied to literature even as the contemporary dialects of England before Chaucer; and the literary speeches of Toledo and Lisbon were but in process of birth. In the absence of agreement as to the lineage and inter-relations of the Arthurian texts, in the want of critical editions and philological studies, and perhaps by the irretrievable loss of earlier models, it is hardly possible to fix the precise *patois* of the original translations; but the same doubts should make us doubly averse from a division or distribution radically at variance from that of the extant texts. The share of Leonese may have been greater, and Galician may have intervened in prose, but the modern antithesis of Portuguese and Castilian can only be applied with some impropriety. With these reservations as to dialect, however, we seem to learn from the romances their general history, guiding inspiration, and channels of distribution, nor do we find these alien and unconnected with the Peninsular mission of Castile. The texts, studied as a whole, offer the only sure hope of an advance in our knowledge; nor will this work be futile if only it point courageously to their paramount authority.

The Portuguese-Castilian novels form a group which can only be considered on the evidence of both literatures; but the Catalan translations ascend independently to immediate French originals. They were executed, so far as we can learn from the available evidence, at a comparatively late period and as the result of a specific impulse; while, on the other hand, Catalan territory enjoyed a more extensive and prolonged circulation of the untranslated foreign matter. But the influence and consequence of the *matière de Bretagne* was more or less uniform in all the Iberian kingdoms, even as their mode of introduction and permeation of society has been found uniform.

The least of these results was the justification of William of Newburgh's forebodings. The Arthurian legend obscured the features of our nation and history, and presented a ready-made answer to all the questionings of the stranger. What is the common lineage of Portuguese and English kings? That of Brutus and Troy. What was the enmity between England and France? That of Arthur and Frollo. What were the manners of English knights? Those of Gawain or of Brehus sans pitié. How do English women behave? Like the damsels of the romances.

What is the scenery of the island? Glades, forests, castles, and an enchanted haze. It is not, of course, certain that the mediæval Castilian would have felt any inclination to inform himself of the elements of our past, even were he free from the Arthurian mirage; for we commonly judge of foreign nations in the terms of some legend, and our own "romantic" and "black" accounts of Spain are even now hardly less removed from history and observation than was the Arthurian account of our mediæval state.[1] In Scotland's case,[2] where no mists intervened, a complete indifference is maintained by the authors of Spain. None the less, the chivalresque convention provided a fatally easy explanation of all English phenomena; and of all the branches of Anglo-Latin literature it is only that of history which is wholly lacking in mediæval Spain.[3] Even the Venerable Bede, whose educational and theological writings enjoyed a wide repute in the lands south of the Pyrenees, was hardly able to introduce his *Ecclesiastical History* to Spanish scholars before Juan Luis Vives (*d.* 1540).[4] From a foreign source Fernán Pérez de Guzmán obtained for his *Mar de Historias* notes on Alfred, Alcuin, Lanfranc, and Anselm, as well as Merlin, and the Grail;[5] but

[1] The "romantic" legend of Spain is dissected in E. Martinenche, *L'Espagne et le Romanticisme Français*; the other has given *Westward Ho!*

[2] First mentioned, so far as we know, in Bernáldez, cap. 245. He has forgotten the Scoto-Franco-Castilian alliance of the whole Middle Ages.

[3] The library of the Marquis of Astorga contained three volumes of these, printed at Frankfurt in 1601.

[4] Vives, *Opera*, v. p. 398. F. Columbus bought a copy at Cologne, printed in 1521. Bede's eschatological paragraphs were known, probably in a detached form. *Cf. Visió de Trictelm* (ed. Miquel y Planas, *Llegendes de l'altra vida*), and Clemente Sánchez de Vercial, *Libro de los exenplos*, Nos. 130 and 241.

[5] Pérez de Guzmán, *Mar de Historias*, capp. 58, 97, 106, 107, 96, 104; Diez de Games, *El Vitorial* (Bibl. Nac., Madrid, MS. No. 17648, fols. 74r–94v, 105r–154r).

Alfonso X. inserted the *Historia Regum Britonum* in his world history, and D. Pedro de Barcellos joined it to *Lancelot* when treating of Peninsular lineages, leaving neglected and unfilled the gap between the last Briton and the first Norman; and Gutierre Diez de Games meanders through an extraordinary sequence of fables in the attempt to give a fundamentally honest account of the Hundred Years' War. The same mind continued into the reign of Philip II., whose notions of English history and Scottish geography were suckled on Geoffrey; save that his contemporaries derived their fantasies principally from the *Amadis*. The chronicles of England had warranted so many absurdities in *Oliverus y Artus*, *Tablante de Ricamonte*, *Roberto el Diablo* and *Palmeirim da Inglaterra*, that the members of the suite which accompanied him to Queen Mary and Winchester could with difficulty see the country for the legendary haze. Juan de Varaona[1] names Insola Firme and Mongaza when he means Wight and Man, and he judges that English beauty has many Mabilias and few Orianas. Andrés Muñoz[2] avers that "some say they would rather live on the mud-heaps of Toledo than in the forests of Amadis," and after citing Lisuarte of the Round Table (from *Lisuarte de Grecia*), Merlin, Brutus, the giants and Arthur, he adds:

> He who invented and composed the books of Amadis and other books of chivalry of that sort, imagining those flowering fields,

---

[1] Juan de Varaona, *Viaje de Felipe II. a Inglaterra cuando fue a casarse con la Reina dona Maria*, in *Col. de docs. inéd. para la historia de España*, i.

[2] Andrés Muñoz, *Viaje de Felipe II. a Inglaterra*, Madrid (Soc. de Bibliófilos Españoles), 1877.

pleasure-houses, and enchantments, before so describing them must indubitably have seen the customs and amazing usages of this realm. For who ever in any other kingdom saw women riding about alone on their horses and palfreys, and actually putting them to the gallop at times with all the dexterity and assurance of a man well versed in the art? So, sir, you may well believe that there is more to be seen in England than is written in these books of chivalry, for the pleasant country-houses, banks, hills, woods, delightful meadows, fair strong castles and fresh springs at every step (for this realm is profuse of such) assuredly deserve a glance, and are, especially in summer, very pleasant.

On the social order of the Iberian kingdoms the Arthurian romances exercised a deep and permanent influence, which was yet more securely impressed on the nation by the successors of *Amadis*.[1] As early as the time of their first introduction Alfonso X. compared his loves to those of Iseut and Tristan, and he introduced into the *Siete Partidas* the definition of the perfect *caballero*; and the next of the same name instituted an order of chivalry and cultivated knightly practices.[2] The great nobles of the fourteenth century read the novels with secret pleasure and hypocritical regrets, and Breton names were in repute among the baptismal registers.[3] The Portuguese Order of

[1] Consult "The Prevalence and the Decline of the New Romances in the Spanish Peninsula," in Dr. H. Thomas, *Spanish and Portuguese Romances of Chivalry*.

[2] *Cronica de Alfonso XI*., cap. 97 (Institution of the Orden de la Banda), and cap. 99: "Et porque venian estonce muchas gentes de fuera del regno en romeria a Sanctiago, et pasaban por Burgos por el camino frances, el Rey mandaba estar omes en la calle por do pasaban los romeros, que preguntasen por los que eran caballeros et escuderos, et decianles que veniesen jostar: et el Rey mandabales dar caballos et armas con que jostasen."

[3] In the later comedias Lanzarote, Tristan and Galban have sunk to lackeys. In Fernam Mendez Pinto's *Peregrinação* both names are frequent among Portuguese emigrants. But the strangest derivative of the Arthurian legend was King Lancelot of Pulo Hinhor, an islet off Tenasserim, who was a communal vender of fish!

the Honeysuckle ascended equally to the *Lai du Chèvrefeuille* and the English Garter;[1] and the Lovers' Wing or *Ala dos Enamorados* held one side of the square at Aljubarrota (1385) in striking contrast to the hired mercenaries of the other wing. The character of Galahad was splendidly realised in the life and conduct of the Constable Nun' Alvares Pereira; and the tragedy of Cornwall mingles with that of D. Ignez de Castro. The latter inspired some passionate lines of the Lusiads which every schoolboy knows; and the life of the former from the pen of Fernam Lopes can be considered as, in a sense, the finest effort of Arthurian prose. Disappointed of physical virginity this "second arm of the realm's defence" knew that in singleness of heart, temperance, courtesy and truth lies the invincibility of the soul.

> He was of honest customs and well instructed in acts of chivalry. For if courage be a strenuous desire of reaching great results through the endurance of profitable toil, this man, recking not of hard nights or days of repulse, fearlessly exposed himself to whatsoever adventure, if so be he might obtain victory over the enemy. Like the Star of the Morning he was clear in his begetting; his life was honest and his deeds honourable, and therein were seen the grave manners of great heroes of old. Women and gambling allowed he to none, so that his camp seemed no host of warriors, but a body of devout defenders. When he was incensed against any, his chiding was gentle, so that of the clouding of his serene brow men had reverence rather than fear.[2]

---

[1] Martorell (*Tirant lo Blanch*, ed. Aguiló, cap. 77), giving the legend of the Garter from Portuguese information, says that the heroine's name was "Madresilua."

[2] F. Lopes, *Chronica del Rei D. João I.*, i. cap. 193 (ed. Braacamp Freire, pp. 373–5); *cf.* p. 60: "Liia ameude per livros destorias, espeçiallmente da estoria de Gallaz que falla da Tavolla Redomda. E porque en ellas achava, que per virtude de virgiindade Gallaaz acabara gramdes e notavees feitos, que outros acabar nom podiam, desejava muito de o semelhar em alguuma guisa; e muitas vezes cuidava em ssi, de seer virgem se lho Deus guisasse."

It is but fair to quote this passage in illustration of the idealism of chivalry, because it has pleased certain critics—Milá y Fontanals, and yet more, Menéndez y Pelayo—to fasten on the *matière de Bretagne* the responsibility for the profligacy and disorganisation of society during these two centuries.

In addition to this feverish poetry of amorous delirium the tales of the *matière de Bretagne* conveyed into modern literature a new ideal of life, well expressed by the term *knight-errantry.* The impelling motives of the heroes of the German, French and Castilian epic were rational and solid, given the ideas, customs and beliefs of their times; they were altogether logical and human within the social state of the heroic ages. But the motives directing the Knights of the Round Table are, in general, arbitrary and futile, their activity is exercised, or rather consumed and wasted, among the chimæras of a dream; the instinct for the life adventurous, for adventure for its own sake, draws them on with an irresistible attraction; they fight for the pleasure of fighting; they cross land and sea, cut off the heads of goblins and monsters, free captive princesses, give and quit crowns, for the mere pleasure of the action, to afford themselves the spectacle of their own overbearing prowess. But no serious aim, national or religious, guides them; the *Quest of the Holy Grail* itself is far from possessing in Breton poems the deeply mystic meaning gained in Wolfram von Eschenbach. The action of the heroes of the Round Table is individualistic, egoistic, anarchical. . . . The novels all describe a chivalresque and courteous world, certainly not that of the rude and barbarous Celtic tribes who provided the germ of this poetry, but that of the twelfth century's ideal, when the French poems were written, and that of the thirteenth, when they were transferred to prose; an ideal world created largely by the *trouvères* of Northern France, not uninfluenced by the poetic courts of the South, where before all other there flourished also the casuistry of love, and where spread the vicious foliage of adulterous gallantry. But if the theory of the *amour courtois* and its incompatibility with marriage was current coin of the *troubadours* and exalted ladies of Provence, it is certain that this lewd tendency freely united with the British fictions, in which the flame of guilty love almost always burned.

In no case can these frivolous imaginings be confounded with the intense, rending passion which the Celtic soul alone seems to have felt in the dawn of modern nationality. Accessories, decoration, refinement of good manners, descriptions of palaces, feasts and deeds of arms, representations of King Arthur's court where all elegance and gallantry has its seat—that is the original contribution of their imitators; and from these it ascended to the life of high society, which was polished, adorned and unmanned in the fashion we note in the fourteenth and fifteenth centuries. The new heroes are as far different from the epic as are in history the Cid and Suero de Quiñones; and they came to be even more absurd in life than in books, for the paladins of the later Middle Ages did not possess either the nebulous, imaginative excitement or the unconquerable and predestined passion, or the mysterious destiny lent by the Breton legends to their own,—emotions which are never wholly absent even from the most degenerate versions.[1]

Let us further add the novelty and strangeness of the manners, the appearance of the exotic type,—so far as we were concerned,—of the Knight-Courtier; the conception of honour, so often false and sophistical; and above all the new feminine ideal, woman's continual intervention, no longer as an obedient wife or queen of the hearth and home, but as a half-divine, half-diabolical creature, served with an idolatrous cult, to whose passions and whims the stern realities of life were sacrificed. And then there is the perpetual sophistry which erected the sentimental order into a moral discipline and confounded manly activity with a dream of art and love.[2]

Something must, however, be deducted from the generous heat of these observations, which have a range wider than that of the Arthurianism of Spain. The pedestrian vices and virtues of the Peninsular translations amounted to much less than a feverish poetry of amorous delirium, nor were they capable of producing revolutionary consequences save under the direction of external tendencies. The old epic massiveness still survived in part, and is illustrated

[1] Menéndez y Pelayo, *Orígenes de la Novela*, i. p. 165.
[2] *Ibid.*, i. p. 170.

as well by the *Coplas*[1] of Jorge Manrique as by the *Poema del Cid*. There had been no lack of destructive passion in the Urracas and Lambras of the old tales, though it was bestial and ungarnished; and long before the Arthurian impact the Cid's gravity and sobriety had tailed off into the anarchy and insolence of the *Mocedades* and the futile violence of the *Cronica Rimada*. The old cast of society was shattered with the passing of the heroic conditions of the Reconquest; the new-found wealth and peace demanded a new culture and a new ideal; for civilisation is but the measure of the excess of luxuries over necessities, of the adornments over the practicalities of life. Nor were the new heroes wholly futile. Against Suero de Quiñones, defending his bridge against all comers (1434), or Hernando del Pulgar, or Garcilaso de la Vega and the Granadine Muza, it is but just to set Cortés and his men, who saw the palaces of *Amadis* in the roofs of Tenochtitlan, and those who named California from a figment of romance; against the royal and guilty lovers of the fourteenth century who may have pleaded the example of Tristan, but with more justice the practice of their own lineage, one sets the chastity and religion of the Holy Constable. The British conventions, whatever their extravagance, were educating a new society of adventurers and enthusiasts, of loyal and courteous gentlemen, who

[1] For example:

"E sus villas e sus tierras
Ocupadas de tiranos
Las hallo,
Mas por cercos e por guerras
Y por fuerças de sus manos
Las cobro."

In this *copla* neither the sentiment nor the language has altered much since the Cid "gained his bread" before Valencia.

were demanded and employed in the marvellous era of discoveries and the Golden Age of Spain and Portugal.[1] Tropical emprise in four continents found, even as it required, more fortitude and faith, more reckless courage and unrewarded loyalty, amid perils from man and nature more unwonted, insidious and vast, than were conceded in the licence of fiction.[2]

In the main, however, the romances are a contribution to literature, and it is in literature that their principal consequences should appear. We shall not be deterred by the circumstance of their being translations; translations, too, are the chronicles and other works of Alfonso X. and the books of Juan Ruiz and D. Juan Manuel. Chaucer deals in transla-

[1] Some of the unemployed energy of Castile is recalled by name in Pulgar, *Claros Varones*, ed. 1789, tit. 17, pp. 106–7: "Yo por cierto no vi en mis tiempos, ni lei que en los pasados viniesen tantos caballeros de otros reynos e tierras estrañas a estos vuestros reynos de Castilla e de Leon por facer armas a todo trance, como vi que fueron caballeros de Castilla a las buscar por las otras partes de la Christiandad. Conosci al conde D. Gonzalo de Guzman e a Juan de Merlo: conosci a Juan de Torres y a Juan de Polanco, Alfaran de Vivero e a Mosen Pero Vazquez de Sayavedra, a Gutierre Quixada e a Mosen Diego de Valera; e oi decir de otros castellanos que con animo de caballeros fueron por los reynos estraños a facer armas con qualquier caballero que quisiese facerlas con ellos, e por ellas ganaron honra para si e fama de valientes e esforzados caballeros para los fijosdalgos de Castilla."

Cf. also the *Vitorial* (D. Pero Niño), *Libro del Passo Honroso* (Suero de Quiñones), and the *Cronica de D. Juan II.*, passim.

[2] Until the year 1492, the conditions of chivalrous literature were still mediæval, prose romance being chiefly represented by the Arthurians and *Amadis*. In that year Montalvo's preface shows the influence of the capture of Granada; and many of the greater discoveries had been made before the new romances were initiated in 1508. The *conquistadores* of Mexico were fired by *Amadis* and its first sequels, but the greater number of caballeresque productions were of the nature of imaginative commentary on the advance of arms and the Faith. It is, thus, fair to claim the educational period for the Arthurians. For the new romances see Dr. H. Thomas, *op. et loc. cit.* In *El Sentimiento del Honor en el Teatro de Calderón* (Barcelona, 1882), A. Rubió y Lluch assigns that code to the suggestions of chivalresque fiction. The point is contested (*Revista de Filología Española*, iii.), and the fact is too distant to be treated with the *matière de Bretagne*.

tions; translation and imitation in all the countries of Europe mark the path of progress in letters and life. Nor will we be influenced by the dull feebleness of some of the versions. Were they all originally of a uniform deadness with the *Baladro del Sabio Merlin*, they would not have fallen much below the average of expression, and would have had power to produce their same effects; for in an immature literature the material resources of style were of more significance than any personality. "Le style c'est l'homme" is the maxim of an adult and self-conscious culture; but before the "man" could be expressed, save with naïveté or unpretentious realism, the Peninsular literatures had to obtain the tools of subtlety in thought and expression, mastery over co-ordination and subordination, the distinction of illation, causation and adversitives from the indiscriminate "and"; they must learn to bind relative and antecedent, introduce cadence into the phrase, discover repetition without identity, conquer synonyms and adjectives; they had to invent and join paragraphs into chapters, chapters into episodes, episodes into books; they had to make books the servants of the author's thought and of the readers' pleasure. For these consequences, they must needs recur to the copy-book headlines of style, which they found in the *matière de Bretagne*.

It is a more grave imputation against these works that they are in general faithful translations, and have been influenced too little by the free operations of the translator's mind. They possess, in consequence, few individual merits of construction. The principal source for alterations in the texts has been error, loss of folios, mistakes of pagination or rubrication, transposition, and similar mechanical trifles. Only in the Castilian *Demanda* do we detect, and, to a less extent, in the writers who draw on Geoffrey's *Historia*, even so elementary a resource as the contamination of different originals. Yet when the Arthurian situations are transferred into ballad form, a higher grade of inventive talent is found; the lengthy and embroidered descriptions disappear, the action becomes rapid, the speeches direct and fiery, the situations dramatic, and the characters alive. The duenna Quintañona in a single phrase links herself to a whole province of the popular mind, and is more real than all the go-betweens of Arthurian fiction; and the Cornish lovers are unmistakable in a few masculine strokes of concentrated pathos. In the prose romances the merits of invention belong to the *Caballero Cifar* and the *Amadis de Gaula*; the former being tentative and unsuccessful, while the latter has absorbed all the new methods in fiction. The principal figures stand out clearly from the crowd; their adventures are pleasingly diversified by secondary characters, who give breadth to the action and relief to the interest; the sublime or marvellous affords a constant source of surprise; peril and triumph alternate, while worth remains constant; the descriptions are long and rich; the stately manners of knights and dames, and the delicate touch for the fluctuations of sweet passion, these were attractive and educative novelties for all ranks successively of Peninsular society.

It is in contrast to the other literature of the times that these qualities, passive and inherited in the

Arthurian translators, active and creative in the authors of *Amadis* and *Cifar*, become most readily apparent. Our extant texts belong almost entirely to the latest fifteenth century and the first portion of the sixteenth, which is the period of their decay; but their impact with greater volume and fresh expression was upon the ideas and culture of the late thirteenth and early fourteenth centuries. The epics, for defect of art, had fallen under the censure of the clerics; the clerics wrote enormous narratives in quatrains that jogged and creaked like springless carts. Literature in prose was embryonic and of limited powers, —lives of saints, chronicles and annals, apologues, works of a childish erudition or devotion. In the prosifications of certain national and foreign epics the imagination had taken its highest flights; but these narratives did not exist for themselves, nor was their direct and honest exposition the needed school of prose. Their success was deduced from that of the Castilian epics, magnificent tories which pleased because they set no store by pleasing, but whose successors were degenerating into ballads, and leaving the halls for the market-places. Less profound or heroic, but more varied, pliable and polished, the Arthurian prose responded more exactly to the demands of a subtler culture; they refined, embellished, introduced subtle distinctions among similar things—sophisticated, if you will; they analysed more curiously if less grandly. Their plots were sometimes effective, and always diversified; their characters less instinctive and fundamental, but more numerous and qualified; their language less nervous, but more graceful and polite. The same tendencies were served by some of the early sentimental novels like *Flores y Blancaflor*, which scored, it may be, even greater individual success; but their weight was not equal to that of a corpus, united in intention and manner and in many subtle inter-relations of detail, in virtue of which the cycles of Arthur and Amadis are the principal feature of the *belles lettres* of the Spanish Middle Age.

Their influence was multiplied by the transcriptions, whose number we can but vaguely compute from the evidence of their decadence. The original versions, which we cannot now attain, were, perhaps, very imperfect in their execution, and largely dependent on their originals for what merit they possessed; succinct and effective in the *Tristan*, garrulous and careless in the *Merlin y Demanda*. As an original expression of a gifted mind, the first *Amadis* can hardly have lacked style, though it is equally improbable that it possessed the sixteenth-century eloquence of Montalvo's version. But as the romances passed through the hands of successive scribes, alterations were made in order to bring the vocabulary into line with the changes of taste, or to restore order in passages that were corrupted or involved; and, in exchange, each scribe left a goodly crop of his own errors. Sometimes a more thorough reformation may have been undertaken by an editor who criticised his text with an eye to greater perfection; and passages, or whole groups of passages, may have been rehandled nearer to the heart's desire. From the errors and the infidelities of copyists spring our different redactions. We note their verbal corrections in every case in which it is possible to collect a sufficient number of texts of the same thing; as when we compare the single fourteenth-century folio of *Tristan* with the corresponding chapters in the editions of 1501, 1528 and 1534, or when we collate the Lancelot fragment in manuscript 2–G–5 with the Vienna manuscript and the Castilian *Demandas* of 1515 and 1535. The prologues and epilogues with which Juan de Burgos has decorated his editions of *Tristan* (1501) and the *Baladro* (1498) raise the suspicion that the lucidity of these issues may owe something to him, and the suspicion is deepened when the edition of 1498 is set alongside of that of 1535; and in the conclusion of *Don Tristan de Leonis* the identity of the French and Castilian descriptions of Iseut in point of matter is as evident as the complete *españolismo* of the details and phrase. It is this last refinement which Montalvo applied to the *Amadis*, which he rephrased throughout in a prose that was contemporary, easy, varied, sententious, self-confident, and rich; and the whole long process—extending from the paratactic naïveté of the primitive versions to the fullness of his inspiration—illustrates the rise and education of that large, periodic eloquence which is now regarded as classic through its perfection in *Don Quixote*.[1]

The claims here made for the Arthurian novels are neither extensive nor exclusive. By an existence and repetition over a considerable number of years, they supported agreeable against didactic literature, encouraged and guided the imagination of a practical people, exhibited at all times a model of construction,

[1] Menéndez y Pelayo, *Origenes de la Novela*, i. cap. v., discusses the style of *Amadis*. The criticisms of Renascence writers will be found in Dr. Thomas, *op. cit.* We have not drawn upon them, because their basis is the "new" chivalry; they are generally ethical.

and helped to build up that prose style that was most akin to their nature. Other causes co-operated in the same effects. Internally, the advance of civilisation required, and was met by, the advance of prose style, and the achievement of each generation was the starting-point of the next. The progress of letters in France, which had been watched in Spain long before the *Poema del Cid*, continued to react on the Peninsular literatures. The intensive study of Latin authors favoured purer ideas of style. The *Cronica del Rey D. Pedro I.* by Pero López de Ayala is a demonstration of Livy's superiority over Orosius, Trogus, Rodericus Toletanus and other scribblers who lie behind the *Primera Cronica General*; the chancellor uses speeches to indicate policy, selects and arranges events to produce a prearranged effect, and marks his interpretation in an artful climax. Yet this climax he imitates not from his Roman model, but from the *matière de Bretagne*. There is a certain sombre dignity in the invention of the Moor Benihatin of Granada, who expounds remorselessly the sevenfold meaning of Merlin's condemnation of the tyrant, only half concealing the chancellor's Trastamaran rancour. In his youth Ayala had read the romances of *Amadis* and *Lanzarote*, and he was, no doubt, well acquainted with the *senificanças* of the trilogy; but the immediate suggestion for this device was probably the passage from the *Poema de Alfonso Onceno* in which Rodrigo Yáñez unsuccessfully endeavoured to produce a climax of feeling by capping the battle of Río Salado with the gibberish of Don Anton. In the *Cronica de D. Pedro I.*, too, the passage is flogged and wearisome and the impression now ludicrous or dull;

but of such defeats victory is born, and each is eloquent of the confidence fourteenth-century Spain felt in the emotional value of the British fiction.

For Fernam Lopes these romances were old nursery tales, and he is the biographer of a second Galahad. Any of the chronicles of the fifteenth century bear witness to the progress and hold of chivalresque ideas and activities; nor is it illicit to attribute their increased fluency and picturesque content of phrase to the same source of suggestion. The *Cronica de D. Juan II.*, for instance, is one which recurs continually to chivalrous interests; "for what concerns the style" it was judged by the sensitive and exacting Juan de Valdés, who admits having qualified himself by a ten years' acquaintance with the new romances, to be in the same category as *Amadis*, *Palmerin* and *Primaleon.*[1]

The final product of chivalresque fiction in the Spanish Peninsula is also the most original expression of the genius of Castile; nor can we end better than by hearing Cervantes' testimony to the Arthurian romances. No novel of this cycle figured in the library examined by the priest, from which circumstance we might infer that they may have fostered the idealism of Don Quixote, but not his lunacy. No romance of the Round Table seems to have been directly accessible to Cervantes. Merlin, a popular figure of the masquerades, is prominent in the second part. He is the proto-enchanter of enchanters; the presiding genius of the Cave of Montesinos; the fashioner of Clavileño; and a figure of fun

[1] Cited by Dr. H. Thomas, *op. cit.*, p. 154: "pero, a mi ver, se puede leer *para lo que pertenece a la lengua* despues de Amadis de Gaula, Palmerin y Primaleon."

impersonated by the witty steward, and dire to the back of Sancho Panza. The Carolingian ballads supplied Montesinos, who also appears in the secondary Arthurian *Tablante de Ricamonte*, from which Cervantes could obtain the names of Arthur, Lancelot, Tristan, Palomades, the Chevalier sans Peur, the Chevalier à Deux Espées, Sagramor and Branor, as well as Merlin, whom he nationalises French. There, too, are the Tabla Rotonda, *Baladro de Merlin* and *Demanda del Sancto Grial*; and the *Anales e historias de Inglaterra* are cited in many chivalresque prefaces. Arthur, called Artús or (from the Italian) Arturo, was remembered also for his enshrinement among the Nine Worthies, whose *Triunfo* he had doubtless read; but Cervantes cares only to put it on record that the king "is now turned into a crow, and they expect him momently in his kingdom." The loves of Tristan and Iseut, Lancelot and Guenevere, whose verity the Knight of La Mancha defends with heat, might give us pause, but the addition of the duenna Quintañona refers us to the ballads, the sole living relics of Arthurian inspiration. Quintañona involves her companions in her comic downfall: she is the "best wine-strainer that Britain ever possessed"—a fact attested by "persons who *almost* remember having seen her"; she and Guenevere in league would not suffice to overcome the chastity of the hero, who naturally surpasses the purity of all the characters of fiction. Lancelot, too, is fallen; he is a precedent to compel duenna Rodriguez to stable Sancho's ass, or for the revelation of Don Quixote's name; and there is even talk of "the necessity of accommodating the old ballad of Sir Lancelot to our present purpose" (i. ch. 2).

The great novel arose, in fact, from a desire to parody a Carolingian ballad; and this has caused the mention of the three Arthurians as well as sustained the Carolingian paladins in such prominence throughout the story.

We need not share Paulin Paris' regrets that Cervantes did not know the superior merits of Arthurian fiction. Parody does not require the best models, even were they preserved in Spain. So far as he had knowledge of the *matière de Bretagne*, Cervantes made excellent use of its humorous possibilities, leaving notes of an interesting little comedy—Arthur the crow and the expectant Britons, Guenevere the unsuccessful seductress of Don Quixote, Lancelot and Sancho's ass, the steward Merlin who distributes whippings, and above and in all, the autochthonous figure of the duenna Quintañona, that seductive centenarian and strainer of wine. But let us ask Don Quixote what is knight-errantry,[1] and he replies:

> Have you not read, Sirs, the annals and histories of England, wherein are handled the famous deeds of King Arthur, whom we in our Castilian vernacular are wont to call King Artús? of whom it is an ancient and common tradition that he died not, but by the art of enchantment was turned into a crow, and that as time goes on he is to reign again and recover his kingdom and sceptre; wherefore it will not be found that from then to now any Englishman has ever killed a crow. Well, it was in the time of this good king that the celebrated chivalrous Order of the Knights of the Round Table was instituted, and the loves therein recounted of Sir Lancelot du Lac and Guenevere occurred, no jot failing, their intermediary and accomplice being that honourable duenna Quintañona; whence comes the ballad so well known and often sung in our Spain of
>
> "Ne'er was knight by courtly dame
> Served, as when from Britain came
> Bold Sir Lancelot,"

[1] *Don Quixote*, i. chap. 13.

along with that soft, sweet progress of his love and mighty deeds. And thereafter that Order of Knighthood went on extending from hand to hand and spread over many sundry parts of the earth, and therein were famous and noted for their feats the valiant Amadis of Gaul and all his sons and grandsons to the fifth generation, and the brave Felixmarte of Hyrcania and the never-as-he-ought-to-be praised Tirant the White, and in our own days we have almost seen and conversed with and listened to the invincible and valiant cavalier Sir Belianis of Greece. This then, gentlemen, it is to be a Knight-Errant, and what I have said is the Order of his chivalry; in the which, as again I have said, I, though a sinful man, have made profession; and that which the knights before-mentioned professed, that same profess I.

APPENDIX

APPENDIX

Since the completion of the manuscript of this work three contributions have been made to the study of Spanish Arthurianism. The corrections, or rather correction, necessitated by them have been entered on the proofs, but it seems further advisable to give them a more extended notice in this Appendix. The late Professor J. D. Bruce's *Evolution of Arthurian Romance* (2 vols., Göttingen, 1923), though it contains a summary bibliography of the Spanish novels, is chiefly of service to the Hispanist as offering a well-read and exceedingly cautious outline of recent Arthurian research. In his chapter dealing with the Pseudo-Robert de Boron and with the *Conte del Brait* the Castilian and Portuguese evidence is of unusual weight and authority.

Professor Karl Pietsch's *Spanish Grail Fragments* (vol. i., Chicago, 1924—vol. ii. is in the press) brings near to a conclusion a philological task undertaken in 1897. The leading interest of this book when completed will lie in its stores of linguistic information, while the literary and historical aspects, which principally affect our study, are to the author no more than incidental. Linguistically we must take account of the affirmation that MS. 2–G–5 is now shown to be written in a mixed language, of which the fundamental basis is Castilian, strongly influenced by Portuguese and Leonese dialectal elements; for by this statement the evidence of language supports that of textual criticism and literary history. But Professor Pietsch's principal service to us is his discovery of the name of Juan Bivas, already known as the translator of Boron's trilogy of the Holy Grail, in the body of the

Portuguese *Livro de Josep Abaramatia*, and by a strange irony he has made this discovery, not in the unread manuscript of this novel, but in one of Klob's notes which has hitherto escaped the eyes of all Klob's readers and of Klob himself! We still require a formal description of Juan Sánchez's manuscript before it can be regarded as the property of scholarship, but we need no longer hesitate to assign it, even apart from the evidence of two etymologies offered by Professor Pietsch, to the progeny of the Castilian translation of the Holy Grail. The date (1313) which Sánchez offers is not to be accepted lightly as the date of the original translation, which was produced, as we have seen, in circumstances somewhat different from those of this manuscript. Sánchez is rather to be taken as a redactor attached to the circle of D. Juan Manuel and D. Affonso de Portugal, or as the Portuguese translator of part of, or the whole of, the Castilian trilogy. As regards its contents, whereas Klob had insisted on the divergences between the *Livro de Josep Abaramatia* and the manuscript of the Palace Library, Professor Pietsch now insists on their identity wherever comparison is possible. The Portuguese story is from start to finish an orthodox *Estoire del Saint Graal.* Even in the cyclic romance of Sir Lancelot that goes under the name of Walter Map this first branch is attributed to Robert de Boron, and as such it was naturally transcribed by the later romancer styled the Pseudo Boron, who wished to displace the Vulgate romances by pretending to be their source. The only contradiction between the *Estoire del Saint Graal* and the later trilogy is that the former assigns the Dolorous Stroke to Brulans and the latter to Balin le Sauvage. We are not yet informed whether the Portuguese manuscript refers to Brulans. The Castilian fragment is reprinted by Professor Pietsch, in addition to the extracts from the *Merlin* and *Demanda* which were already sufficiently well known. It is an abstract, somewhat fuller than the other sections, covering the events of the

Vulgate *Estoire del Saint Graal* from vol. i. p. 12, line 30 of Sommer's *Vulgate Version of the Arthurian Romances* to p. 46, line 17, and from p. 47, line 4 to p. 48, line 30; between these two sections headings are sandwiched, which cover allusively the matter of pp. 46–66. The narrative omits the introduction and details here and there, shows a preference for the readings of H. O. Sommer's later manuscripts (*e.g.* i. p. 20, n. 10, p. 30, n. 5, p. 47, n. 6; in one case, at least, the Portuguese version coincides), and sadly disfigures proper names and even common nouns (*e.g.* "Barfano," "Polo," "Mays," "al rrey Damasco," "Betatira," "canes," "diziseis," for "de Cafarnaon," "Apolin," "Martys," "au roy de Damas," "Betanie," "sarrasins," "lxv.").

In *El Lanzarote español del manuscrito* 9611 *de la Biblioteca Nacional* (published in the *Revista de Filología Española*, xi. pp. 282–297) Sr. Bohigas Balaguer gives a better account of this manuscript than has hitherto been put into print, as well as reprinting the important Tristan paragraphs. He has not, however, attempted to collate the Spanish version with the standard French texts, and is, on the whole, less concerned with the *Lanzarote* than with Wechssler and Brugger's hypothesis that it formed a single cyclic romance with the Grail trilogy of the Pseudo-Boron, thus expanding the work of this writer from three parts in its extant redactions to six in its hypothetical complete form. Sr. Bohigas is of the opinion that the Spanish text never formed part of such a compilation, though he forgets the allusion on fol. 310 to the episode of the Knight of the Two Swords in the *Baladro del Sabio Merlin*. In this he is certainly right. The Wechssler-Brugger hypothesis took its rise in G. Paris' view that the Holy Grail story of the Pseudo-Boron was anterior to the version current under the name of Walter Map and indissolubly attached to the *Lancelot*. But A. Pauphilet has proved, by the least controvertible demonstration in the history of Arthurian studies (*Romania*, xxxvi.), that the Pseudo-Boron is no more than a *rifacimento* of Map. The plagiarist found Map's first book resting on the authority of Robert de Boron; he transcribed it and part of the *Merlin*, and then invented the *Suite du Merlin* as well as a refashioned *Queste del Saint Graal*, covering himself by fresh citations of Robert de Boron. He did not desire to transcribe the *Lancelot du Lac*, which would have disturbed the symmetry of his work (*Merlin en Prose*, ii. p. 57); but, a knowledge of Lancelot's career being necessary for the comprehension of any *Quest* in which Galahad was prominent, he impudently declared that the book of Sir Lancelot ought to be considered part of his work. All allusions to Lancelot in the trilogy are satisfied either by Map's *Lancelot* or by the Lancelot sections of *Tristan*, so that the Wechssler-Brugger hypothesis is quite without foundation.

Lest this Appendix end on a note of dogmatism, let us consider some things that remain to be done. Spanish-Portuguese Arthurianism still requires descriptions of the *Livro de Josep Abaramatia* (Portuguese text), *Baladro del Sabio Merlin* (1498) and *Historia de Lanceloto, Leonel y Galvan*, as well as textual and linguistic studies. While in the thesis presented by this book we have principally considered the possible influence of our Plantagenet monarchs, there are also some hints of a special relation between the Spanish stories and the Italian. When we consider the close relation established between the Norman rulers of England and Sicily and their successors, it is clear that the two influences are not exclusive. The leading facts seem to be these: (1) the Spanish texts depend on texts written in the French language, but quite possibly written in Italy or, at any rate, in close agreement with such versions; (2) the Spanish *Tristan* seems to form a special sub-group with two Italian versions and two works written in French by Italians; (3) the *Baladro del Sabio Merlin* uses an original distribution of Merlin's prophecies that especially resembles their distribution in two

Italian texts, and all *Prophécies de Merlin* are traditionally derived from the French text presented by "Richard of Ireland" to Frederic II. in the year 1228; and (4) Torroella's *Faula* is demonstrably a Norman-Sicilian tale. The problems before us are, perhaps, as many and interesting as those that lie behind.

THE END

INDEX

INDEX